Celebrating Poetry

West – Spring 2006

Creative Communication, Inc.

Celebrating Poetry
West – Spring 2006

An anthology compiled by Creative Communication, Inc.

Published by:
CREATIVE COMMUNICATION, INC.
1488 NORTH 200 WEST
LOGAN, UT 84341

ISBN 10: 1-60050-058-7
ISBN 13: 978-1-60050-058-9

Foreword

Welcome! Thank you for letting us share these poems with you.

This last school year we surveyed thousands of teachers asking what we could do better. We constantly strive to be the best at what we do and to listen to our teachers and poets. We strongly believe that this is your contest. Several changes were made to this anthology as we adapt to what was requested.

In this and future editions of the anthology, the Top Ten winners will be featured on their own page in the book. Each poet that is included in this book is to be congratulated, however, the Top Ten Poets should receive special recognition for having been chosen as writing one of the best poems. The Top Ten Poems were selected through an online voting system that includes thousands of teachers and students. In a day and age where television programs use viewer voting to determine which contestant is the winner, it is appropriate that our poetry winners are chosen by their peers.

Over the years we have had many parents contact us concerning the privacy of their children. The comments focus on the fact that publishing a poet's name, grade, school name, city and state with each poem is too much information. We want to address these concerns. In the Fall 2005 edition of the anthology, we made the decision to only list the poet's name and grade after each poem. Whereas we received many calls and letters concerning the issue that we were publishing too much information, we received thousands of calls and letters requesting that we again publish more information to include a student's school name and state with each poem. Therefore, for this and future editions we will publish each student's name, grade, school name and state unless specifically instructed not to include this information. Just as this information is included in a school yearbook, we provide this information in this literary yearbook of poetry. This decision hopefully makes it easier to find classmates in the book and brings appropriate recognition to the schools.

We are proud to provide this anthology. In speaking to the poets in our anthologies we have found that our anthologies are not stuffy old books that are forgotten on a shelf. The poems in our books are read, loved and cherished. We hope you enjoy reading the thoughts and feelings of our youth.

Sincerely,
Gaylen Worthen, President
Creative Communication

Enter Our Next Poetry Contest!

Why should I enter?
Win prizes and get published! Each year thousands of dollars in prizes are awarded in each region and tens of thousands of dollars in prizes are awarded throughout North America. The top writers in each division receive a monetary award and a free book that includes their published work. Poems of merit are also selected to be published in our anthology.

Who may enter?
There are five poetry contest divisions that include almost everyone. Poets in grades K-3, 4-6, 7-9, 10-12, and adults may enter the contest.

What is needed to enter the contest?
You can enter any original poem 21 lines or less. Each entry must include the poet's name, address, city, state and zip code. Student entries need to include the poet's grade, school name and school address. Students who include their teacher's name may help the teacher qualify for a free copy of the anthology.

How do I enter?
Enter online at:
www.poeticpower.com

Or, *Mail your entry to:*
Poetry Contest
1488 North 200 West
Logan, UT 84341

If you are mailing your entry, please write "Student Contest" at the top of your poem if you are in grades K-12. Please write "Adult Contest" at the top of your poem if you are entering the adult contest.

When is the deadline?
The contest deadlines are December 5th, August 15th, and April 5th. Poets may enter one poem in each contest.

Are there benefits for my school?
Yes. We award $15,000 each year in grants to help with Language Arts programs. Schools qualify to apply for a grant by having a large number of entries of which over fifty percent are accepted for publication. This typically tends to be about 15 accepted entries.

Are there benefits for my teacher?
Yes. Teachers with five or more students accepted to be published receive a free anthology that includes their students' poems.

For more information please go to our website at
***www.poeticpower.com**,*
email us at editor@poeticpower.com or call 435-713-4411.

Table of Contents

Spring 2006 Poetic Achievement Honor Schools

* Teachers who had fifteen or more poets accepted to be published

The following schools are recognized as receiving a "Poetic Achievement Award." This award is given to schools who have a large number of entries of which over fifty percent are accepted for publication. With hundreds of schools entering our contest, only a small percent of these schools are honored with this award. The purpose of this award is to recognize schools with excellent Language Arts programs. This award qualifies these schools to receive a complimentary copy of this anthology. In addition, these schools are eligible to apply for a Creative Communication Language Arts Grant. Grants of two hundred and fifty dollars each are awarded to further develop writing in our schools.

Acacia Elementary School
Vail, AZ
Claire Jacobson*

Academy of Charter Schools
Westminster, CO
Mrs. Laughlin*

Briargrove Elementary School
Houston, TX
Robin Abair*
Mrs. Callender*
Mrs. Emerson*
Mrs. Parrow*
Mrs. Porter
Mrs. Sawyer
Marcy Thompson

Brush Creek Elementary School
Eagle, CO
Ms. Givens
Elizabeth Ronzio
Jenna Walsh

Camptonville Academy
Chico, CA
Lori A. Josifek*

Carlthorp School
Santa Monica, CA
Dr. Leslie Johnson*

CLASS Academy
Portland, OR
Teresa Cantlon
Justice Evans
Leslie Huffman*

Coeur d'Alene Avenue Elementary School
Venice, CA
Joyce Koff*

Community Children's Center
Desert Hot Springs, CA
Danyel Grandmain*

Crestview Elementary School
Waco, TX
Anita Stubblefield*

Criswell Elementary School
Forney, TX
Theresa Hale*
Luanna Johnson
Mrs. Lane
Laura Smith*

Daly Elementary School
Hamilton, MT
Sandy Auch
Kerry Hanson
Jane Hollibaugh
Mrs. McConnell
Mrs. White

Daves Avenue Elementary School
San Jose, CA
Mrs. Louthian
Nancy Ringsted

DeQueen Elementary School
Port Arthur, TX
Mrs. Farmer
Gwen E. Simmons
Israel Taylor
Maybelline Washington

Edison Elementary School
San Diego, CA
Jennifer Oliger*

Eton School
Bellevue, WA
Dr. Debra Gessert*
M. McGrath
Patty Sorenson*

Fir Grove Elementary School
Roseburg, OR
Debra Allen
Lynn Schnoor

Fort Vannoy Elementary School
Grants Pass, OR
Jim Kriz*

Fort Worth Country Day School
Fort Worth, TX
Kim Davis
Darlene Ignagni
Michael Parker
Donna Rubin
Edwena Thompson*
Mary Kay Varley

Four Peaks Elementary School
Fountain Hills, AZ
Kathleen Calhoun*
Mrs. DeWitte
Barbara Geiges
Linda Ness*
Madeleine Smith*
Mrs. Willim

Frontier Valley Elementary School
Parker, CO
Patrick Allen
Carrie Merrill
Carol Sotebeer
Sue Sporer

Gause Intermediate School
Washougal, WA
Jim Schroeder*
Connie Vernon*

Gold Canyon Elementary School
Apache Junction, AZ
Michelle Sobkoviak
Judy A. Youngren*

Grace School
Houston, TX
Sally Charlton
Jamie Heinrich
Suzanne Kircher
Sally Kollaer
Debbie McColloch
Claire McMullin*
Kim Peters
Pat Runkel
Teri Walker
Anne Williams*
Betsy Wolter

Heatherwood Elementary School
Boulder, CO
Jolie Kasynski*

Hollister SDA School
Hollister, CA
Mrs. Dalton
Joan Hacko
Emily Wagner

Horn Academy
Bellaire, TX
Shirley A. Wright*

Jackson Elementary School
Sanger, CA
Joyce Braun
Debbie Galloway
Ms. Keck
Mr. Luginbill
Mr. Mimura
Mrs. Reetz
Mrs. Santos
Mrs. Woodward

Katherine Delmar Burke School
San Francisco, CA
Joelle Auberson
Nayo Brooks
Alexander Lewis

Kyrene De Las Brisas School
Chandler, AZ
Ruth Sunda*

Lincoln Elementary School
Hanford, CA
Jaime Camacho
Angela Gonzales
Sarah Hoisington
Christina
      Rodriguez-Padilla*

Little Scholars School
San Jose, CA
Mrs. Castle
Mrs. Nayak
Mrs. Rahman

Lorenzo De Zavala Elementary
School
Baytown, TX
Denise Morgan*
Jennifer Wade

Montessori Learning Institute
Houston, TX
MyLe Nguyen Vo
Lekha Worah

New Emerson School
Grand Junction, CO
Michelle Hooker
Paula Martin
Terry Schamlz
Carrie Wertz

Northridge Elementary School
Highlands Ranch, CO
Maureen Holland*

Notre Dame Elementary/Jr High
School
Chico, CA
Stephanie Beyers*
Caroline Howard

Open Charter Magnet School
Los Angeles, CA
Anne Granick
Dena Vatcher

Orchard Elementary School
Orem, UT
Marcia Parrish*

Our Lady of the Snows School
Reno, NV
Mrs. Burke*

Paonia Elementary School
Paonia, CO
Carol Beers
Jodi Simpson

Phoenix Metro Islamic School
Tempe, AZ
Fatima Abdel Hag
Alia Al-Taqi
Hind Hania
Mootaz M. Koriem
Badrun Nahar
Veronica Ramirez

Pinnacle Charter School
Federal Heights, CO
Mrs. Ladouceur
Mrs. Spencer
Zack White

Polk Elementary School
El Paso, TX
Karen Alvarez*
Susan Ayers*
Kathy Bogas*
Laura Fox*
India C. Graves*
Peggy Kovan*

Presbyterian School
Houston, TX
Mary Pat Christou*
Gail Kirkconnell

Reid School
Salt Lake City, UT
Kim Aulbach
Meagan Black
Paulette Evans
Jill Gammon
Cheri Israelsen
Mindyn Mullinix
Rose Palmer
Michelle Peterson
Shauna Tateoka

River HomeLink Program
Battle Ground, WA
Tonia Albert
Ryan Anderson
Sherri Gassaway
Julie Sperry

River Oaks Baptist School
Houston, TX
Dana Machen
Diantha Sneed

Robinson Elementary School
Robinson, TX
Michelle Chudej
Margaret Evans
Sherilyn Nering

Sangre De Cristo Elementary School
Hooper, CO
Lorrie Jacobsen*
Sandy Rogers

Scenic Park Elementary School
Anchorage, AK
Cindy Forsyth*
Mrs. Hill
Mrs. Kueter

Solana Santa Fe Elementary School
Rancho Santa Fe, CA
Christy Campbell
Cara Curran
Mrs. Khattar
Mrs. Lugo
Sharon O'Brien
Ms. Shea*
Mr. Taunt
Angie Tremble

Spring Creek Elementary School
Laramie, WY
Sherilyn Berube
Andrea Hayden
Mark Williams

St Dorothy School
Glendora, CA
Julie Coughlin*

St Mark's Day School
El Paso, TX
Clara Griswold
Mrs. Groover
Mona Mehta

St Raphael School
Santa Barbara, CA
Mary Faria
Carol Fritz*
Barbara Malvinni*
Diane McClenathen

Stanbridge Academy
San Mateo, CA
Maggie DeLoach
Brenda B. Fitterer
Melissa Myers
Katie Riggs

Summit Elementary School
Smithfield, UT
Carla Cox
Mrs. Shaffer

Sundance Elementary School
Sundance, WY
Connie Green
Tammy Needham

Sunnyslope Elementary School
Hollister, CA
Josie Hernandez*
Lynn Parsons

The Mirman School
Los Angeles, CA
Jocelyn Balaban
Candace Corliss*
Wendy Samson*
Jane Shimotsu*

The Pegasus School
Huntington Beach, CA
Mrs. Deen
Mrs. DiCato
Denise Lessenger
Mrs. Moore

Thomas Edison Charter School
North Logan, UT
Tanya Bidstrup
Mr. Packard
Mären Wendel*
Lee Ann Wilkins*

Turner Elementary School
  Willis, TX
    Kathy McLemore*
    Cassie Read*

Twin Lakes Christian Academy
  Cedar Park, TX
    Cheryl Barnett
    Rachel Edwards
    Aimee Herst
    Sue Johnson
    Lockie Kirksey
    Lee Vandenhouten

University Park Elementary School
  Dallas, TX
    Laurel Arnold
    Mrs. Johnson
    Phyllis Mabus
    Miss Morrow
    Becky O'Donnell
    Mr. R. Schlender

Westwood Charter Elementary
  School
    Los Angeles, CA
      Joyce Koff*

Wonderland Avenue Elementary
  School
    Los Angeles, CA
      Zachary Earl*

Woodcrest School
  Tarzana, CA
    Mrs. Martin
    Luanne Paglione

Writers in the Schools Program
  Houston, TX
    Ms. Brown
    Kiki Przewlocki

Language Arts Grant Recipients 2005-2006

After receiving a "Poetic Achievement Award" schools are encouraged to apply for a Creative Communication Language Arts Grant. The following is a list of schools who received a two hundred and fifty dollar grant for the 2005-2006 school year.

Acushnet Elementary School – Acushnet, MA
Admiral Thomas H. Moorer Middle School – Eufaula, AL
Alta High School – Sandy, UT
Alton R-IV Elementary School – Alton, MO
Archbishop McNicholas High School – Cincinnati, OH
Barbara Bush Elementary School – Mesa, AZ
Bellmar Middle School – Belle Vernon, PA
Bonham High School – Bonham, TX
Cool Spring Elementary School – Cleveland, NC
Douglas Elementary School – Liberty, KY
Dumbarton Middle School – Baltimore, MD
Edward Bleeker Jr High School – Flushing, NY
Emmanuel/St. Michael Lutheran School – Fort Wayne, IN
Floyds Knobs Elementary School – Floyds Knobs, IN
Fox Creek High School – North Augusta, SC
Friendship Jr High School – Des Plaines, IL
Gibson City-Melvin-Sibley High School – Gibson City, IL
Hamilton Jr High School – Hamilton, TX
John F. Kennedy Middle School – Cupertino, CA
John Ross Elementary School – Edmond, OK
MacLeod Public School – Sudbury, ON
McKinley Elementary School – Livonia, MI
Monte Cassino School – Tulsa, OK

Language Arts Grant Winners cont.

New Germany Elementary School – New Germany, NS
North Beach Elementary School – Miami Beach, FL
Paradise Valley High School – Phoenix, AZ
Parkview Christian School – Lincoln, NE
Picayune Jr High School – Picayune, MS
Red Bank Charter School – Red Bank, NJ
Sebastian River Middle School – Sebastian, FL
Siegrist Elementary School – Platte City, MO
Southwest Academy – Baltimore, MD
St. Anthony School – Winsted, CT
St. John Vianney Catholic School – Flint, MI
St. Paul the Apostle School – Davenport, IA
St. Rose School – Roseville, CA
St. Sebastian School – Pittsburgh, PA
Sundance Elementary School – Sundance, WY
Thorp Middle School – Thorp, WI
Townsend Harris High School – Flushing, NY
Warren Elementary School – Warren, OR
Washington High School – Washington Court House, OH
Wasilla Lake Christian School – Wasilla, AK
Woodland Elementary School – Radcliff, KY
Worthington High School – Worthington, MN

Young Poets Grades K-3

Note: The Top Ten poems were finalized through an online voting system. Creative Communication's judges first picked out the top poems. These poems were then posted online. The final step involved thousands of students and teachers who registered as online judges and voted for the Top Ten poems. We hope you enjoy these selections.

Top Poem Grades K-3

I Know a Little Green Frog

I know a little green frog,
That hides up in the trees,
It lives in tropical forests,
And hides behind the leaves.

Its red eyes are for protection,
To scare its enemies away.
The sticky pads upon its feet
Help it to climb and play.

It lays its eggs among green plants
That have water droplets in them.
When the eggs hatch, tadpoles come out
To drink the water in them.

From one half to two inches long,
The adult frog will grow.
And usually on its underside
Yellow or blue may show.

So if you're in the rainforest,
Listen carefully,
And you might hear a little song
By a green frog up in a tree.

Joshua Barbur, Grade 1
Montessori Christian Academy, TX

Top Poem Grades K-3

Ballet

First we do a grande plié,
Now let's do a releveé.
Stand up straight as you sauté.

Onto the barre, I place my hand,
And on my demis-pointes I will stand.

I love doing échappés.
But do I love them more than chassé?

Now some pirouettes across the floor.
I'm sad when class is over as I bourreé out the door.

Madelyn Carter, Grade 3
Castle Dale School, UT

Top Poem Grades K-3

My Dream

When I was just a little girl
I had a wonderful dream
I walked in a field of clover
And sat beside a talking stream
While I looked for the lucky four
From the sky came a Pegasus white as snow
When I turned around she stood beside me
And told me that we should go
I held out my green charm just for her to eat
She thanked me and lifted me on her back
We flew above the clouds and down to my house
And before my parents even noticed my dream had faded to black

Asia Cowen, Grade 1
The Pegasus School, CA

Top Poem Grades K-3

In November

In November
the leaves fall
with colors
as if a rainbow
has grown inside of them.

In November
the bare trees
are lit up by the moonlight
as if the moon
has hidden inside of them.

In November
a river flows
as if the wind is taking it
down the dirt path.

In November

Riley Douthit, Grade 3
McGaugh Elementary School, CA

Top Poem Grades K-3

Winter's Blast

Wind whips furiously,
Snow blows hard,
Cold temperatures drop,
Snowflakes slither down slick roads,
And I am on black ice.

Jason Duvall, Grade 3
Sundance Elementary School, WY

Top Poem Grades K-3

Snow Feelings

When I feel snowflakes
I feel like I am a white snowbird
flying in the clear blue sky.

Or a bunny hopping in the deep snow.

Sometimes I feel like a horse
trotting in the snow
and the snowflakes are gently falling on my back.

Sterlyng Ellis, Grade 2
Frontier Valley Elementary School, CO

Top Poem Grades K-3

Daydream

I stare at my half-eaten zucchini,
imagining it as if it were a half-eaten soldier.
Not literally,
but as if emotions were half-eaten,
debating whether the bloodshed he had caused was sin,
or if it was a patriotic act.

To make my scenes more sketched with pessimism,
I imagine him cradling his gun,
knowing the chaos he caused.

I think about this cruel knowledge
for a few moments,
then push away my zucchini plate,
losing my appetite.
I then walk away,
filled with pity...

Jackson Kinder, Grade 2
Prospect Sierra School, CA

Top Poem Grades K-3

When I Think of Winter...

When I think of winter...
I can hear the leaves falling off the trees,
the birds flying south for the winter,
and the snow falling on the icy ground.

I can taste the snow drifting from the puffy clouds
that look like cotton candy,
the falling water of icicles hanging from our roof,
and the minty red and green stripes of Christmas candy canes.

I can smell the steam of chocolate chip cookies
that Mom just popped out of the oven,
the smoke from the chimney gracefully gliding across the field,
and the fresh-baked bread in the oven from the store next door.

I can see the cold frosty roses in the field by the school,
the bear's footprints leading to a cave so he can have a long winter nap,
and the leaves floating through the air and falling in my hair.

Caitlyn Oppermann, Grade 3
Red Rock Elementary School, TX

Top Poem Grades K-3

Butter Flies

Where is the butter
In a butterfly?
Why they named it this
I don't know why!
In beetles,
Where did they hide the beets?
Where's the dragon
In dragonfly? Jeeps!
Why only a queen
Is the thing!
In an ant colony
Where's the king?
How can a ladybug
Be a male?
Where on a snake
Is the start of its tail?
In school I can spell them,
So I guess I'm winnin'…
But all these silly names
Sure have my head spinnin'!

Margaret Rausch, Grade 2
Mohave Accelerated Learning Center, AZ

Top Poem Grades K-3

My Snake

I have a friend who has no legs,
Soft and leathery are its eggs.
Its body is as long as a rope,
If you feel it, it's as slippery as soap.
It attacks its enemies with a bang,
With poison it stores in its fangs.
If you see him don't you shake,
For my friend is a snake.

Aastha Shah, Grade 2
Little Scholars School, CA

Scarlet
Scarlet looks like your cheeks blazing up in embarrassment.
Scarlet feels like apple pie fresh from the oven.
Scarlet feels like rosy red roses.
Scarlet tastes like raspberries.
Scarlet sounds like fire crackers shooting out sparks.

Julia Todderud, Grade 2
Bridlemile Elementary School, OR

What I Remember
I remember my grandpa singing me one special song
I remember him making his coffee and there I heard nonstop singing
I remember thinking in my head "Jacqueline do not ever forget that song"
I never did
I remember me sitting on his lap and telling him things
I just wanted him to know
I remember the warmness of his hands and him saying
"I will live forever"
I remember the hats he would let me use that would go over my head
I keep them in my backpack so I can remember him
I remember the day he passed away I was in Boston, Massachusetts
I asked a wish fifteen seconds later a snow blizzard started
I was amazed
I remember my family's favorite baseball team
Did not win the World Series for 86 years
I remember when my grandpa passed away at 86
and that year his favorite baseball team
Won the World Series for 2004 now we know why they won
I remember my grandpa

Jacqueline Blumsack, Grade 3
Coeur d'Alene Avenue Elementary School, CA

B Is For...
B is for a ball that you play with.
B is for Brianna, which is my name.
B is for brown, black, and blue, which are colors on a stormy day.
B is for boots that you put on.
B is for the butterfly that flies in the spring.
B is for the birds that also fly too.
B is for baby that is just so cute.
B is for the bumblebee that leaves you with a sting.

Brianna Maldonado, Grade 2
Lincoln Elementary School, CA

A Scaly Dragon

I am a scaly dragon.
I wonder how high I can fly in the blue sky.
I hear the wind blowing over the mountains.
I see a red-spotted dragon egg in a big nest.
I want to fly across the sea.
I am a scaly dragon.

I pretend I am a large friendly bird.
I feel free as I soar in the white clouds.
I touch the fish I caught with my claws.
I worry if there is trouble and if I can help.
I cry when another dragon is wounded.
I am a scaly dragon.

I understand the dragon ways.
I say, "I will live forever."
I dream of being a good and helpful dragon.
I try not to blow fire to harm anyone
I hope I will always be free.
I am a scaly dragon.

Scott Miller, Grade 2
Grace School, TX

By a Stream

In the forest there was a rock
By the river I took off my sock
I dangled my toes in the cold, cold river
It was freezing and I started to shiver

Lena Ballard, Grade 3
Cubberley Elementary School, CA

Fire Red

"Flash!"
"Swoosh!"
Sparks of sapphire flying everywhere!
Scratching against my face.
Like a thousand bees stinging my face.
I get out of the fire bushes
that had stung my face like a thousand pins.
I feel the fire bushes against my back,
Burning,
Burning.

Amanda Lingle, Grade 2
Brush Creek Elementary School, CO

My Dog

My dog
Darkish yellow
Runs fast and chases cats
He's kind and loves my family
Good boy!

Lainey Chenoweth, Grade 1
Grace School, TX

The Grandfather Clock

Tick tock, tick tock,
goes the grandfather clock.
If you want it to stop,
throw a rock at the clock.
If that doesn't stop the clock,
there's only one thing to do…
Throw it off the dock!

Andrew Zhuo, Grade 3
Vine Elementary School, CA

Cobras

Cobras are fierce.
Cobras are defiant.
Cobras will bite you,
and slither up to you.
Cobras are venomous.
Cobras are killers.

Ethan Angel, Grade 2
New Emerson School, CO

Gardens

Sweet aromas
Beautiful flowers
Bright colors
Sparkling dew
Green grass
Apple trees
Ripe fruit
Golden sun rays
Blue skies
Glimmering ponds
Wonderful feelings
Twinkling joy

Patricia DalBello, Grade 3
Grace School, TX

California

C andy shops everywhere
A ll day fun
L ay in the sand all day
I love it there
F ish and crabs in the water
O ysters and clams and mussels on shore
R iding the waves in the water
N othing but fun
I t is beautiful
A big ocean

Brianna Nelson, Grade 3
Four Peaks Elementary School, AZ

Love

Love
If love were a color it would be pink,
As a flower in the meadow.
If love were a taste it would be delicious,
Like a baked apple pie.
If love were a feeling it would be happy,
As my mom when she sees me,
If love were a smell it would be sweet,
Like my grandfathers cane.
If love were a sound it would be peaceful,
As a bird that sings.
Love

Kyler Beaton, Grade 2
Grace School, TX

Why Not to Go on the Oregon Trail

O bstacles block your way.
R ivers are hard to cross.
E xtra hard to get fresh meat.
G ross food.
O xen don't eat everything.
N o trees to cut down to make a raft.

T here are bad Indians.
R attlesnakes are poisonous.
A lkaline water is very poisonous.
I t's not easy.
L eave too late and you're goners for sure.

Erica Deines Schumacher, Grade 3
Four Peaks Elementary School, AZ

Dogs

Dogs need to rest for energy.
Back again on the sled.
Dogs have to face the cold.
People may drop dogs.
Wear booties to keep their feet warm.
Sleep on straw.
Sometimes get hurt or die.
Pass the finish line.
Too tired to bark when over.

Diana Marquez, Grade 3
Briggsdale Elementary School, CO

The Mysterious Thing

I'm thinking of something
that has a pole, a ball, and a rope.
When I first saw it,
It was very, very magical.
When I saw a bright light
shining on the ground
the light was very, very bright.
A gray light touching
magically the pole.
I hear "ting, ting"
when the ball hits the pole.
I wonder if it is safe or if it is fun.
Do you know what it is?
You're gonna find out!

Leslie Renteria, Grade 3
Edison Elementary School, CA

Fall

The leaves will fall down.
Some are big, and some are small.
I really like fall!

Tony Tripodo, Grade 3
Grace School, TX

Art

I love art
It's colorful and pretty,
and when you hang it on your wall
it goes chink!

Alaric Martinez, Grade 3
Summit Elementary School, UT

The Raven

She swoops down like a black pearl,
caws like a silent shadow.
She flies free in the breeze,
as much as she will please.
The raven…

Agnes McGinnis, Grade 2
Calvert Home School, ID

Wishing for Grades

I wish this year would be no fear,
I wish myself the best for the TAKS test,
I wish to get good grades,
And learn first-aid.

Elaina Espinoza, Grade 3
Turner Elementary School, TX

Earth

Earth
Enormous, spherical
Living, turning, floating
Home of the USA
Living Planet

Alexander Comerci, Grade 3
Four Peaks Elementary School, AZ

Mythical Magic

griffins
proud, swift, dangerous
soaring, fighting, flying, biting
griffins soar their heads held high
full of pride that they can fly
buck beak

Catalina Niessen, Grade 3
Montessori School of Ojai, CA

Things I Love Best

Beaches white with sand dollars,
The rain's fresh smell,
Snowboarding on sparkling snow,
The smell of red flowers,
Feeling green grass on my bare feet,
These are what I love best!

Lauren Rolfe, Grade 3
Four Peaks Elementary School, AZ

Nature
I smell a tiger in the jungle.
Nature smells pretty like roses.
Nature looks as pretty as a bird.
Nature tastes like dirt in the woods.

Lizceth Hernandez, Grade 1
Robert L Stevens Elementary School, CA

Spring
In Spring, bunnies come out and play.
When spring comes the grass becomes green.
The wind comes up us and
people are happy and glad.

Melissa Delgado, Grade 3
Midland Elementary School, CA

Guinea Pig
G osh, do I like to run,
the whole **U** niverse should have guinea pigs!
I am easy to take care of,
N o one wants an expensive pet.
E veryone says I'm adorable,
A nd also say I'm cute!

P eople always love me,
I always keep my temper,
G osh, everyone loves me!

Allison Malone, Grade 3
St Raphael School, CA

Spiders
Spiders have eight long, skinny legs.
They lay hundreds of tiny eggs.
All spiders eat flies.
They're quiet as spies.
A spider loves to spin.
I see a web near a trash bin.
Black spiders are the color of ashes.
When an enemy approaches, the spider dashes.
Spiders do not carry much weight.
But they catch a lot of bait.
Do not step on a spider and be a fool.
Spiders are cool!

Blake Fisher, Grade 3
Froid Elementary School, MT

Places
School
fun, cool
running, testing, reading
Rachel, Mrs. Shoaff, TV, movies
jumping, playing, cleaning
safe, warm
Home
Carly Taylor, Grade 3
Rogers Elementary School, NV

The Adventure
First we go to China
Then we go to Spain
Hey how dare it rain
Well the adventure has to end
So it might as well now.
Lindsey Leigh, Grade 1
Criswell Elementary School, TX

Horses
Horses come in many colors:
Polka dot, gray, brown, and black.
You can ride a horse,
But they can run very fast.
Don't forget to hold on
Or you might fall off!

Horses can be your pets.
You can put them in a barn
And feed them hay.
Give them water to drink.
They are so pretty,
You can comb their hair.
Hannah Wilhite, Kindergarten
Twin Lakes Christian Academy, TX

Zebras
Zebras
White, black
Eating, playing, kicking
Zebras are striped.
Horses
Amanda Gomez, Grade 1
Myatt Elementary School, TX

Things About My Mom
She makes me shut off the TV,
I think it won't hurt me.
She washes the laundry,
I have to do it for free.
She makes me clean my room,
Right when I grab the broom.
My mom goes to work,
To teach about the world.
She is a good teacher,
Because I want to be her.
My mom is clean,
When she uses the washing machine.
Skylar Ann Green, Grade 2
Manzano Christian School, NM

Summer and Winter
Summer
Pretty, fun
Swimming, fishing, playing
Hot sun — cold snow
Sledding, snowing, playing
Cold, ice
Winter
Jessie Solorio, Grade 3
Turner Elementary School, TX

Humpty Dumpty Had a Ball
Humpty Dumpty dancing at the ball.
Humpty Dumpty dancing with a pig!
Humpty Dumpty.
Alexia Wong, Kindergarten
Jacob Wismer Elementary School, OR

Money
I like money.
Do you like money?
Is money made out of honey?
I like dimes too.
I like pennies and quarters!
I like dollars too.
Twenty-dollar bills are great!
I can't wait for more money!
Alonzo Gutierrez, Grade 3
Honey Hollow Elementary School, CA

A Tree

A tree
Is as still as an
Empty playground.
A tree
Is as silent as a
Turtle.
A tree is tall as a
Dinosaur.
A tree
Is steady as a
Statue.
A tree
Is like a
Little sound
Of wind.
Hector Benitez, Grade 3
Edison Elementary School, CA

Piano, Piano, Piano

Graceful notes and
music.

Different songs
every
time.

High pitch
Low pitch.
You can play.

Eight
notes
in one
octave.

Different colors
black
or
white.

I love piano. I play
day and night.
Sage Thomas, Grade 3
Acacia Elementary School, AZ

Ocean

An ocean is so big! Why? I don't know.
Oh yeah I know because it's deep!
Why it's deep. I don't know.
Oh yeah I know.
People dig.
Why they dig? I don't know.
You tell me.
I will not tell you anymore. Okay.
Mohammed Luqman Ahmed, Grade 1
Phoenix Metro Islamic School, AZ

Axis Deer

It has a black nose,
and the axis deer is big
with white dots on it.
Niki Gonzalez, Grade 3
Lorenzo De Zavala Elementary School, TX

Nature

Nature smells like flowers.
Nature looks like worms.
Nature feels hard.
Nature tastes like dirt.
Daniela Trejo, Grade 1
Robert L Stevens Elementary School, CA

Parents

Mom
friendly, happy
cooking, cleaning, working
female, lady, gentleman, male
typing, driving, writing
serious, helpful
Dad
Robert Ocampo, Grade 3
Kathy L Batterman Elementary School, NV

Russy the Walrus

Russy the walrus saw some rain,
So he ran to a glacier,
But slipped off because of the rain.
Then Russy the walrus had to stay in the rain.
Tersa Soria, Grade 3
Sunnyslope Elementary School, CA

If I Were Colors

If I were purple I would be grapes on a tree.
If I were red I would be a rose or an apple.
If I were blue I would be a lake of water or a blue ocean.
If I were pink I would be a bouncy ball.
If I Were yellow I would be a banana or the sun.
If I were green I would be a green bush or grass or leaves.
If I were orange I would be an orange or a goldfish.
If I were light blue I would be a shark.

Victoria Ledezma, Grade 2
St Dorothy School, CA

Mensur

M agnets are my favorite things
E ager to read books
N eighbor of Asha
S aber-tooth tiger is my favorite mammal
U mpires are my favorite coach like Br. Abdud Sabur
R eptiles are my favorite creatures

Mensur Aliye, Grade 2
Phoenix Metro Islamic School, AZ

I Hope Santa Doesn't Care

When we were putting on our gingerbread house a gumdrop on the door...
All of a sudden it splattered on the floor!

The peppermints flew on the ceiling, and the lollipops on the wall...
The marshmallows stuck to the windows, and the icing began to fall!

The chocolates stuck to the chimney, and we couldn't get them out! I swear!
So when Christmas Eve comes, I hope Santa doesn't care!

Michaela Cherry, Grade 3
Grace School, TX

Grandpa

My grandpa is a funny old man,
He likes me a lot. He gives me a hand,
When we exercise together to stay in great shape.
I jump up when he bends down,
And when we are finished we take a ride to town.
We have lots of fun right from the start,
I love my grandpa with all my heart!

Elizabeth Burnett, Kindergarten
Presbyterian School, TX

Coconut

The saddest thing I ever did see
was a dog biting a coconut tree,
he would tug and tug 'till he came to see
he was biting a tree!

Sean Farrell, Grade 3
Hood Case Elementary School, TX

I Am a Cooking Machine!

I am a cooking machine
I cook and cook and cook all day
I love to cook spaghetti
Yummy! Yummy! Yummy!
I love spaghetti don't you
oh and I forgot to tell you I like pizza too!

I like lots of cake like
chocolate and vanilla and strawberry
I like the smell of cakes
Yummy! Yummy! Yummy!
and I forgot to tell you I like pizza too!

Don't you hear that?
Sizzle Sizzle Sizzle!
That's the sizzling of the steak
oh and I forgot to tell you I like pizza too
oh forgot to tell you I like pizza too!

Mycahe Dillard, Grade 3
Briargrove Elementary School, TX

My Friends and Family

My family is sweet,
My friends are kind.
When we are on the teeter-totter,
They sure are kind.
When we're on the monkey bars,
They're more encouraging.
I like my friends and family!
I like it when they come over.
We play lots and lots of fun games.
Like Twister, now that is fun!
I also like going over to my friend's house.
My friends and family.

Megan Young, Grade 3
Kootenai Valley Christian School, MT

Me
Me
Exciting, fun
Nice, crazy
Sometimes I'm sad
Sweet
Samantha Moody, Grade 3
Gold Canyon Elementary School, AZ

Sweet
The stars are bright
And so are you
Flowers are sweet
And so are you

A radio is loud
And so are you
The brightest things are
So bright just like you

A tree is green
And so is a bird's wing
A bracelet is cool
Just like you

The world is special
And almost like you
The things I do are
Just like you

Fruit is good as you can be
Almost the thing you can do
After night I look up at
The sky and see someone's pie
Brandy Ruiz, Grade 3
Los Padillas Elementary School, NM

Candy
My cotton candy is pink.
I will eat it in a wink.
So you better watch out,
Because I might pout.
If you make a batch that stinks.
Crystal Condado, Grade 2
C C Hardy Elementary School, TX

Christmas
Santa, cold, toys,
Green, red, yellow,
It is Christmas
Audrey Johansen, Grade 1
Thomas Edison Charter School, UT

Deadly Cupcakes
Cupcakes are
deadly,
they choke you, they make you hyper,
sticky.
One day they will take
over the world.
Watch out for cupcakes.
Brycen Jones, Grade 3
Acacia Elementary School, AZ

Volcanoes
Volcanoes
Dangerous, destructive
Shooting, running, exploding
Volcanoes make new land
Exploding mountains!
Andrew Cooper, Grade 3
Four Peaks Elementary School, AZ

My Little Brother
My brother is cute
When I play with him
He laughs
He smiles
When I say Boo!
He laughs
And when I Say peek-a-boo!
He laughs
Sometimes I make him smile
Sometimes he gets scared
Then he cries a little bit
And sometimes
He cries a lot
sometimes he licks his toys
I love my brother a lot
Ricardo Hernandez, Grade 3
Edison Elementary School, CA

The Park
The park is a wonderful place to go.
Children going down slippery slides,
or playing tag.
Squishy sand going through your hands,
Singy swings going up, down, and around.
Warm monkey bars going side to side.
The park is a wonderful place to go,
you should go too!

Jade Huerta, Grade 3
Vine Elementary School, CA

Footballs
F antastic
O utstanding
O utrageous
T he
B est
A ll star
L iving
L egend
S port

Cole Goldklang, Grade 3
Solana Santa Fe Elementary School, CA

The Cat and the Man
There was a cat and a man.
They both were named Dan.
The man worked in a barn.
And the cat played with yarn.
For dinner, they ate tuna out of a can!

Ezana Foster, Grade 3
Wonderland Avenue Elementary School, CA

Chickens
Chickens are cool,
Chickens don't drool,

Chickens run 'round,
Pecking at the ground.

Chickens go cock-a-doodle-doooooooo!!!
While the cows go moo!

Javan Bridger Zadrozny-Hier, Grade 2
New Emerson School, CO

Candy
Pink, blue
sticking, eating, fluffing
soft, sweet, fluffy, sticky
Cotton Candy
Emily Dimas, Grade 2
C C Hardy Elementary School, TX

My Cousin Willian
My cousin Willian
Likes to play Playstation
If you want to play Playstation
With him he will say "Yes"
He will play for one whole hour
When he comes to San Diego
He plays Playstation
He doesn't have one at
his house
He likes car games.
We have a game that has
amazing cars on it
he likes fantastic cars
I like my cousin.
Christian Mendez, Grade 3
Edison Elementary School, CA

Letting My Heart Be
My heart tells me
if it is right or not.
No more fighting
with friends.
I'm letting my heart be.
My heart is the boss
of my mind.
It is fun listening
to my heart.
Alexis Gonzales, Grade 1
Lee Richmond Elementary School, CA

Butterflies in the Wind
In the blustery wind
butterflies fly in the breeze
at the streaming river.
Sammi Ferrato, Grade 3
Four Peaks Elementary School, AZ

Spring
I love spring
and I love bugs.
I like fresh air.
My mom plants flower seeds
and in three days you see
the beginning of flowers.
Frank Infante, Grade 3
Midland Elementary School, CA

Bunnies
They have big, long ears.
They are fluffy, with big teeth.
And they love veggies.
Sonia Arredondo, Grade 3
Hood Case Elementary School, TX

One Night*
The night has come.
A potato bug lands on a flower.
A skunk walks in the forest.
It is very beautiful.
The stars are shining
on a chain of moon.
Skunk darts behind a tree,
comes out from behind it.
The skunk is fuming "odorously."
It is very beautiful
by the still pond.
Skunk waits,
skunk stands quiet.
The sun comes up.
It is very beautiful.
Natasha Lasky, Grade 3
Carlthorp School, CA
*Inspired by Guillaume Apollinaire.

Stars
S leeping in the night
T rying to catch the moon
A s they stand on your arm
R ising to the sky
S hining like the sun
Michael Ramirez, Grade 3
Emerson Elementary School, TX

Rainbow

Red is the color of love for my mommy.
Orange is the color of the good-smelling rose.
Yellow is the color of a smiley face.
Green is the color of the grass in the spring.
Blue is the color of the sky in the morning.
Purple is the color of my favorite crayon.

Kinsey Hartung, Grade 1
Grace School, TX

Friends

My best friend Zack!
He likes to play tag,
But he can't catch me,
I am fast as can be.
When I come out he wants to fight,
So I run to the right.
And he yells, "I quit!"
I tell him to come on friend just look up,
You can find me behind the truck.
Off we go to find a new adventure,
Just me and my friend Zack.

Ben Powitzky, Kindergarten
Presbyterian School, TX

Volcano

Volcano
Exploding, destructive
Burning, erupting, booming
Volcanoes have melted rock called lava.
Exploding mountain.

Ryan Wood, Grade 3
Four Peaks Elementary School, AZ

Summer

Summer, summer
I love summer.

Summer is when you grow flowers.
Summer is when my birthday is.

Summer is when you go swimming.
Summer is when the sun is shining bright.

Marissa Hoeck, Grade 2
Frontier Valley Elementary School, CO

Cymbals
Go cymbals, go!
Twirl in the twilight.
Spin things,
rattle things,
make things move.
Crash your golden body.
CRASH!
BANG!
CRASH!
BANG!
crash,
bang.
Martha M. Pirtle, Grade 3
Writers in the Schools Program, TX

Pebble
My
P
e
b
b
l
e
Is black
Not white
It is hard
Not soft
Brooke Jones, Grade 1
Fir Grove Elementary School, OR

My New Friend
On the desert it was a sunny day
It was any trip…so far away
It met a cactus who waved his arm
His cactus stickers meant me no harm
Bailee Brookshire, Grade 3
Cubberley Elementary School, CA

Shark
Toothy, translucent
Shark is very mean to me and
I run from the shark.
Garrett Colton Dews, Grade 3
Our Lady of the Snows School, NV

Joy
Joy is the color of brown.
It sounds like a party.
It smells like brownies.
It tastes like truffles.
It looks like the sunshine's rays.
Joy feels like kisses and hugs.
Fiona Wilcox, Grade 1
CLASS Academy, OR

How to Score a Homerun
I'm up next of course I will do it.
The pitcher pitches
Crack crack crack.

I made it. I made it. I think I am
I'm running as fast as I can
Run run run

A tear just swishing off of my face.
Will I? Do I run to home base?
Go go go.

I slide and I glide and I slide
I think I made it
Just waiting for the dust to clear off.

I hope I won't
Cough cough cough

Yay yay yay
I won. I won
But now that I noticed,
It's 3 to 1.
Tony Talushllari, Grade 3
Briargrove Elementary School, TX

Snake
S lithering across the ground
N ow trying to
A pproach
K eeping quiet to catch its prey
E ating it at the end.
David Robles, Grade 3
Emerson Elementary School, TX

Hummingbirds
Hummingbirds flying
Really fast, eating nectar
And enjoy playing
Kristen Lynem-Wilson, Grade 3
Wonderland Avenue Elementary School, CA

Thankful
Roosters cock-a-doodle-dooing,
Pumpkin pie right when you wake up,
Touching sticky, raw meat for meat loaf,
Coyotes howling at night...
These are things I'm thankful for!
Tim Schlum, Grade 3
Four Peaks Elementary School, AZ

Roses...Are Friends
Roses are red...violets are blue,
I lick a sweet candy and you lick it, too.

'Cause we are friends...do not drool,
You helped when I almost failed school.

Friends are people...I can depend on, too,
My friends are so cool they'd like even you!!
Summer Latimore, Grade 2
DeQueen Elementary School, TX

If I Were a Color
If I were light blue
I would be a fresh ice water.

If I were red
I would be a tasty raspberry or a cranberry.

If I were pink
I would be a flamingo or salmon.

If I were yellow
I would be a sour lemon or lemonade.

If I were orange
I would be delicious orange juice.
Raquel Ledezma, Grade 3
St Dorothy School, CA

Iguana
Little iguana,
very cute with lots of scales
has greenish long tail

Brittany Mathis, Grade 3
Lorenzo De Zavala Elementary School, TX

Flowers and Lemons
Nature feels like it is cold.
It tastes like crusty crabs.
Nature smells like yellow flowers
and yellow lemons.

Fabian Campos, Grade 1
Robert L Stevens Elementary School, CA

Pets
Dog
cute, playful
running, barking, biting
Golden Retriever, bone, mice, feline
climbing, scratching, chasing
ugly, flexible
Cat

Kyle Feng, Grade 3
Kathy L Batterman Elementary School, NV

In the Summertime
Why are the children playing all day?
Today is the first day of summer.
It is a sunny Saturday.
There will be no loud thunder.
All the happy children are at the beach.
Their mothers are watching them play.
Their teachers can't wait to teach.
Soon it will be a fall day.

Anthony Maximov, Grade 2
St John of San Francisco Orthodox Academy, CA

Lion
The lions are the kings of the jungle.
They roam fearlessly in the jungle.
They hunt in packs and they protect their cubs.

Xavier Pulikkathara, Grade 2
Montessori Learning Institute, TX

Winter

Winter is a glistening time,
It's hours of gliding down hills in a line.
Slippery ice under our feet,
A blizzard is what we soon will meet.

Glistening snowdrifts on a frozen hill,
Powdery snowflakes give us a chill.
The blizzard will be freezing
Without a doubt.

But while the children play
The snowdrifts begin to melt away.
And some children may pout about this frosty land,
But soon winter will again be at hand.

Jenna Wisniewski, Grade 3
Marshdale Elementary School, CO

Excitement

Excitement is hot red.
It sounds like opening presents on Christmas day.
It smells like everything.
It tastes like barbecue sauce.
It looks like people waving their arms and kicking their legs.
Excitement feels like my nerves jumping up and down.

Piper Williams, Grade 1
CLASS Academy, OR

Active Jack

I'm a brother, I'm a cousin, but when I close my eyes I know I am more.
I'm a wound up puppy.
I'm a donkey kicking out of anger.
I'm a kickball flowing in the air.
I'm a clock ticking slowly.
I'm a math packet full of math problems.
I'm a mean, grumpy tiger hunting meat.
I'm a wave collapsing on the shore.
I'm a hockey stick slapping pucks in the goal.
I'm a frantic kid looking for my lost homework.
I'm a glove trying to catch a Yankee ball off a home run.
I'm a bald eagle soaring in the air.
When I open my eyes I'm more than that.

Jack Lutsky, Grade 2
Open Charter Magnet School, CA

Albuquerque's Drought
The roadrunners run
The rattlesnakes rattle
Mother Earth's throat is dry
From Father Sun
Sasha Held, Grade 3
Georgia O'Keeffe Elementary School, NM

Shocked
Shocked
If shocked were a color, it would be yellow
As yellow as a star in the sky.
If shocked were a taste, it would be lemon
As sour as a lemon can be.
If shocked were a feeling, it would be surprise
As you feel when you get an unexpected gift.
If shocked were a smell, it would be stinky
As garbage in the garbage can.
If shocked were a sound, it would be "buzz"
As the sound that a bee makes.
Shocked
Daniel Baudin, Grade 2
Grace School, TX

Dreams
D o whatever you want in a dream
R un with wild animals fly with an
E agle you never realize that it is
A mazing when you dream good, bad, and
M agnificently and boom to awaken
S o surprised to see it is just a dream.
Karen Olivas, Grade 3
Emerson Elementary School, TX

The Mud
The mud is gooey, it's very sticky.
I can't get out of this mud!
I'm jumping, climbing, clawing, and falling,
But I still can't get out of this mud!
I have to be calm, very, very calm
So that I can get out of this gooey, gooey mud.
Will I grow old in this mud?
Will I? Will I?
Turner Patrick Givens, Grade 3
Writers in the Schools Program, TX

Dolphins
Dolphins
Slick, blue
Jumping, splashing, swimming
Dolphins have blowholes.
Porpoises
Bailey Clark, Grade 1
Myatt Elementary School, TX

Red
Red, red
Hello red.
Welcome to the bright red.
Red, red
Let's cheer for red.
Red rose,
Red balloon,
Red raspberries,
Red stop signs.
Yeah, let's hear it for red!
Rahyl Nathoo, Grade 2
Grace School, TX

Spaceships
Flying through the air
like an enormous
bird of prey.
Stewart Aslan, Grade 3
New Emerson School, CO

Sun
Sun is bright and warm.
It is a wonderful gift.
It's truly the best.
Elizabeth DalBello, Grade 3
Grace School, TX

Spring Is Here
Spring is here,
I love how the
Butterflies come out
And watch the flowers bloom
In color.
Jack Breen, Kindergarten
The Presentation School, CA

Planet
If I were a planet
I'd see the stars
I'd float in space
I'd go around the sun
If I were a planet

Jeremy Hochberg, Grade 1
Solana Santa Fe Elementary School, CA

My Dad
My dad is the best
he has black hair and brown eyes.
When we're ready to go to school he takes us.
"Good bye" I said.
The best thing about my dad is that he loves me
he likes when I give him hugs and kisses
but sometimes we dance.
When we go to stores he buys me anything
"What do you want sweetie" he asked
"No thanks dad just buy what you need
and save the rest for the bills." I said back.
Whenever I feel lonely he cheers me up.
I do the same when he feels lonely.
We love each other with our hearts.

Edith Perez-Toledo, Grade 3
Lincoln Elementary School, CA

Under Sea Life
Huge, heavy shark swimming quickly;
Giant squid floating calmly;
Salty green water making waves creatively;
Long jellyfish gliding gracefully.

Alex Smith, Grade 3
Fox Elementary School, CA

What Is Blue?
Blue is the color of the sky and blue as the sea.
Blue is like a little stripe of the rainbow
and blue is like a shirt that I wear.
Blue is like some paper
and like the bird that flies around.
Blue is the color of a book.
I like the color blue.

Marisela Escobar, Grade 2
Lincoln Elementary School, CA

Wouldn't It Be Funny?

Now, wouldn't it be funny
If the school were upside down,
And everyone in the school
Made no sound?
And wouldn't it be funny
If you wrote upside down,
And you would go to the principal
From school, you'd be bound?
And wouldn't it be funny
If we read upside down,
When we were reading
All we'd read were nouns!

Sophia Ortega, Grade 3
River Oaks Baptist School, TX

December

December is fun!
December is cold.
December is special.
The 25th of December is Christmas.
You get presents
And have a great big feast!

Jaymz Kirkpatrick, Grade 3
Crestview Elementary School, TX

Frosty Morning

Snow covers the ground
White sugar sprinkling
Morning dew
The frozen lake
The deer come out
To see winter beauty
The sky is blue
In the white wintery world.

Beth Strutz, Grade 2
Blue Oak Elementary School, CA

Basketball

Hoops, run
Shoot the ball
Feeling like a winner
Basketball

Jay Paul Rauscher, Grade 3
South Shore Montessori School, TX

Baseball

Baseball, baseball, baseball!
Baseball is fun!
I play baseball.

Baseball is the best!
I love it.
I am on the Cubs.

I am going to hit a home run!
I got hurt two times.
Home runs are hard to hit.
Baseball, baseball, baseball!

Raoul Lopez, Grade 3
Honey Hollow Elementary School, CA

Stars

The stars are twinkling
in the sky.
They are beautiful
when they twinkle.
They are so beautiful
like diamonds.
They sparkle
in the night.
I get out of bed.
I see them in the sky.
They twinkle in the night
SO bright
that they make me smile.
I'm so happy
when they twinkle.

Leslie Negrete-Martinez, Grade 1
Lee Richmond Elementary School, CA

Math and Language

Math
Difficult, hard
Adding, dividing, multiplying
Trick questions — writing words
Spelling, writing, challenging
Educational, hard
Language

Kyle Backhus, Grade 3
Turner Elementary School, TX

In My Dream

In my dream I was talking to God
In my dream I was saying
How my life would be and
How long I would live in my life
In my dream I saw the stars
And the moon at night
In my dream I was playing with God

Emani Black, Grade 3
Coeur d'Alene Avenue Elementary School, CA

Spring

Spring is the time of the year
when you go and play soccer, baseball,
or maybe even basketball.
In spring, you mow your grass
or water your plants.
Maybe clean your house and dust.
The animals come out from hibernation.
Trees, flowers, and roses start blooming.
Grass starts turning green.

Kale Alton, Grade 2
Walsh Elementary School, CO

1,200 Pounds

Bump
    Bump
Bump

1,200 pounds coming toward me.
What could it be?
    I will go see
An elephant coming right in front of me.

Rosio Aguilar, Grade 3
Lincoln Elementary School, CA

Snake Streams

I saw a stream with a snaky smile,
Its glowing eyes staring at me,
Squeezing through the rocks,
Slithering and sliding though the valley
Shedding its waves like skin,
Why are we afraid of it if it is afraid of us?

Joseph Park, Grade 3
Kyrene De Las Brisas School, AZ

Christopher
Brother
Blonde hair, blue eyes
Loves to play basketball
It's fun to chase him all around.
Fun boy
Sara Wray, Grade 1
Grace School, TX

A Water Fountain Sounds Like...
When it is raining
It sounds like a waterfall
Flushing the toilet
It sounds like a fish splashing
A rock splashing
It sounds like a roller coaster
Throwing rocks in the water
Breaking a branch
Loren Hergenrether, Grade 3
Fort Vannoy Elementary School, OR

Dolphins
Dolphins,
Helpful and smart
Leading the fisherman
  to a school of tuna
Can you spin and swirl?
Can I go with you?
Felicity Audin, Grade 1
Paonia Elementary School, CO

My Sister
My sister, she gave me a blister.
I wanted to sell her.
But instead, I kept her,
Because I love her!
Sophia Johnson, Grade 1
St Mark's Day School, TX

Spring
I go outside and swing,
I feel warm,
The rainbow makes colors in the sky.
Alex Molesworth, Kindergarten
The Presentation School, CA

Stumpy My Sweet Dog
Stumpy was sweet
Stumpy was calm
Stumpy like to run and play tag
Stumpy is in Heaven
And he was an angel
And he still is!
Ashton Fisher, Grade 2
New Emerson School, CO

Dogs
Sometimes furry
Sometimes biting
And all the time barking
And just being lazy
My dogs' names are Tula and Lucy
And I like it that way
Kelcee Mael, Grade 3
Gause Intermediate School, WA

School
S omething nice
C ool teachers
H omework is good
O f all good things
O ur special place to learn
L earn and teach
Nick Tagliarini, Grade 3
Four Peaks Elementary School, AZ

Time
Time is time
And a lime is a lime
There are
Minutes,
Seconds,
Hours,
And years
If you want to
Find out what
Time it is
Then just look at
A clock!
Isobel Curtin, Grade 3
Katherine Delmar Burke School, CA

Switzerland

S o cold up there
W hite snow up there
I like snow
T he ice is hard
Z innias are beautiful
E verybody stays in their houses
R eally icy
L iving there is ok
A nd if you step in the water you will freeze
N ever step outside
D aisies are not allowed to be picked

Natalie Burgermeister, Grade 3
Four Peaks Elementary School, AZ

Watermelon

Watermelon, watermelon nice and juicy,
It was all over my shirt,
I'm about to burp!
Watermelon so yummy it's already
Down in my tummy!

Bobbie Buchanan, Grade 3
Hood Case Elementary School, TX

The White Tiger

White tiger, white tiger,
did you put sugar on your face?

White tiger, white tiger,
did you hide your sugar in the snow?

White tiger, white tiger,
why does your body look like a white cotton?

Grace Kim, Grade 3
Cahuenga Elementary School, CA

Faith

Faith is light blue.
Faith sounds like ripples in the water,
Faith tastes like a warm cup of hot chocolate,
Faith smells like brownies cooking in the oven,
Faith looks like roses blossoming in the spring,
Faith makes me feel good and warm inside.

Cheyanne Miller, Grade 3
Highland Elementary School, CO

Horse
Runs on open plains
through the sparkling mountains.
It's as soft as silk
and sparkles in the wind.
It's pretty when it gallops
under diamond moons.
Shannon McNatt, Grade 3
Grace School, TX

Spring
Spring
Budding leaves, breezy winds
Roses blooming, growing, lovely
Leaves that feed the tree with nutrients
Wet, foggy season
Of cloudy skies
Jennifer Day, Grade 3
Morningside School, MT

I Have
I have a cat I like to hold.
I have a tooth made of gold.
I have a hat that is really old.
I have some food with mold.
I have a dog that has a cold
That is all I have.
Craig Nash, Grade 1
Thomas Edison Charter School, UT

Stallions
Stallions can run fast in water.
Stallions can have spots.
Stallions can be in books.
Stallions are pretty.
I like stallions.
Audrey Hudson, Kindergarten
Grace School, TX

Dogs Are…
Dogs are funny
Dogs are lazy
Dogs are fun!
Dogs are droolers
Dogs are bad
Dogs are good
Dogs are big
Dogs are small
Dogs are loud
Dogs are quiet
Dogs are playful
Dogs are naughty
And that's what dogs are.
Chelsea Bowers, Grade 3
Fort Vannoy Elementary School, OR

My Cat
My cat has a nose,
His name is Lowes,
He is fat,
He ate a rat,
And he has all of his toes.
Jason Koenig, Grade 3
Turner Elementary School, TX

My Senses
I like to taste sweet juicy peaches.
I like to see hairy animals at the zoo.
I like to hear the ocean waves.
I like to smell crunchy burned bacon.
I like to touch little baby bunny rabbits.
Eddie Hepburn, Grade 1
Grace School, TX

Summer
Summer is when you can…
go to the pool, play baseball,
play soccer, ride a bike and…

HAVE FUN!!!
Karli Behrens, Grade 2
Frontier Valley Elementary School, CO

Grandma Helen
Grandma
Baby-sits me sometimes
White hair, likes red
Miss her when I am not with her
Helen
Klayton Simonette, Grade 1
Grace School, TX

Many Cats

Cats, cats, there are mean cats
And nice cats, fat cats and skinny cats.

There are white cats and brown cats
Night cats and morning cats.

Cats, cats, all different kinds of cats.
Wild cats, mom cats and dad cats.

Dirty cats and clean cats
Cute cats and ugly cats.

I like cats!

Melissa Bower, Grade 2
Sangre De Cristo Elementary School, CO

My Cat Baby-Girl

My cat Baby-Girl loves to hide under the couch.
 loves to lick the inside of the toilet
 loves to be lazy and
 loves to eat.
She sometimes gets up to fight
 and run or to eat and
 move to another spot.
She hates other cats that don't live with her
 and likes to play with string
 and pony tails.
She climbs the curtains and goes
 on the top of the windows.
As you can see, she does funny things
 but that's not all.
 there's much, much more!

Sabrina Real, Grade 3
Acacia Elementary School, AZ

Dogs

Dogs are playful,
They are nice,
They are good listeners,
They are sweet and cute,
And they help all of the
People in the world.

Armine Gulyan, Grade 3
Tca Arshag Dickranian Armenian School, CA

Boots

Today is like any other warm spring day.
But it's that day, that very special day of my boots
Coming in from a long superior journey.

Shining bright like horse hooves clip clopping
Trying to win the race like a speeding rocket
Waiting to win
New smells flying through each corner of the house
Try and catch the smells or you'll miss it.
Speeding back down to the ground

Designs of curves and lines everywhere
Tapping to all the beats
All over the Earth.

Let me wear them for a year or two.
Let me clip them and clap them.
Let me follow them where we go
Let me

Let me wear them.

Haley Abramson, Grade 3
Horn Academy, TX

My Closet Is the Galaxy

My closet is the open galaxy
White shirts are asteroids
Multi-colored pants are the planets
The shorts are the moons
One of the hangers is a planet's ring
My closet is the endless galaxy.

My belts are the sun
Flying asteroids are like balls bouncing around everywhere
In my closet and in outer space
Some of the planets are bigger and some are smaller
Yet all of them are enchanting.

The sun is like a handful of fireflies
Both the sun and fireflies are incredibly bright
My enchanting closet is the vast galaxy!

Michael Swerdlow, Grade 3
The Mirman School, CA

Draco Lizard

Draco lizard flies
flies with wings that touch the sky
red, brown, green, and black

Marcos Herrera, Grade 3
Lorenzo De Zavala Elementary School, TX

He Stood

A light breeze blew in dandelion fluffs.
Some caught in his dark chocolate fur.
But on he stood, majestically.
The only sounds heard,
Were leaves and fluff,
Flying in the air.
The wind, softly blowing,
Wild geese honking, as they fly south.
And soft steps of squirrels,
Searching for food.
Finally, night came.
The Great Dane left,
Leaving the autumn world behind,
As he walked home.

Poorvaja Rajagopalan, Grade 3
Sexton Mountain Elementary School, OR

Toucans

Toucans are large birds.
They have multicolored beaks.
They live high in trees.

Tara Bevers, Grade 3
Lorenzo De Zavala Elementary School, TX

Maisy

She made me happy every day,
She romped and romped and loved to play
She never ever got tuckered out,
She was small, short and stout.
We loved each other there's no doubt
When she left I had to pout.
I just couldn't let her go,
So when she did I cried "OH NO!"
I think about her all the time.
That's why I wrote this special rhyme!

Alison Artzberger, Grade 3
Namaqua Elementary School, CO

Arctic Foxes

Arctic foxes with
snowy white fur and sharp teeth
hunt for white rabbits.
Gianna DasGupta, Grade 2
Northridge Elementary School, CO

Corretta Scott King*

Wife of Martin Luther King, Jr.
Mother of four children
Widow in her early years.

Dedicated to peace
Loved her children
Wanted white people to be friends
With black people

Fighting is never right
People need to get along
We work together every day
Never fight, ever!

We are all on the Earth
We need to share
And take care of others.
The best way is to treat everyone
The way you want to be treated.
Tyler Kirk, Grade 3
Garden Lakes Elementary School, AZ
*Dedicated to George Bush
and Mrs. Torrejos

Oh the Food We Can Eat!

Pumpkin soup,
Pumpkin pie
All the things I wonder why?
The corn, the bread
We have been fed

I love Thanksgiving

My friends and family love it too
With all the food that's fed to you!
Natalia Valentine, Grade 2
Foothills Elementary School, CO

Rock On!

I am
World traveling, soccer kicking,
French toast eating, cool boy.

I am
Sports playing, science
experimenting,
Baseball throwing, smart boy.

I am
Kickball pitching, reading person,
Family loving kid.

I am
Freeze tag tagging, hoop shooting,
Soccer saving, genius kid.

I am
Math testing, science balancing,
Football catching, little boy.

I am
Basketball fouling, math dividing,
2 square bobbling, sports champion.
Zach Saville, Grade 3
Briargrove Elementary School, TX

My Mom

My mom is nice
She can cook rice
We watch TV together
Sometimes we like the weather
American Idol is what we like
She has loved me since I was a tike
Paige Miller, Grade 2
Cottonwood Montessori School, NM

Seal

The seal is slow
They lay and swim in water
They eat fish
They sleep on the sand
Ahmed Husanovic, Grade 1
Phoenix Metro Islamic School, AZ

Sad!

I
once had
a puppy named
Shorty. But we had
to give her away to
my momma's friend at work. Now,
she is gone and I'm all alone.
Will I ever get another sweet little puppy?

Jesus Granja, Grade 2
C C Hardy Elementary School, TX

My Lovely Sunshine

You look like a rose
just getting ready to bloom
in early spring.

You look as pretty as an angel
in the sky.

You smell like dandelions and blossoms
in a field of love and kindness.

You make me feel like a warm angel
soaring to the bright light
ahead of me.

You sound like a red robin singing
more beautiful than anyone else could.

I know you will always be with me
because when I look at the sun and stars
I see your face.

Sean Parker, Grade 3
Wills Elementary School, TX

Baseball

Baseball is my favorite sport.
I like to bat and hit home runs.
I swing my arms and jump up high,
To catch a ball that comes flying by.
A good eye is all you need and lots of speed.
Baseball is the game for me!

Joseph Cummins, Kindergarten
Presbyterian School, TX

Football

If I were a football...
I'd hear people cheering,
I'd fly through the air like a helicopter,
I'd be so dizzy every day,
If I were a football...

Michael Antonorsi, Grade 1
Solana Santa Fe Elementary School, CA

The Face Creation

Draw my face as round as a pearl.
Paint my hair as light as the moon.
Paint my skin as tan as a donut.

Color my eyebrows as black as the galaxy.
Color my eyelashes as black as a tuxedo.
Shape my eyes as an oval as the oval itself.

Color my nose as pink as a flower.
Draw my mouth as wide as a candy bar.
Draw my teeth as black as a gorilla.

Draw my neck as blue as a blue jay.
Draw my ears as pink as bubble gum.

Benjiman Stiskin, Grade 3
Briargrove Elementary School, TX

Nature

Birds singing a song
Animals hunting for food
A cold windy breeze

The sun shines on us
The season I love the best
To swim and enjoy

Shivering branches
Colorful leaves flying high
Like dancing party

Trees bare like cold bones
Playing in the cold wet snow
Having lots of fun

Annie Ching, Grade 3
Purple Lotus International Institute, CA

Ladybugs

Ladybugs have lots of spots.
Ladybugs can land on you.
Ladybugs fly up high.
Ladybugs are good luck.
I like ladybugs.

Elizabeth Cole, Kindergarten
Grace School, TX

Fireflies

Fireflies
Nice and beautiful
Shine your light
Pretty as Christmas
I wish people didn't hurt you.
Fireflies

Madelyn Carlson, Grade 2
Grace School, TX

Cats

Cats
Furry, soft
Purring, meowing, scratching
Cats like to play
Kitties

Nate Montalvo, Grade 1
Myatt Elementary School, TX

Tigers

Tigers
Striped, soft
Hunting, running, scratching
Tigers eat meat
Cats

Fernando Miranda, Grade 1
Myatt Elementary School, TX

Jesus

J ustice
E verywhere
S in saver
U nbelievable
S avior

Lauren Lloveras, Grade 3
Grace School, TX

Page 53

I Can Fly Through the Wind

The wind takes me over the trees
Over and over and over the trees
It takes me over the garden
I see lots of houses, too
It takes me over the mountains and back
I see snowy peaks, yes I do;
It takes me over the rainbow
And the wind slows down;
Then I slide down the rainbow
And I walk back home
Thinking, what a wonderful day!

Angela Takahara, Kindergarten
La Patera Elementary School, CA

Spring

The warm sun rising
Lighting everything up
Spring is coming soon

Nathan Lopez, Grade 3
Wonderland Avenue Elementary School, CA

My Little Sister

My sister's hair is soft as fur.
She chases me like a cat.
When we go to the store
She says "It's beautiful like me."
We go outside
The sun shined as we passed by.
It shined like fireworks.
When my mom buys her glitter
She puts it everywhere.
She is as cute as a butterfly.
We play hide and seek
And all the games that she likes.
When tears start going down her cheeks
She comes to me.
She puts her arms on my shoulders
And gives me a kiss.
I give her one too.
She always says "I love you"
So I say the same thing.
We also do the same thing.

Jessica Hernandez, Grade 3
Lincoln Elementary School, CA

My Dog
I mportant
S pecial
A mazing
B eautiful
E xciting
L azy
L oving
E xcellent
Blake Busta, Grade 2
Frontier Valley Elementary School, CO

Spring
Splish splosh splish splosh splish.
Spring is wet and windy weee!
Good for flying kites.
Calvin Miksell, Grade 3
Summit Elementary School, UT

Planes
Fly, fly, fly…
I look up to the sky
And hope to see a plane pass by.

Planes came to be
On Kitty Hawk in 1903,
With a dream to be free
And soar over the sea.

In the early years,
Pilots had no fear,
And the children would cheer,
When the planes flew near.

I've been in a plane before
And there is nothing I like more
Than watching the world below,
Living and moving so slow.

As the engines push it far,
Faster than a car,
The rocket reaches to the stars,
Trying to reach Mars.
Kyle Ruggaard, Grade 3
Four Peaks Elementary School, AZ

God and Jesus
You love me
And I love you too.
You fight the devil
There are lots of people
who help you.
God and angels
help you too.
Nick Foster, Grade 1
Lee Richmond Elementary School, CA

Seals
Seals can do tricks
sometimes with sticks

When the trainer calls
the seals will do tricks with balls

When seals play cards
it gets real hard

Watching seals is cool
especially when they're in the pool.
Laura Roberson, Grade 3
Robinson Elementary School, TX

Star
S hiny bright diamonds
T wirling in the sky
A lone as the sun
R ises.
Aileen Chacon, Grade 3
Emerson Elementary School, TX

Thankfulness
I am thankful for my dad
Because he's never bad
He always like to play
And listens to music every day
He likes to talk
And go on walks
Dad has big feet
He eats a lot of meat
Moses Leon, Grade 2
San Jacinto Elementary School, CA

Where Has My Soccer Ball Gone?
Oh where, oh where, has my soccer ball gone?
Oh where, oh where, can it be?
I played with it last night while watching rugby.
Oh where, oh where, can it be?
Oh where, oh where, has my soccer ball gone?
Oh, have I reason to dread?
Yes, I just remembered where it lies now —
Oh yes, it's under the bed.

Jeremy Colvin, Grade 3
River Oaks Baptist School, TX

Running
When the gun sounds the people take off.
Some run, some jog, some walk.
Wind blows as runners pass.
Hands clap and snap at runners.
Mouths on people yell and scream.
Dogs bark
People whistle
Cow bells ring
Suddenly
The race ends
As the last person crosses the finish line.

Natasha Schepps, Grade 3
Horn Academy, TX

Bamboo
Bamboo is dark green,
They are so tall and sturdy,
Leaves shoot out like swords.

Hannah Blume, Grade 3
Wonderland Avenue Elementary School, CA

Flowers
Oh flower oh flower my precious little thing
How I adore your colors and your wing
Your petals shine at night
Glistening and glittering what a wonderful sight
I love the way you smell like fresh air at night
And the way you twinkle during my sight
Oh you're the one for me
Oh flower don't you see

Matilda Donovan, Grade 3
Solana Santa Fe Elementary School, CA

Two Friends

They are my best friends
Their names are Nathan and Nick
They make me happy
David Larragueta, Grade 3
Our Lady of the Snows School, NV

Stars

Stars
Twinkle in the sky
How I see it
They are up high
Over our heads
They help us
Sleep and snooze and doze
Stars, stars
Kennedy Von Halle, Grade 1
Scenic Park Elementary School, AK

Dear Snow,

You fall to make
A nice soft blanket of
White
Then it all piles up
To make
A snowman
Then when the glistening
Sun comes out
It melts and waters
The grass
But it was fun to play
While you were here
Like sledding and
Skiing.
Weston Rasmussen, Grade 2
Heatherwood Elementary School, CO

Winter

Winter
Cold, dark
Shiver, play with the snow, slide
Snow is like crystals from the clouds.
Icy
Seong Yun, Grade 3
Zuni Elementary Magnet School, NM

The Deer

Deer can fight.
Deer can run.
Deer can jump.
Deer can stab with their horns.
I like deer.
Jake Van Dorfy, Kindergarten
Grace School, TX

Sun

Glowing ball of gas
Temperature really hot
Keeping us awake
Eduardo Martinez, Grade 3
Willard Elementary School, CA

Sports

Basketball with a hoop.
Baseball with a hard swing.
Football 100 yards.
Soccer — get the kick.
Those are just a few.
Ballet — let's dance.
Gymnastics — let's do the splits.
There's a couple more.
Swimming — going down.
Running — let's go! Come on!
Golfing — hit it soft, hit it hard.
Volleyball — lots of scratches.
Tennis — hit it across the court.
Skating — don't fall!
Rock climbing — that's a long way up.
I love sports.
Ashley Fuelts, Grade 3
Acacia Elementary School, AZ

The Desert

Come and explore the desert
Can you hear the snake slithering?
Can you see the scorpion stinger?
Can you taste the salty sand?
Can you smell the cactus blooms?
Can you feel the cactus thorns?
Jobim Powers, Grade 1
Paonia Elementary School, CO

Nature Feels Good
Nature smells like flowers and leaves.
Nature tastes like dirt.
Nature feels like soft animals.

Antonio Andrade, Grade 1
Robert L Stevens Elementary School, CA

Baseball
It is another typical Saturday afternoon in July
The sun is high in the sky burning up Houston
It is so hot and humid with no breeze

There's a large crowd to watch the big game
The crowd is getting steamed and hot
But not matter
They are so excited, noisy, nervous
They get hot and sweaty and very thirsty
Cold drinks refresh the crowd

The players race around the field
They appear confident and powerful
As they throw and hit

Now the game is winding down
One team will go home as the winner
And the other team will be exhausted
And disappointed

I love baseball

Andy Asano, Grade 3
Horn Academy, TX

Monkeys
Sweet little monkeys jump
around high in the trees.
I wish I was there.

Melanie Flores, Grade 3
Lorenzo De Zavala Elementary School, TX

Tree Frog
Slimy small tree frog
silly, sticky, colorful
beautiful, squishy

Shelby Lowell, Grade 3
Lorenzo De Zavala Elementary School, TX

Happiness

Happiness looks like the bright, hot, shining sun coming down on me.
Happiness sounds like a crowd cheering after a competition.
Happiness tastes like warm, tasty chocolate chip cookies right out of the oven.
Happiness feels like a newborn chocolate colored puppy.
Happiness smells like a beautiful red rose blooming out.

Erika Mullen, Grade 3
Canyon Rim Elementary School, CA

I Walk

I walk by the beach as lonely as can be.
I hear the waves crashing hoping that someone talks to me.
I finally meet someone but she goes away forever and ever.

Aubrey DelaRosa, Grade 2
Creslane Elementary School, OR

The Best Hamster in the World!

My hamster Lily, died on the 20th of March,
she was my best friend.
My mom said not to get a new one in a long time.
I liked to snuggle with her,
she felt like velvet,
I loved to play with her, she always won.
She died in her food bowl,
my mom said she was probably thinking of food when she died.
I want her back here with me,
I remember her cute little face,
she was so calm.
I got her Christmas 2004,
I read dwarf hamsters live up to 2 years of age,
maybe she is doing good in Heaven,
she never bit,
I miss her so much.

Hannah Barlow, Grade 3
Patton Elementary School, TX

Basketball and Football

My first favorite sport is football.
Second is basketball.
My favorite football player is Champ Baily.
Then my favorite basketball player is Allen Iverson.
My favorite football team is the Denver Broncos.

Bernard Chavez, Grade 3
Academy of Charter Schools, CO

Lucy

My eyes are as bright as rubies.
My smile is as cute as a flower.
My teeth are as bright as the sun.
My fingernails are as beautiful as Ms. Cantlon.
My hair is as soft as silk.

Lucy Roberts, Grade 2
CLASS Academy, OR

Pets

Pets are always sweet!
But they jump on my knee.
I don't know why.
But I'd also like to try!

Araxi Gindzhikyan, Grade 3
Tca Arshag Dickranian Armenian School, CA

Spring

Spring reminds me of flowers.
Flowers remind me of green grass.
Green grass reminds me of blue skies.
Blue skies remind me of beautiful blue birds.
Beautiful blue birds remind me of rainy days.
Rainy days remind me of spring.

Mackenzie Mitchell, Grade 3
Wiederstein Elementary School, TX

Pink

Pink is the color of tulips.
Pink is the color of a heart.
Pink is the color of lipstick.
Pink is the smell of the tulip.
Pink is the color of a bunny's nose.

Emily Yates, Grade 1
Solana Santa Fe Elementary School, CA

Fall

Leaves rustle under your feet
as people hurry by in a hustle and bustle.
The smell in the air is smokey,
as people inside are warmed by the fire.
Fall is breezy, windy too.
I like fall, but then again, I like spring, too!

Kaitlyn McLaren, Grade 3
Daves Avenue Elementary School, CA

Blue

Sad is blue
like running water.
It flows through my head
like a ball.
It makes me feel gushy
like an apple.
It makes me want to cry.

Caleb Grabendike, Grade 2
Northbridge Elementary School, CO

School

I love to play in the grass
Especially with my class
I like to have a fun day
School makes me want to stay
I love my school
Because I think it's cool
At school kids are smart
In the play we all have a part

Barbara Martinez, Grade 2
San Jacinto Elementary School, CA

If I Were a Whale

If I were a whale,
I'd swim in the deep blue sea.
I'd eat lots of krill, and
Dolphins would swim with me.
I'd spout water through my head,
And flip my flippy tail.
Oh, I wish I were a whale,
But I'm a kid instead.

Graham Nickel, Grade 2
New Emerson School, CO

Harriet Tubman

H arriet Tubman escaped
A nd she was born in 1820
R ailroad which was a secret network
R an looking for her freedom
I ndustrialization helped save slaves
E very day she worked as a slave
T ubman

Lester Flores, Grade 2
Pinnacle Charter School, CO

The Fish

Fish flying over the sky
Wishing to go back in the water
Trying to reach down in the water
But they couldn't reach down
So they had fun in the sky, flying

Sang Mee Ahn, Grade 3
Cahuenga Elementary School, CA

Thankful

The smell of California salt air
In the morning
On the porch
Fine sand running to the water
The feel of green grass on my feet…
That is what I'm thankful for!

Nicholas Larson, Grade 3
Four Peaks Elementary School, AZ

Winter's Night

Snow so icy,
so crunchy and cold,
snow flakes are falling,
with sleds and snow balls rolled.
We sleep in our beds,
during this wintertime,
listening for reindeers,
and bells to chime.
I wish for health,
and happiness for all,
and a happy New Year,
One and all!

Gabriela Marie Goffman, Grade 1
The Pegasus School, CA

If I Was in Charge of School

If I was in charge of school,
I'd chop off people's hair.
If I was in charge of school,
I'd tape you to a chair.
If I was in charge of school,
I'd smash a pumpkin on you
Then I'll be shouting…YAHOO!

Stajah Blue, Grade 3
Elmira Elementary School, OR

Change

Change has many meanings, such as:
In the morning, every morning,
I watch and wait
and see a burst of color
spurting out of the mountain...
and the color changes.

It becomes blue
with fluffy white marshmallow clouds
breezily dancing to a bird's melody all day...
and the feeling changes.

Then the darkness of night
comes falling down from the sky
like a feathery blanket
muffling the sounds of the city.
The hush spreads like a disease...
and the noise changes.

Clare Maloney-McCrystle, Grade 3
Daves Avenue Elementary School, CA

The Drum in the Orchestra

The drum in the orchestra is
louder than any other instrument
with its blanket of skin
on top.
Drum noise pops out
band-boom-boom-boom!
The ring of the bells
is hardly heard at all.
The drums *band-boom-boom-boom*
their wonderful noise
band-boom-bong-boom!

Erina Szeto, Grade 3
Carlthorp School, CA

A Golden Retriever

I wish I were
Golden
I would be at my house
Playing with my owner's friends and family,
smiling at them all!

Chris Reedy, Grade 2
University Park Elementary School, TX

School

I see my friends every day
When we get popcorn we pay
We play in the grass
And learn in our class
We always try our best
When we take a test
Each day we get better
And write nice letters

Joceline Pedraza, Grade 2
San Jacinto Elementary School, CA

Sad

Sad is blue
like rain water.
It sinks through my skin
like hot lava slowly oozing
from a volcano.
It feels like rain drops
are falling from my eyes.

Hannah Hitchcock, Grade 2
Northridge Elementary School, CO

The Flute

I like the flute,
Sounds very neat.
It only plays in my head magically.
So I like it.

Alina Kim, Grade 3
Cahuenga Elementary School, CA

When Leaves Change Color

When leaves change color
to red, orange and brown,
don't frown,
because fall is coming.
Bright colored leaves that
match the sun;
you will have great fun,
jumping in piles of Autumn leaves.
And when you are done,
you will have a plentiful feast
on Thanksgiving Day.

Jake Harrison, Grade 3
Notre Dame Catholic School, CA

Look at This

I am a
dog caring,
teeth brushing,
help teaching,
kid

I am a
paper making,
color drawing,
hard working,
kid

I am a
book writing,
cool making,
pencil writing,
kid

Atalie Lopez, Grade 3
Briargrove Elementary School, TX

My Dog

My dog
Is the coolest!

My dog jumps
When I tell him

My dog
Eats pancakes
On Sunday

My dog's
Eyes glow
In the dark

My dog
Is as white as
Snow White

My dog
Is a boy
That plays with a toy

Joseph Barragan, Grade 3
Los Padillas Elementary School, NM

Where, Oh Where?

Oh where, oh where, have my Skittles gone?
Oh where, oh where, can they they be?
I ate one last night while feeding the dog.
I ate one while seeing the sea.
Oh where, oh where, have my Skittles gone?
Oh where, oh where, can they be?
Yes, I have a reason to want more.
Oh yeah, they're on the kitchen floor!

Emma Taylor, Grade 3
River Oaks Baptist School, TX

Cupcake

If I were a cupcake…
I'd taste like frosting,
I'd smell like chocolate,
I'd be happy,
If I were a cupcake…

Katie Farhood, Grade 1
Solana Santa Fe Elementary School, CA

Dear Ice,

Why are you slippery
when I am walking.
You are covered with snow
but when the wind starts to blow
you shimmer and shine on the ground.

You are a very pale blue with a dab of white.

Did you know you shine like the moon
and you're the only thing like you.
You're one of a kind.
That's what you are.

Anna Colman, Grade 2
Heatherwood Elementary School, CO

I Dream of Shopping

I dream of shopping.
I dream of a mall where everything is on sale.
Malls that carry a lot of shoes.
Malls that sell everything you need.
I dream of shopping.

Brittany Nelson, Grade 3
Daly Elementary School, MT

Brown
Brown is the color of my hair.
I like brown bears.
I love when little brown bunnies hop.
I like brown.

Jacqueline Tullie, Grade 1
Solana Santa Fe Elementary School, CA

Pineapples
Pineapples are like hills with grass on them,
Bumpy like a roller coaster,
When I slice into it the juice comes oozing out
like lava from a volcano,
My taste buds wake up to the sweetness
like lemonade,
Book me a flight to Maui
I love pineapples

Jonathan Forsman, Grade 3
Daves Avenue Elementary School, CA

Martin Luther King Jr
M ade a speech called "I Have a Dream."
A boy, he was a boy.
R eally wanted people to love others.
T ried to help other people
I think all should love others he said.
N ever was mean.

L oved to help people
U nder danger people hated him.
T eenager — went to college
H e had a boycott.
E arned a lot of money
R eally wanted whites to love blacks.
Never hurt people.

K ind and nice he was.
I love all people he said.
N ever stopped loving others.
G uided boycott.

J unior was his last name
R eally wanted to help people

Lerae Trujillo, Grade 2
Pinnacle Charter School, CO

Sunset to Dusk from Dawn to Day

Darkness slowly covers the shining air.
It darkens the air to a point where you breathe out foggy mist air.
The shadow of your body disappears but not before saying goodbye before disappearing in the darkness.
I watched as quiet darkness spread and roamed the trees through the forest.
I looked through the dark shining window, I saw light come up and start to make morning shine.
As the little light started coming through the sky it soon made light in the house.
That's when day came like it suddenly went up to make daylight.

Jacob Maline, Grade 3
Lincoln Elementary School, CA

Winter Is

Winter looks like a season with bare trees,
And you can see people having fun.

Winter feels like a breeze just passed you,
And it also feels like you're in the opposite of summer.

Winter sounds like a happy season,
Because you can hear the joyful laughing of children playing.

Winter tastes like warm delicious hot chocolate,
And it also tastes soft like snowflakes.

Winter smells like a warm delicious smell,
If you walk around your neighborhood.

Aida Sidi, Grade 2
Hedgcoxe Elementary School, TX

Talking About Rosa Parks

R osa was born Feb. 4
O ctober met a guy.
S he really loved her mother.
A rrested for not giving her seat to a white person.

P arks had a lot of friends
A nice girl and famous
R osa expected respect
K icked off the bus
S he worked for civil rights

Kelby Jones, Grade 2
Pinnacle Charter School, CO

I Am

I am nice and friendly.
I wonder about the world.
I hear the birds chirping in the early morning.
I see the fading horizon in the dark.
I want a good world.
I am nice and friendly.
I pretend to fly far away in the sky.
I feel happy like it's Christmas.
I touch soft fur.
I worry about my dog if he runs away.
I cry about my family.
I am nice and friendly.
I understand my friends.
I dream of world peace.
I try not to be a whiner.
I am nice and friendly.
I am Ian.

Ian Kearns, Grade 3
River Oaks Baptist School, TX

My Friend

he is my best friend
he makes me really happy
he has a doggy
Giancarlo Franchesco Perano, Grade 3
Our Lady of the Snows School, NV

The Honest Days of Honest Abe

Abe was a very young lad
But he was terribly sad
His mom had died from milk of a cow
And now he is left with his dad

As he grew up with his charm
He had a romancing arm
Then he married a girl named Mary Todd
And he never meant any harm

There was a girl named Grace Bedell
She thought Abe was very swell
She inspired him to grow a beard
And he ran for President as well
Samantha Rose Abrams, Grade 3
Canyon Rim Elementary School, CA

Butterflies

I like butterflies!
Butterflies can fly in the air.
Butterflies can connect nectar.
Butterflies are different colors.
Butterflies make me happy.
I like butterflies!
Nicholas Sion, Kindergarten
Grace School, TX

Springtime

Petals fall softly,
Sun flows in,
Crunch, crunch, crunch,
Deer run through the woods.
Flowers spring up with pride,
Petals fall softly down, down
Drip drop drip drop
Spring is lovely.
Jack Murray, Kindergarten
The Presentation School, CA

Puppies

Very playful
Sometimes tame
Always there
Great friends
Different barks
Sometimes scratching
Great smell
Good hearing
Wonderful puppies
Trenton Telge, Grade 3
Grace School, TX

The Stars

Are the sun and moon's kids
Who stay in the sky
Forever and ever
Looking down from heaven
Twinkling and sparkling
Like shiny ice.
Kyler Newton and Christian
Schenker, Grade 1
Juneau SDA School, AK

My Mom
My mom is so sweet,
she tucks me into bed.

I feel so safe and warm,
when she holds me tight with all her might.

My mom.
Alyssa Jasso, Grade 2
Lincoln Elementary School, CA

Hummingbirds
Two green humming birds
Fly on the sea of blue sky
Near paper white clouds.
Gabriel Fields, Grade 3
Wonderland Avenue Elementary School, CA

My Home
When I come home,
I hear welcome home.
I see my mom and dad and sister.
And my dog coming up to me.
I smell a big feast.
I smell candles lit.
It feels great to be home safe and sound.
I love hugs and kisses
And my dog licking my face.
Hailey Straub, Grade 3
Four Peaks Elementary School, AZ

The Army
In the old days,
They fought with swords, staffs, daggers,
Bows and arrows.
They rode horses.
They protected our country.

Now, they wear camouflage clothes.
They fight with all sorts of weapons.
They drive tanks, airplanes, jets,
Helicopters, boats, jeeps.
They protect our country.
Andrew Wilhite, Grade 1
Twin Lakes Christian Academy, TX

Black Cat
I saw a black cat
It was super fat.

I saw a black cat
It ate a rat.

I saw a black cat
The cat was a brat.
Alex Smith, Grade 3
Four Peaks Elementary School, AZ

Blue Jay
The song of a Blue Jay,
Fills joy in the air.
The sound,
The song,
Mixes together,
That forms a delightful air.
With love you must keep
It safe with care,
Close with you,
And the air.
It will sing a song,
That adores your care.
Just as long as you,
Remember the Blue Jay.
Brooke, Grade 3
Katherine Delmar Burke School, CA

Fall
The summer moves on
Beautiful leaves cover earth
Rays of sun peek through.
Jack Romo, Grade 3
Lanai Road Elementary School, CA

I Wish...
I wish I were a cloud,
making different shapes,
when I get full I rain,
nothing cheers me up,
even if people are happy.
Eve Javey, Grade 3
Daves Avenue Elementary School, CA

Zoo on Wheels
Have you seen the zoo?
It's like my mom's car.
It has dust-bunnies,
Lint-rhinos,
Straw-elephants,
Paper-monkeys,
But the Jelly-stain-giraffes
Are for me.
A.J. Hampton, Grade 2
Criswell Elementary School, TX

Teacher
Teacher
Nice, sweet
Helping, caring, doing
Very nice to us
Helper
Johnny Rodakis, Grade 3
Four Peaks Elementary School, AZ

Baseball in the Spring
Baseball is a fun springtime sport.
They don't play baseball on a court.
At a baseball game you get to bat.
You wear a helmet as a hat.
Batting is very fun.
You can get a homerun.
There are seven minutes in an inning.
The Redhawks are winning.
I would like to learn to pitch.
Maybe someday I could get rich.
Dustin Portra, Grade 3
Froid Elementary School, MT

Noorhan
N oorhan is good at running.
O ften does art.
O r plays games.
R eads very well.
H elps people a lot.
A lways tries her best.
N ever hurts kids at school.
Noorhan Monther, Grade 2
Phoenix Metro Islamic School, AZ

October

October October
I like October.
October is cooler.
In October leaves are falling to the ground.
October has some colorful things.
People are trick or treating in October
Because it is Halloween in October.

Madeline White, Grade 2
St Mark's Day School, TX

Snails

Hard shells,
Slimy body,
Barely seeing night and day.
Moving slowly,
Down the pathway.
As they go along their way.
They're nocturnal and use antennae eyes,
Due to not having ears.
I am fascinated with these little creatures,
And watch them often at night.

Cooper Braverman, Kindergarten
Presbyterian School, TX

As I Look Outside My Window

As I look outside my window
the bare winter trees seem to glow
As I look outside my window
the frost piles on the window glass
while everyone dreams
through the night
As I look outside my window
the millions of stars brighten the sky
As I look outside my window
I see the faces of my beloved ones
who had their last word
As I look outside my window
the snow skips down from the sky
As I look outside my window
my eyes start to doze
and I crawl into my bed
and dream of another night like this.

Rachel Savage, Grade 3
Westwood Charter Elementary School, CA

Mountain
We live on a mountain.
We drink from a fountain.
And we eat the meat
That we tenderize with our feet!
Trey Taylor, Grade 3
Sundance Elementary School, WY

Brother
Brother
Sweet, kind
Loving, caring, playing
I love my brother
Boy
Kylee Poole, Grade 3
Four Peaks Elementary School, AZ

Bunny
He nibbles my heels
he needs to eat off brown wheat
Like a cotton tail.
Connor Brewster, Grade 3
Our Lady of the Snows School, NV

Boys and Girls
Boys
Rough, climbing
Running, sports, loud
Hyper, brother, sister, sensitive
Pretty, nice, shopping
Clean, sweet
Girls
Kate Conklin, Grade 1
Armstrong Elementary School, TX

Grizzly Bears and Polar Bears
Grizzly Bears
Brown, black
Running, climbing, growling
Standing, huge, hibernating, swimming
Fish, white, Arctic
Iceberg, camouflage
Polar Bears
Coco Murchison, Grade 1
Armstrong Elementary School, TX

Soccer
Coach is great.
I can't wait.
Saturday the big game.
Pass back and forth.
Score a goal.
This is the best of all.
Keeper guards the goal.
It is great.
I can't wait.
Saturday the big game.
Janet Toller, Grade 3
Acacia Elementary School, AZ

Confusion
Confusion is steaming green.
It sounds like a train.
It tastes like raw fish.
Looks like a white room.
Confusion feels like blowing up.
Alex Itkis, Grade 2
CLASS Academy, OR

Four Seasons
In spring there are many flowers
Some are pink and blue.
Most of them smell very good
They all look fresh and new.

In summer I have a lot of fun
Even though it's very hot.
Sometimes I eat ice cream
But in summer I eat it a lot.

In fall it's very windy
Leaves are scattered on the ground.
The leaves are pretty colors
When they fall they don't make a sound

In winter it is very cold
And there's a lot of snow
You go sledding down the hills
And hope the wind won't blow.
Emily Gilbertson, Grade 3
Woodcrest School, CA

God

God is great.
God is the greatest in the whole world.
God is the most powerful person on Earth.
He created the Earth.
He made you and me.
He made our parents.
He is my Father in Heaven.

Eli Alspaw, Grade 3
Kootenai Valley Christian School, MT

My Home

The birds singing a poem just for me.
They are so happy I am home.
The sights look beautiful,
More beautiful than the woods.
The sun is a bright light through the windows.
The dinner tastes delicious, nice warm bread.
Feels like people hugging me,
Dog licking my face,
And knocking me over.
Just feels like finally I am HOME!

Cory Kukkola, Grade 3
Four Peaks Elementary School, AZ

The Seasons

In winter the icy wind
kisses your face like the first sight of love.

In spring the sun shines on you
like a star at night.

In spring when you look at the leaves
they start to bloom.

Devon Catindig, Grade 3
Northgate School, WA

Halloween Ghost

Halloween ghost are with us.
They see whatever we do.
Some of them are humans that turn into ghosts.
Some ghosts are nice but some are mean.
Danny Phantom is the ghost who is very nice.

Faria Ara Putal, Grade 3
Cahuenga Elementary School, CA

Grandparents

G randparents are fun to be with
R eads a lot to me
A good person to be with
N ever is mean
D oes a lot of fun things
P erfect people
A lways nice
R espectful to me
E xperienced a lot of things
N ice people
T rustworthy

Jalin Yoder, Grade 3
Four Peaks Elementary School, AZ

Bear

When I see a bear I think of the roar.
I sense danger
As it runs through my mind.
Black Bear

Kole Schell, Grade 3
Sundance Elementary School, WY

Mom

Mom looks like a rose,
Getting ready for spring,
Mom smells like blossom,
And looks like one too,
Mom sounds like a bird singing,
Like it is having a baby,
Mom tastes like a chocolate ice cream,
She always feels happy for her family.
Latonia

Brenna Nez, Grade 2
Ganado Primary School, AZ

The Mermaid

Prettily,
Beautifully,
Amazingly,
The mermaid
Was sitting on a rock.
— Ooh!

Kadiesha Watts, Grade 1
Fir Grove Elementary School, OR

Hawaii

H appy place to be
A good place to relax
W aves crashing in the background
A fun time to run around
I like playing games
I t's cool to look at the seals

Reid Sanchez, Grade 3
Four Peaks Elementary School, AZ

Mom

Smells nice like a rose,
Pretty like a blue bird,
Singing in a tree,
Her laugh is like
A happy voice,
Sometimes it is an angry voice,
Her hair is like a pillow made from
A sheep fur,
It is soft like a blanket,
Tastes like a banana,
Smells like a strawberry.
Sheryle

Marshall Begay, Grade 2
Ganado Primary School, AZ

Oceans

The ocean is zooming
rushing and rolling
with the waves
they are mixing
with the loud noise
the waves are going
90 m.p.h. like a car.

Kyle Baker, Grade 3
Lincoln Elementary School, CA

Spring Flowers

Spring flowers are red and blue.
They look like they like you.
They are tossing and turning
when the wind is blowing.
Then I think it's snowing.

Tashina McMaster, Grade 3
Academy of Charter Schools, CO

Abstract Art

Enormous lion eating and attacking;
Minuscule, small-brained person watching;
Immense tree standing and waiting;
Long branches engraving trees.

Thomas Babb, Grade 3
Fox Elementary School, CA

Tree

oh tree do
you ever get tired of
standing all day with your
leaves falling off to the ground
oh tree do you ever get cold
in winter or hot in summer
or tired of the rain in
spring or do you get tired
of your leaves falling
off in autumn
I wonder
of these
things
how
do you
survive
with all
of this?

Joanna Walsh, Grade 3
Wonderland Avenue Elementary School, CA

Wouldn't It Be Funny?

Now, wouldn't it be funny
If the humans were the pets,
We would be fed outside
If you got away, the animals caught you in nets?
And wouldn't it be funny
If animals told you to fetch
They threw a ball very high
It would be hard to catch!
And wouldn't it be funny
If they took me on a walk
They would take me to a park
The animals would know the words we talk!

Jackson Irby, Grade 3
River Oaks Baptist School, TX

I Try

I try not to anger my friends.
I don't disturb my parents
when they're talking.
I don't disturb my sister.
I don't shove a person
out of the way.
I know Jesus is watching
the same as my parents.

I never say, "Give me it now."
I say, "May I please have it?"

And I do say that.

Austin Barthel, Grade 3
Briggsdale Elementary School, CO

Dear Blizzard,

You look like
Hundreds of sprinkles
Shimmering
In the moonlight
And you make
A sparkling white
Thick blanket
Of snow

Catherine Kuhn, Grade 2
Heatherwood Elementary School, CO

I Am a Hawk

I am a hawk.
I live in the mountains.
I live at the top.
I live in a cave.
I have brown, black and white feathers.
I spot a gray dot in the valley below.
I take off to get it.
I fly like the wind but I have to stop.
I land like a plane by the meadow.
I catch that gray dot, then I fly away.
I go to the mountains.
I land at the top and eat the gray dot.
I am a hawk.

Claire Fitzgerald, Grade 2
CLASS Academy, OR

Places

School
fun, boring
teaching, working, learning
teacher, student, Adam, Justin
playing, running, jumping
fun, cool
Home

William Hunt-Webster, Grade 3
Rogers Elementary School, NV

Snowflakes

Big ones
Small ones
Skinny ones
Fat ones
Snowflakes
Everywhere
In my hands
On my pants,
On my big fat coat.
Snowflakes dark
Snowflakes light.
Heavy ones
Light ones.

Allison Hamel, Grade 2
Frontier Valley Elementary School, CO

Books

Big books
Small books

Thin books
Thick books

Chapter books
Cool books

Weird books
Adventure books

Everywhere there are books
Every kind of book is cool.

Taylor Hooten, Grade 3
Robinson Elementary School, TX

Monsters

M onsters
N ibble
O n
P aper
Q uilts

Eric Oh, Grade 3
Wonderland Avenue Elementary School, CA

Statue of Liberty

S tanding tall to welcome,
T elling people freedom,
A lways looking for people to come to America
T o persuade people to come.
U nited States rocks!
E verything is cool, especially the Lady Liberty.

O nly the Statue of Liberty, a symbol of America,
F reedom for everyone.

L ive peacefully in America,
I slands to see.
B eautiful places.
E veryone is nice.
R etake your life and stay.
T all Lady Liberty to welcome
Y ou can be part of America!

Jefferson Lieu, Grade 3
Lafayette Elementary School, CA

My Garden

My garden has lots of flowers.
And we are planting them today.
I know what it looks like,
It looks like flowers on stems and some trees.
It's so beautiful!

Jadyn Ngai, Kindergarten
Jacob Wismer Elementary School, OR

Springtime

I like spring because trees and flowers grow.
The smell is so fresh when we plant.
There are a lot of bunnies in the springtime.

Esteban Hernandez, Grade 3
Midland Elementary School, CA

Like

A picture is like a painting coming to life in a dream
A flag is like a kind king that represents our country
Stars are like fireflies still in the sky
A home is like the owner that keeps you nice and warm and especially safe
Hair is like a blanket to keep your head warm, dry, and soft
Books are like entertaining words that keep us from television and chores
(Well, maybe not chores!)
Earth is like a home we will never leave and explore "forever"
Pluto is like a planet made of chilly, chilly cold, cold freezing, freezing ICE
A pencil is like a pen that can be erased with an eraser on the other side.

Sarah Works, Grade 3
Fort Vannoy Elementary School, OR

Macaroni and Cheese

Macaroni, macaroni, macaroni in a cheesy pot
fresh and cheesy and chewy.
Macaroni, macaroni, macaroni in a cheesy pot and very yummy.
Macaroni, macaroni in my tummy
rumbling grumbling in a tummy.
Macaroni and cheese!!!

Raynor Goh, Grade 3
Briargrove Elementary School, TX

My Closet Is...an Aquarium

My closet is an aquarium,
The aquarium is a magical world,
The plastic storage boxes are the fish tanks,
The shoes in the boxes are the fish,
The fish glitter in the golden water, which is really the closet light,
My socks are the sea urchins,
My shirts are the colorful sea plants covering the bottom of the aquarium,
My pants are the coral swaying with the water,
My sweatshirts are the evil sharks trying to eat the fish,
My shorts are the friendly dolphins swimming and playing,
My bathrobes are the puffer fish inflating and deflating,
The blue water in the aquarium is as shiny as silver,
I can hear the water move, "Swoosh,"
The light in my closet makes the aquarium glow,
As I step out of my magical closet,
The fish disappear.
This is my favorite room in the house.

Daniel Birnholz, Grade 3
The Mirman School, CA

My Sister, My Best Friend

My sister is my best friend
She makes me feel better when I am sad
She may have fights with me but
I still love her no matter what
She sometimes thinks I am annoying
But I think she is great
I love it when my sister plays with me
Because she never wins
I like my sister with all my heart
I do not know where I would be
Without her
My sister is perfect in my eyes
I would never make her a sacrifice
Like others would do to their sister
I want to be just like my sister
Because she is a wonderful person

Aleena Barash, Grade 3
Desert Mountain School, AZ

My Favorite Fish

My favorite animal is a fish,
The way I got it was,
I made a wish,
It is the best fish,
He knows how to make a wish,
And wash a dish.

I looked at him with my eye,
He looked like
He was going to die.

Menua Yesayan, Grade 3
Tca Arshag Dickranian Armenian School, CA

Not

I am nice, you are not
I am hot, you are not
I am cool, you are not
I am having fun, you are not
I am cold, you are not
The Earth is cold, the stars are not
The sun is hot, Pluto is not
He is cool, I am not.

Tristan Feniak, Grade 3
Delphi Academy of San Francisco Bay, CA

Cafeteria Food

The pizza's full of mold.
The drumsticks are moving.
The bread is as hard as a rock.
The lasagna has fungus.
The hamburgers have mushrooms.

The next time you go to school,
bring your own lunch.

Hayley Bruck, Grade 3
Carlthorp School, CA

The Race

The air feels so sweet like candy
We run like cheetahs
Far and near
Not tired until we fall
Our feet crunch the leaves
While our hands rip the air
We passed places
The air is still
Suddenly
The air feels sour again

Aishat Sadiq, Grade 3
Horn Academy, TX

Spring

Spring is my favorite season
and let me tell you the reason.
There's grass all around,
there are flowers on the ground.
There are kites in the sky
flying so high.
There are people in the park
playing until dark.
I like spring.

Dreydon Smith, Grade 2
Walsh Elementary School, CO

Cats

Cats prancing about
with their feet on the hard ground
licking with rough tongues.

Haley Chavez, Grade 2
Northridge Elementary School, CO

A Loon Who Had a Bassoon

There once was a loon
Who had a bassoon
When he played all day
People ran away
And went to the moon

Caitlyn Cameron, Grade 3
Gold Canyon Elementary School, AZ

Love

Love is fun!
Love, love love!
Love is cool!
I like love!
Love, love, love!
Love is snappy!
Love makes me happy!
Love, love, love!
Love is fun!
I can't stay without love!
I can't stop thinking about love!
Love, love love!
XO, XO, XO, XO, XO!

Marlene Orozco, Grade 3
Honey Hollow Elementary School, CA

Proud

Proud is yellow
like a sunflower.
It runs through my body
like rain falling.
It makes me feel happy.
It makes me want to smile.

Amy Zhou, Grade 2
Northridge Elementary School, CO

The Bird

I gave my bird a fat worm.
It gave a little squirm.
My beautiful bird stands firm.
The bird stands against the worm.
Oh my! The fat worm had germs.
The bird gets rid of the worm.

James Clancy, Grade 1
Montessori Learning Institute, TX

Cats Around the World
I see a fluffy cat
Fat cat, big cat

Small cat, short cat
Long cat, sad cat

Interesting cat, silly cat
Smart cat, dumb cat

Serious cat, mad cat
I see a cat

Around the world

Jonatan Garcia, Grade 2
Sangre De Cristo Elementary School, CO

I Love Spring
I love the weather in spring.
In spring birds will sing.
It rains when the sky is gray.
In the mud puddle I like to play.
The fluffy clouds are white.
The clouds are all right.
Thunder is loud.
Lightning comes from a cloud.
Sometimes the sky is green when I see hail.
This is the end of my tale.

Bailey Christoffersen, Grade 2
Froid Elementary School, MT

My Cat Trigger
My cat Trigger hops
Like he's bigger.

He plays with a key.
He plays with me.

He goes outside
And he plays on the slide.

He likes me
And he sleeps on my knee.

Kyle Freel, Grade 2
Sangre De Cristo Elementary School, CO

What If…
What if we had super powers,
If friendship could never end?
Sometimes I wonder…
How would it feel to lose a friend?

It hurts you, it breaks you,
It tears you apart.
It feels like a life you lost,
That was very dear to your heart.

I wonder how many things we worry about,
That don't mean anything at all?
But a friendship isn't just something…
It's worth more than all.

Samantha Pease, Grade 3
Frontier Valley Elementary School, CO

Love
Love is like a rainbow.
It is kind and beautiful.
It is very helpful and peaceful.
Let's reach out to the victims of the hurricane.
Let's give a hand and help them
And be friends to them.

Paul Andrew Ingram, Grade 3
Montessori Learning Institute, TX

Dear Jesus
Thank You Jesus for this day You gave to me.
Open my eyes so I may see

The stars
The heavens
The mountains
The trees

The wind
The flowers
The animals
The seas

Thank You for this day You gave to me.

Noah Hunter Vandenhouten, Kindergarten
Twin Lakes Christian Academy, TX

Colors
Colors are big
Colors are small
Colors are huge
Colors are nice

Yellow is warm
Red is super
Blue is fantastic
Black is night

Tim McKee, Grade 1
New Emerson School, CO

Anthony
Anthony is great.
I like to watch videos.
I can swim and dive.

Anthony Escarilla, Grade 1
Kimball School, WA

A Mouse
There once was a mouse
He lived in a house
He needed something to eat
So he went to get a treat
Then he sat in his house
And started to eat!

Matthew Chabala, Grade 2
Carden West School, CA

Wind
Rustling leaves fly by.
Beautiful sounds of whistling.
Spirit of the air.

Angela McWhorter, Grade 3
Grace School, TX

My Friend Is Fun
My friend is fun.
He likes to run.
He is a chum.
He likes to chew gum.
He is fun.

Jeffrey Annabi, Grade 1
St Mark's Day School, TX

I Wish

I wish
I were a flower,
Pretty, colorful and smelling good,
Then people will pick me.

I wish
I were a ring,
Sparkling rubies,
Solid gold,
People will wear me.

I wish
I were a paper,
To draw, write on, or print,
I will be thrown away to recycle into paper
To live again.

Jessica Maidman, Grade 3
Daves Avenue Elementary School, CA

Lollipops

Lollipops
Tasty, sticky,
Shrinking, sucking, biting.
Very yummy,
Candy.

Riley King, Grade 2
University Park Elementary School, TX

One Old Owl

One old owl sitting up on a tree.
In the peaceful night.
One old owl staring into the full moon.
One old owl rising up into the sky to fly.

Ashley Seigal, Grade 2
Horizons K-8 Alternative Charter School, CO

A Little Fish

There once was a little fish,
Who made a giant wish.
The wish came true,
Instead of red he was blue.
Then he splashed in the water with a "Splish!"

Emelia Lambros, Grade 3
Wonderland Avenue Elementary School, CA

Snakes
There are a lot of snakes,
like anacondas and pythons.
They are the biggest.
Yellow snakes, black snakes,
Those are just a few.
Poisonous snakes, venomous snakes,
Tree snakes and more.
Snakes are very scary.
Snakes are more scared of you
than you are of them.
Snakes are pretty animals.
How they slither.
There are about 5,200 species.
Angela DiOrio, Grade 3
Acacia Elementary School, AZ

Spring Freedom
Freedom
Glistening days
Shimmering, warming, jubilant
Mint-green grass blankets of flowers
Cover the garden.
Spring freedom has covered the city.
New season
Hannah Dutro, Grade 3
Morningside School, MT

Mermaid
Oh mermaid what shall we do?
We shall swim in the ocean.
But I cannot swim.
But we can play ball in the sand.
She said I cannot go in sand I will die.
I got her in the sand.
My great friend died.
Hannah Dobrott, Grade 3
Katherine Delmar Burke School, CA

Arctic Fox
Chasing rabbits fast
tails white and fluffy covered
chasing squirrels fast too.
Tristan Stomm-Hartford, Grade 1
Highland Park School, MT

Birds
Yellow beaks peck seed
Fine feathers sway with lightly winds
Strong wings fly swiftly
Annie Chen, Grade 3
Fox Elementary School, CA

Fairy
Oh fairies, oh fairies what nice wings,
How you fly, what marvelous things!
They are so beautiful and light,
Oh yes, and very bright!
Oh how you flutter and spin,
If there was a contest you would win!
Darien McMillan, Grade 3
Katherine Delmar Burke School, CA

Playing
Playing, playing all day,
Butterfly in green life,
Forest, nature, world.
Avery Hersom, Grade 3
Turner Elementary School, TX

The Flower
Cutely,
Sweetly,
Preciously,
The flower
Is growing in the field.
— Lovely!
Haley Burgan, Grade 1
Fir Grove Elementary School, OR

Baseball
I won the strikeout!
I'm the best hitter.
I hit a homerun.
Baseball is fun.
I like to bat.
I wear my hat.
Yea! A homerun.
Makes baseball so fun!
Daniel Sanchez, Grade 3
Honey Hollow Elementary School, CA

The Hungarian Horntail
I like the Hungarian Horntail
It has an eye that's evil looking.
Its flames will turn you to ash,
it will kill you with one slash.
It will destroy anything in its path,
a tree would never last.
A dragon as fierce as a vampire,
building up its fire,
and it will come through its mouth.
Then a thing will happen,
it will burn down Florence Sabin.
It rages all your fears,
you're its dinner,
I'd run,
I'd hide,
I'd do everything I can.
But I'm already dead so I'm happy to say,
that if you don't do as I say you'll be as I, dead,
under a gravestone by I.

Sidney Brown, Grade 3
New Emerson School, CO

Wish List
I wish I had all the money,
I wish I had a cool bike,
I wish I was the fastest boy in the world.

Joel Smith, Grade 3
Turner Elementary School, TX

Parrots
Beautiful colors,
parrots flying through the trees
in the rain forest.

Shelby Flowers, Grade 3
Lorenzo De Zavala Elementary School, TX

My Life
Santa Rosa is home.
It feels perfect
but not just perfect.
It feels warm
and just like life.

Sayra Barajas, Grade 1
Robert L Stevens Elementary School, CA

Stingray

In case you haven't heard,
stingrays live in the seas and oceans all around the world!
Near the shore to the sea beds,
you will find rays with eyes on top of their heads.
Stingrays come in different shapes, colors and sizes.
They are full of surprises!
The biggest stingray of all is the Manta Ray,
Just seeing one would surely make your day!
Round stingrays look like dinner plates.
And yes, rays do have mates.
Blind electric rays are almost totally blind.
They use their radar-like sense to find.
Stingrays move by rippling their fins to flee.
They are very graceful; in fact, swimmingly.
Some rays can leap out of the water.
Why bother?
Rays hide and blow sand for their food.
Hopefully, you will find them in a good mood!
Stingrays have a poisonous spine
to defend themselves, just fine.

Alexandra Cooke, Grade 3
Four Peaks Elementary School, AZ

Colors

If I were red I would be a big juicy apple.
If I were orange I would be a beautiful flower.
If I were green I would be a blade of grass.
If I were blue I would be a dolphin in the ocean.
If I were pink I would be a flamingo in the water.
If I were purple I would be a hair band in my hair.

Mira Serrato, Grade 2
St Dorothy School, CA

Window

Through my window I see a beautiful ocean.
I see the birds flying and pretty shells.
I see the sun setting in the west.
Through my window I see palm trees.
I see children playing and people wading in the sea.
I see my dress waving in the wind.
Through my window I see my world.

Yolanda Strickland, Grade 3
Daly Elementary School, MT

Pets

I wish I had a fish.
I do not want a dog.
I want a pet that is not big.
My mom wants a guinea pig.
I don't like furry pets
and I don't want my mom to get a guinea pig.
It has fur on it.
My dad likes bats.
His favorite color is black.
That is why he likes bats
because his favorite color is black.

Rayford Mitchell, Grade 3
Garden Lakes Elementary School, AZ

Tiger

Tiger — swiftest cat
It is striped, black, and orange
Cat in the jungle

Timothy Porter, Grade 3
Lorenzo De Zavala Elementary School, TX

My Senses

I like to taste candy from party favors.
I like to see my dad when he comes home.
I like to hear a siren from a fire truck.
I like to smell hot food out of the oven.
I like to touch my legos when I build robots.

Mason Cherry, Grade 1
Grace School, TX

Summer

When the sun shines in the summer day
The wind is getting lower and lower
Until it disappears
It is getting hot and hot
During each day
Each year summer comes
It's hot
Hot
And hot
Finally
Summer is over until next year

Charlie Tellez, Grade 3
Horn Academy, TX

I Love the Moon
I love the moon
So beautiful and bright

So beautiful and bright
in the night sky

When the moon is up
it has a gleaming
which stretches across the heavens
from east to west
What a beautiful full moon tonight
Lily Gordon, Grade 3
Grattan Elementary School, CA

Black
Shadows looming in the darkness,
Rich black monstrous skies,
The depths of the ocean
A black panther looking for a victim,
Vampire bats swooping down for a kill,
Who will be its next target?
Black is death,
Waiting, waiting, waiting
John Parsons, Grade 3
Daves Avenue Elementary School, CA

The Wonderful Park
Trees wiggle
The park is bright
Why are there
A lot of people
In the park?
If this day
Is bright
Why are people
Yelling really loud?
I feel happy
Because I'm playing
On the swings
With kids.
The sky is blue,
It is so colorful.
Erik Ledezma, Grade 3
Edison Elementary School, CA

Hail
H ard balls of ice
A fter the storm everything
I n the world
L aying outside gets dented
Justin Perry, Grade 3
Emerson Elementary School, TX

6 Teddy Bears
Bears here,
bears there.
One on the stairs.
One in a tree.
One on the swing.
One in a box.
One on the bed.
And one just for me!
Genesis Valdez, Grade 3
Lincoln Elementary School, CA

Changing Seasons
Winter is here
It is nice and cool in the winter
I was drinking hot chocolate
It was hot and bright brown
As winter blows it turns to sun
My cold hands would be focused
I would watch winter turn to spring
Suddenly winter was gone
When the sunshine butterflies fly
Some blue, some green, some pink
As soft air rushes through the sky
Everything is still, spring is here!
Jackie Marie Budde, Grade 3
Horn Academy, TX

Fishes on Dishes
When you go to see some whales,
he might eat something with scales,
if you ever see a fish,
you'll want him on a dish,
please don't eat the fish,
or a whale will have you on his dish!
Nicholas Risma, Grade 3
Academy of Charter Schools, CO

Saturn's Rings

Saturn has rings beautiful as can be.
Saturn has rings going round and round.
Saturn's rings are such a sight to see.
Saturn's rings so beautiful.

Jonathan Davis, Grade 2
Lincoln Elementary School, CA

Love

I love my dad he makes me glad.
I love my mom she helps me with my math.
I don't like bees because they sting.
I love my sister she helps me think.
But you make me sing, when bells ring.
Give me a hint about love because I love you.

Emily Nguyen, Grade 2
Little Scholars School, CA

Book

If I were a book...
I'd read to myself,
I'd tell people to pick me
when they came by,
I'd live in a library,
If I were a book...

Stephan May, Grade 1
Solana Santa Fe Elementary School, CA

Pets

Dogs
fuzzy, loud
running, playing, biting
dog house, Golden Retriever, cat food, lion
eating, purring, sleeping
lazy, sharp
Cats

Fadi Azar, Grade 3
Kathy L Batterman Elementary School, NV

Python

Slithery python
dangerous, long constrictor
digests its victims

Malik Broussard, Grade 3
Lorenzo De Zavala Elementary School, TX

Animals Are Cool

A nimals are very cool
N eat but don't swim
I n pools.
M ammals give birth to baby
A nimals.
L ots of food to eat.
S o my favorite animals are cats.

A llah made animals
R ead about animals so you can learn.
E very animal can have babies.

C aring about their family.
O tters live in the lakes, ocean
O r the sea.
L ots of animals are happy or sad

No matter what I still like animals.

Nuraida Azhar, Grade 3
Phoenix Metro Islamic School, AZ

Python

The most exciting thing
I ever did
was when I held a python.
It was the best
when we looked eye to eye, knowing
he was not going to bite me.
The reason I did it
is because I especially like
to take my chances
with any type of snakes.
Have you ever done that?

Deryl Storck, Grade 2
Acacia Elementary School, AZ

Thankful

The salty water of the ocean,
Like shiny, clear glass,
Twinkling stars that you wish upon,
Writing stories with a glittery pen,
That's what I'm thankful for!

Enmorrea DelaCruz, Grade 3
Four Peaks Elementary School, AZ

Beautiful*

The flowers are shining
in the moonlight.
In the forest there is beauty.
One moon shines everywhere
to light the way.
Everywhere is so beautiful.
It is too hard to describe.
I'll just have to photograph it.
Everywhere is beautiful.

Yu-Shien Ni, Grade 3
Carlthorp School, CA
*Inspired by Guillaume Apollinaire.

Slavery

Slavery
can be like
chains holding you down
from freedom.
Slavery
is like
being separated from family.
Slavery
is like
being in a house
half-finished.

Alexis Roether, Grade 3
Acacia Elementary School, AZ

Holidays

Green, red, Santa
Jesus, yellow, toys
Soft, candy, cold
Happiness fills the air.

Annie Worthen, Grade 1
Thomas Edison Charter School, UT

Tiger

T igers growl
I trap my food
G rowling is what I do to defend myself
E verything is scared of me
R un, I am coming

Katiana O'Dowd, Grade 3
St Raphael School, CA

George the Dolphin

The blue dolphins swim around
I met one and said, "Hello!"
I gave it a name, called it George
It swam away and I said,
"Please George please don't go away,
Please stay with me and let's have some fun!"

Jessica Lim, Grade 3
Cahuenga Elementary School, CA

Thankful

Winter mountains with sparkling white snow,
The crunchy taste of tacos,
The delicate smell of roses,
The sound of kids' laughter,
The gentle feel of a kitten's fur,
These are things that I'm thankful for.

Zachary Rahn, Grade 3
Four Peaks Elementary School, AZ

Brown Leather

I wish I were brown.
I would be at the football game
looking at the ground
when I am soaring
after players hike me in the air.

Matthew Evans, Grade 2
University Park Elementary School, TX

Freedom

Freedom is…
Happiness,
Peace,
Love,
Spending time with friends (any color),
Doing what you want to do,
Having a right,
Following your heart,
Believing in yourself,
Standing up for yourself,
Black skin is no different from white skin,
We are not different at all!

Alexandria Olafson, Grade 3
Hedgcoxe Elementary School, TX

Benjamin Franklin

B e true
E xciting inventions
N ice person
J oyful person
A wesome
M aking inventions
I ntelligent
N ice

F unny man
R espectful
A good man
N ational hero
K ind
L oving
I nventor
N atural leader

Courtney Callagy, Grade 3
Canyon Rim Elementary School, CA

My Red Kite

My red kite can go up, up, up.
It can fly in the breeze.
It can fly in the sky.
Sometimes I make it fly so, so high,
it almost touches the sun.
Oh no! It's getting burned!
Oh no! Look at it! It is now broken!
Wah! Wah! Wah!

Austin Taylor, Grade 1
First Baptist Christian Academy, TX

My Dog Lola

Peach and white, small and furry,
She likes to chase us every day.
She likes to jump on my bed,
When I wake up to play.
She likes to lick me on my face,
And she likes to eat my food.
She runs so fast, I can't catch her,
And makes me feel like a fool.
Sometimes Lola is very rude!

Paola Sagel, Kindergarten
Presbyterian School, TX

Fall Day

Pine trees here and there
waving in the big strong wind
on a short fall day.

Mikala Edwards, Grade 3
Four Peaks Elementary School, AZ

Nature Girl

She walks with the
Sun, dawn and night
She walks with the
Forest, mountains, valleys
She walks with the
Snow, rain and hail
Therefore she is the
Nature girl

Mikayla Durtschi, Grade 3
Katherine Delmar Burke School, CA

Magic

You have magic!
With magic I can play.
I have toys for my tricks.
I can pull a rabbit from my hat.
I can turn a dog to a cat.
What do you think of that?
Magic!

Emma Rodriguez, Grade 3
Honey Hollow Elementary School, CA

Danny

He is really smart
and likes to play all day
he is funny and nice

Collin Bernard, Grade 3
Our Lady of the Snows School, NV

Imagining October

When I think of October
I begin to see pumpkins with grins.
I imagine skeletons chasing me.
I hear a skeleton, *clickety-clack*
I smell pumpkin pie

Forest Walker, Grade 1
Paonia Elementary School, CO

What Should I Wear for School Today?
What should I wear for school today?
Orange or red or purple or gray
shirt that is bright
jeans are just right
old shoes new lace
a big smile on my face
only who I want to be
is the person who is me.

Oriams Barcenas, Grade 3
Lincoln Elementary School, CA

Summer Around the Corner
Summer around the corner
I cannot wait.
The buzzing sound of honey bees,
pollinating the daffodils.
The sweet sound of little bird hatchlings,
crying for food.
The fluttering sound of hummingbird wings,
going to feed.
Now it is nightfall,
the frogs start their evening chorus.
The bees go back to the honeybee hive,
the little bird hatchlings going to sleep.
The hummingbirds go back to their nests,
and now it is my turn to go to bed.

Jack Stevens, Grade 3
Home School, WA

Science Park
Jumping trees,
Whistling wind,
Plucking plants,
Rushing water,
Placing rocks,
Gallopy grass.
Rushing wind races to the galloping grass.
All of the water drains out the sun.
This is gonna be lots of fun.
The trees in a breeze.
Cotton likes to sneeze!

Blair Rentie, Grade 1
New Emerson School, CO

My Little Dress

I am wearing a dress can't you see,
And it just barely fits me.
You see I have grown so tall,
So I will have to get another dress at the mall.
Maybe I should get some shoes while I'm there,
Oh my gosh! My dress has a tear.
Maybe some earrings to match the dress,
Wow! The shoes cost much less.
That was really fun,
Good bye everyone.

Rayann Blamy, Grade 3
Community Children's Center, CA

Noises

Yesterday, I heard weird noises
Coming from upstairs,
Like…
Bang!! K-Boom! Hissss…
Gong! Muh ha ha ha
The sounds all made me think that
A crazy guy came into my house,
But when I went up,
It was only the radio making…
Very, very, very weird noises.

Michelle Cho, Grade 3
Wonderland Avenue Elementary School, CA

Soccer

I love soccer
Soccer is fun.
I can't wait until we play in May.
When we win we will say, "Hooray hooray."
We will get a trophy.
My teammates will rest.
We will go to a restaurant.
I will be the best!
I like soccer.
Do you like it too?
When you hit the ball into the net.
It feels like the best.
How about you?

Estevan Hernandez, Grade 3
Honey Hollow Elementary School, CA

Make Me!

Draw my head as round as a hot planet.
Create my blonde hair as tiny as a millimeter.
Make my eyebrows as blonde as sand on the beach.
Design my eyeballs as brown as mud.
Make my nose as tan as a palm tree.
Draw my mouth as red as Mars.
Create my teeth as white as pages in the dictionary.
Design my neck as tan as a donut.
Draw my ears as oval as a flat penny.

Joseph LeBlanc, Grade 3
Briargrove Elementary School, TX

Soccer

Playing soccer when you get the ball you pass it to the other player
who is open then you shoot the ball in the goal

Once you shoot the ball you go to your spot
when they kick the ball to you, you get it or let it go out of bounds

When you get the ball you pass it to the person
and that person you passed it to goes for the goal

Once you go for the goal you go back to your spot
and wait for the ball to come to you

Then it is time to go in from recess.
Back to the classroom.

Evan Savoie, Grade 3
Horn Academy, TX

Colors

If I were red I would be a ripe cherry or a juicy raspberry.
If I were orange I would be a juicy orange or a beautiful butterfly.
If I were green I would be a tiny leaf or a big huge tree.
If I were blue I would be the big blue sky or the beautiful sea.
If I were purple I would be a flower or maybe a bucket of paint.
If I were pink I would be a blossom or a big balloon.
If I were silver I would be a silver dollar or a shiny nickel.
If I were gold I would be a bar of gold or a beautiful Christmas bow.
If I were yellow I would be a shooting star or the sun brightening up your day.
If I were all the colors I would be a rainbow way up in the sky.

Michelle Rios-Buza, Grade 2
St Dorothy School, CA

What Is Blue?
Blue is the color of people's eyes.
Blue is the color of the sea.
Blue is the color of the sky without a cloud.
Blue is the color of a crystal ball.
Yarelly Gonzalez, Grade 2
Lincoln Elementary School, CA

Friends
I see my friend everyday
And these are some of the things we say...

Hello!
Hi!
Good!
Great!
Cool!
Awesome!
Hey!
Wow!

We study math, spelling, literature, science,
    social studies and then we play outside.
Finally,
We say...
    Goodbye!
Taylor Sonne, Grade 2
Grace School, TX

I Wonder Why...
I wonder why the seasons change
And why all dogs bark.
I wonder why the grass is green
And why the sky gets dark.
I wonder why birds fly
And why rabbits hop.
I wonder why cows moo
And why snowflakes drop.
I wonder why the Earth's the Earth
And why God created it.
And I wonder HOW
Everything
Works.
Rachel Yanover, Grade 3
Wonderland Avenue Elementary School, CA

Owls
Their wings are ruffling
if ready for flight again
in the darkening night
Carlos Cohen, Grade 3
St Raphael School, CA

Snakes
Snakes are here
Snakes are there
Snakes are absolutely
    Everywhere.

Snakes are slithering
Snakes are biting
Snakes are hissing
So run away!
Riley Perez, Grade 2
New Emerson School, CO

Pigs
Pigs
Pink, fat
Slopping, snorting, playing
Pigs are stinky
Hogs
ZaRian Baylor, Grade 1
Myatt Elementary School, TX

Colors
Black crow
White cloud
Red apples
Green grass
Yellow lemon
Blue pants
Purple grapes
Indigo blueberries
Orange carrots
Violet violets
Gold treasure
Silver medal
Pink pig.
Kaleb Tierney, Grade 1
Ryan Elementary School, CO

Snow

There are two kinds of snow,
The two kinds of snow are yellow and white.
The snow you can eat white,
The snow that's plain out gross is yellow.
You can make snowballs, snowmen,
You can also make snow angels.

Bryce Thomas Samuel, Grade 3
Gause Intermediate School, WA

Cleaning Machine

I've made an amazing cleaning machine.
It cleans the ring on the table.
It got dust off the blanket.
It even cleaned the drum and its cable.

I've made an amazing cleaning machine.
It cleaned up everything just like that.
I'm gonna use it for the rest of my chores,
but I still can't find the cat.

Sabrina Batchler, Grade 3
Carlthorp School, CA

So Many Cats

Big cats, little cats, bob cats.
House cats, black-footed cats.

Good cats, bad cats, wild cats,
Tame cats, silly cats, climbing cats!

Furry cats, strong cats, hungry cats,
Old cats, new cats!

Playful cats and lazy cats.
But to me, any cat is great.

Lexi Lopez, Grade 2
Sangre De Cristo Elementary School, CO

Macaw

Colorful macaw
flying parrots up to trees
rainbow scarlet bird

Stephanie Buenrostro, Grade 3
Lorenzo De Zavala Elementary School, TX

Love

Love is red like roses
in the garden
that are blooming so bright.
It beats through my head
like a heart pounding.
It makes me smile
like bunnies playing in the
grass and cry for joy!

Ashlan Schlehuber, Grade 2
Northridge Elementary School, CO

My Sister Rachel

My sister is caring
she helps me when I need it
she makes me laugh when I am sad
she lets me use her stuff
my sister is strong.

My sister has a good heart
she loves my family and me.
She cleans a lot and helps a lot
her name is Rachel
and I want to be like her.

Maddie Hastings, Grade 3
Patton Elementary School, TX

Poor Norman

There once was a cow named Norman
He went out when it was stormin'
When lightning struck
He got hit by a truck
Some people said he's just snorin'.

Emily Arroyo, Grade 3
St Raphael School, CA

Summer

Summer,
The best!
You can stay up
All night long.
Summer is the best season
Of all, it rocks!

Albert Corona, Grade 3
Turner Elementary School, TX

Little Stars

Stars so small
they glow all night
how beautiful they are in the night.

McKenna Robles, Grade 3
St Raphael School, CA

I Am

I am a boy.
I wonder if dinosaurs were dead
I hear frogs in the meadow
I see hermit crabs on the sand
I want a bird as a pet
I am a scientist.

I pretend to be a soccer player
I feel happy
I worry about not being happy
I touch frog's slimy skin
I cry when I cut onions
I am happy.

I understand my mom
I say, "please."
I dream of a monster
I try to play soccer
I hope I win the soccer game
I am having fun.

Max Castroparedes, Grade 2
Grace School, TX

Spring

Bees, wasps, butterflies
flying around my head.
Hope the bee doesn't sting me
or I will be in bed.
I hope a mosquito doesn't bite me!
If it does I will have a
bump on my head.
If that wasp tries to bite me
I will run for my life.
If that butterfly lands on me
I will be as lucky as a ladybug.

D'Lanee Doyle, Grade 2
Walsh Elementary School, CO

Flowers

Roses are red, violets are blue
wherever you are I will still be with you.
Roses are pink, violets are blue,
why can't they smell like me and you?

Katlyn Nguyen, Grade 2
Sierra Vista Elementary School, CA

Acting

I love acting because you can do fun things
It is very fun and do it with my cousin Emily,
But it can get annoying.

So far, I have done four plays.
They have been fun and hard.
I love acting.
You never know what part you'll get
Only the teacher knows what it'll be.
I love acting very much

I must keep on doing my dream.
I will never stop doing it.

It is hard but I love it.
You don't have to like a lot
But I know I do

Acting, I love

Shelby Brown, Grade 3
Horn Academy, TX

Three-toed Sloth

A small three-toed sloth
grayish, hanging upside down
sleeps on high branches

Juliana Yolland, Grade 3
Lorenzo De Zavala Elementary School, TX

Marlen in the Beach

The beach is orange and blue.
It looks like a bird in the sky.
It looks like a butterfly in the pretty sky.

Marlen Barajas, Grade 1
Robert L Stevens Elementary School, CA

Sister

Sister, sister, play with me.
Sister, sister, eat with me.
Sister, sister, go with me.
Sister, sister, read with me.
Sister, sister, skate with me.
Sister, sister, have fun with me.
Sister, sister, race with me.
Sister, sister, helps me.
Sister, sister, write with me.
Sister, sister, you are fun.
Sister, sister, I love you!

Joseph Kennedy, Grade 1
Lee Richmond Elementary School, CA

Frogs

Amphibians
ribbeting and croaking
leaping from lily pad to lily pad
different colors
cool creatures.

Amanda Strahota, Grade 3
Acacia Elementary School, AZ

Star

I'm like the sun
    in the sky.
I'm kind of big.
I have hot gases
    inside.
I can turn into a comet
    inside.

Francisco Romero, Grade 2
Acacia Elementary School, AZ

Marker and Pencils

Marker
Liquid, colorful
Ink, lids, thick
Thin, messy, drawing, writing
Wooden, lead, erasable
Creative, sharpened
Pencils

Crawford McCrary, Grade 1
Armstrong Elementary School, TX

The Cat and the Pig

The cat chased the pig
the pig ran but the cat was too fast
the pig ran and ran and ran

Stephen Abellera, Kindergarten
Hollister SDA School, CA

Fireworks

Fireworks shoot into the sky
    the lonely moon's eyes
grow bigger and BIGGER

Zach Smith, Grade 1
Fir Grove Elementary School, OR

Blue

Sometimes I just don't have a clue.
What is the color blue?
Is it the color of trees?
Or is it the color of your knees?
Does it match with your skin,
Or does it match a fish's fin?
I'm determined to find out
What the color blue is all about.
It's a mixture of yellow and green,
As you have probably seen.
Blue is found in the sky,
And there's no wonder why.
Blue is the color of a blueberry,
But not the color of a strawberry.
Blue is the color of the ocean.
It is constantly in motion.
Blue is found in the air.
It is found almost everywhere!
I wonder why I never knew
What was the color blue?

Hurlink Vongsachang, Grade 2
San Elijo K-8 School, CA

The March Wind

The wind blows hard in March.
The wind blows soft to me in March.
The wind blows leaves around.
The wind b l o w s .

Demier Golden, Grade 1
New Emerson School, CO

A Song Is a Bicycle
When I think of a slow song I go fast.
I won't use as much of my energy.
The beat sounds like wheels.
The song screeches like brakes.
The tune goes back and forth like gears.
The rhythm's soft like a bicycle seat.

Kennan Davison, Grade 3
CLASS Academy, OR

Penguins, Oh, Penguins
Penguins, oh penguins
You slide on your belly
You dive in the water
I hope you're not smelly
You're black and you're white
You're slick and you're silly
It is true you've come to observe
Our little towns and our big cities
But where you are from
It is freezing it's cold
And here it changes
In the winter the breeze is frosty
In the summer
The breeze is warmly heated by the toasty sun
Don't stay here too long
Mom says — No Pets.

Kimberley Estrada, Grade 3
Robinson Elementary School, TX

Roses Are Red Violets Are Blue/Pink
Roses are red violets are blue
I look good so do you.

Violets are pink
your feet really stink.

Roses are red violets are blue
you lent me your glove so I gave it back to you.

Roses are red violets are blue
when I see you I can't stop thinking of you.

Joseph Bui, Grade 3
Northgate School, WA

Hockey

Lucky me,
My dad takes me to
Rocking hockey games.
Alix Crossley, Grade 3
Summit Elementary School, UT

My Little Sister

My little sister's sweet,
and her name is "Yunnie Kim."
It's cool the way she likes to eat,
it is neat.
I like the way she talks
really cute.
When she looks at clocks,
she likes to study numbers.
She is very curious,
and wants to learn new things.
Sometimes she bothers us
with bling-bling rings.
She likes candy,
and my friend Mandy.
Sometimes Yunnie is a fuss
to us.
She's a good sister,
not a grumpy mister.
I love her,
and she loves me.
Jinnie Kim, Grade 3
Cahuenga Elementary School, CA

Winter

Winter is like hunting.
It comes once a year.
Sledding is like sighting in your gun.
You try it once and do it again.
Matt Barnes, Grade 3
Mound Valley Rural School, NV

The Sun

The sun is big and bright
And such a delight.
But you can't see it at night.
Kyle Wilhelm, Grade 3
Robinson Elementary School, TX

Kids

Boys
cool, athletic
running, playing, jogging
football, baseball, jump rope, dolls
laughing, talking, walking
sweet, nice
Girls
Christopher Manriquez, Grade 3
Rogers Elementary School, NV

The Voice of Hope

The blood of hope fights illness.
The body of our shadow follow us.
The heart of peace is in our spirit.
The soul of harmony flies around us.
The bones of friendship flow in us.
The breath of justice is in the wind.
Hope is a strong feeling.
Maureen Lake Atkinson, Grade 2
CLASS Academy, OR

Janette

J aguars are my favorite animal
A rt is my favorite thing to do
N ightingales are my favorite birds
E el is my favorite fish
T iger is my favorite
T ennis is my favorite subject
E is the last letter in my name.
Janette Flores, Grade 2
Phoenix Metro Islamic School, AZ

Christmas

C is for carol
H is for holiday
R is for Rudolph
I is for icicles
S is for star
T is for Christmas tree
M is for "Merry Christmas"
A is for angel
S is for Santa Claus
Ohidul Mojumder, Grade 2
Sierra Vista Elementary School, NV

Colors

A rain of purple fell on my fence
A smog of red covered an apartment.
A volcano of blue exploded on an ocean.
A tornado of indigo swirled on the sky.
A lightning of brown hit a car.
A sprinkle of gray splashed on an elephant.
A hail of green dropped on a field.
A snow of white fell on a city.
A hurricane of silver spun on a skyscraper.
Colors are cool.

Nathaniel Trobough, Grade 3
CLASS Academy, OR

Green

Green is the color of the beautiful grass.
Green is the color of the stem of a flower.
Green is the color of a frog in a pond.
Green is the color of a person's sweater.
I like green!

Bethany Conklin, Grade 1
Solana Santa Fe Elementary School, CA

Animal Life

The swan swam swiftly through the lily pads.
The snake slithered through the heather brush,
looking for mice to eat.
The mice noticed the slither in the grass
and went away,
hopefully,
to live another day.
Goodbye, Goodnight.

Charlie Blecker, Grade 2
Stanbridge Academy, CA

Earth

Earth is a beautiful place
With war, it's a big disgrace
The president will hide
The children will have cried

Then the Earth will settle down again

Julia Malloy, Grade 3
Delphi Academy of San Francisco Bay, CA

The Bike

I like to ride my bike,
One time when I rode my bike
I went zoom to the right, zoom to the left
And then rrrrt, I turned and while I was turning,
I was falling to the ground, but for some reason
I did not fall, and I continued to ride my bike.

Callisto Havercroft, Grade 3
Briargrove Elementary School, TX

What I Remember

I remember waking up in the morning
listening to all the birds chirping
and the sound of the trees in the breeze
I remember my first taste of milk
running down my cheeks
my little eyes opening to the world

The light shining in my eyes
Smiles lighting up my day
I remember the happiness and joy of my mom and dad
bringing me in this world protected
my first step walking in the world
I remember I first walked on Christmas night
exploring all there is
galloping with my friend's horse
I remember my preschool
the bunk bed there and stuffed animals and play area with bikes
that I would ride on
My birthday at Girl Mania when I turned eight
my flower girl dress that I wore
Getting my hair done
My dog going up there never to be seen again

Drew Barash, Grade 3
Westwood Charter Elementary School, CA

Trick-or-Treaters

Here come the trick-or-treaters with their baskets full of candy
Going to house to house collecting candy.
And after they're done, the little trick-or-treaters dump the candy on the floor
Sorting out the ones they like and the ones they don't like.
And the best part is getting to eat the candy.

Chandler Jordan, Grade 2
St Mark's Day School, TX

April Rains
Tip, tip, tip
It's the sound of rain.
Finally, the rain is over,
But I know it will come again!

Natalie Fedorov, Grade 2
St John of San Francisco Orthodox Academy, CA

The Water Gun Fight
The water gun fight
Ready set go
Squirt
Splash
That is halftime
Okay
Are you ready?
Yes!
Okay!
Splat
Squirt
Squirt
Splat
I'm cold
Let's get a towel
So we get dry

Evan Flint, Grade 2
Horizons K-8 Alternative Charter School, CO

Nature
The most important thing about a life is nature.
It is amazing and free.
It can exhaust and tire you.
It is the most important thing.
But the most important about a life is nature.

Marcus Wuensche, Grade 3
Daly Elementary School, MT

Tigers
Tigers are awesome
with claws and teeth like razors —
very orange fur

Jacob Hellums, Grade 3
Lorenzo De Zavala Elementary School, TX

Basketball

When the ball bounces
The ball made echoes
On the court
The ball was pounding
And rose in the air
As if it were trying to say something
But then suddenly
It hit the backboard
And as it went into the basket
It made a swishing sound
The crowd went crazy

David A. Falloure, Grade 3
Horn Academy, TX

Sunrise

When the sun rises,
It lets out the light,
To tell people that it's time to go,
But most will never follow,
To helpful things,
The sun is the best,
When the rain is here,
Wait a while,
The sun is here,
What I love the most,
Is the sunrise bright and early.

Rachel Quock, Grade 3
Katherine Delmar Burke School, CA

Fairies

Quick as a wink
Sparkle in the air
Fairies
Our little friends
But never in sight
The twitch of wings
Sparkles of all colors
Fairies are always there
From when the burning sun goes up
'Til it goes down
Hair, face, mouth, nose
Fairies

Carson Kraft, Grade 3
Katherine Delmar Burke School, CA

Devil's Tower

D aring to challenge anyone who
E ver stands in its path
V ictory over all
I gnoring all below it
L aughing in the face of death
S earching the land

T owering
O ver all
W earing the face of pride
E veryone admires but fears its
R adiance over all

Claire Lamman, Grade 3
Spring Creek Elementary School, WY

Sharks

These creatures run
And jump about.
Until they hear
A bloody shout.

Feeding on some
Crunchy fish;
Especially if they
Taste delish.

Schools of fish
Squirm in their mouths,
Crunching, chewing,
There's no doubt

Creepy creatures,
Carnivore beasts,
Getting ready by
Preparing feasts.

Logan Weinman, Grade 3
Summit Cove Elementary School, CO

Long

I will stretch like a giraffe
I will stretch like a snake
because I am long

Aissa Mougey, Grade 1
Fir Grove Elementary School, OR

A Rainbow Hummingbird

I am a hummingbird.
I drink pollen from flowers,
That's how I get my powers.
I can fly very, very high.
If you will be my friend
I will give you a piece of my rainbow,
Cherry and strawberry.
Then we'll fly very high and be out of sight.

Katarina Heim and Quinn Gottlieb, Grade 1
Cottonwood Montessori School, NM

Happy Thanksgiving

N ow it is November.
O h, my family is going to eat turkey!
V ery good and yummy. Mmmm!
E veryone in my family eats mashed potatoes.
M y family likes Thanksgiving!
B e a good thanker.
E verything looks delicious.
R emember Thanksgiving is special.

Thanksgiving

Raymundo Cortez, Grade 3
Midland Elementary School, CA

My Dog

My dog
Runs around
At my house
Every day
Because he wants to play.

Sala Yeonhee Oh, Grade 3
Wonderland Avenue Elementary School, CA

A Big Cat

A
B ig
C at
D unks
E very
F erret

Theo Sher, Grade 3
Wonderland Avenue Elementary School, CA

Daddy

D ifferent
A wesome
D arling
D elightful
Y ou would love him.

Jonna Hewitt, Grade 3
Robinson Elementary School, TX

Friends

Friends
super cool
great to have
fun to talk to
terrific

Kacy Francis, Grade 3
Robinson Elementary School, TX

I Wish

I wish I could do math all day.
I wish I could read all day.
I wish I could turn a frog into a dog!

Jason Lewsader, Grade 1
St Mark's Day School, TX

Banana

Banana, banana
You are
so fun
to peel
peel 1
peel 2
peel 3
what fun
now it
is time to eat.

I open
my mouth
and my
white teeth
slice into you
chew chew chew

Sean Guderian, Grade 2
Heatherwood Elementary School, CO

Sunflower

It is green
Tall with leaves
When I see
The sunflower
It makes me glad.
But I don't
Understand
Why it takes
A lot of time
To bloom
When the air
Whistles
It makes a
Beautiful sound
When the sun
Goes down
The shadow sleeps
So the sun
Will wake
The shadow

Emanuel Tapia, Grade 3
Edison Elementary School, CA

Monkey

Monkey.
Very playful.
Very loud.
Climbs trees.
Eats bananas.
Mammal.
Carry babies on your back.
Spider monkey.

Symmony Park, Grade 2
Acacia Elementary School, AZ

In the Woods

Snowy, cold, and windy,
A brown, still cabin,
Warm on top of a hill,
Davy Crockett sipping hot chocolate,
Practicing his speech,
Famous, brave, Texan.

Mary Dade, Kindergarten
Presbyterian School, TX

Football

I like to play football. Do you like football?
I run fast like the wind I fall down
I still have a chance
Goal! Goal! Goal!

Nader Hassouneh, Grade 3
Briargrove Elementary School, TX

Lots of Cats

Large cats, small cats, fat cats,
Little cats, big cats, huge cats.

Skinny cats, mom cats, dad cats,
Baby cats, grandma cats, grandpa cats.

Brother cats, sister cats, silly cats,
Mad cats, happy cats, friend cats.

Funny cats, messy cats, mean cats,
Bad cats, good cats, nice cats.

Wow, lots of cats!

Brianna Molina, Grade 2
Sangre De Cristo Elementary School, CO

March

M y birthday
A nice month
R eally fun
C an be very hot
H oliday is St. Patrick's Day

Taylor Benson, Grade 2
University Park Elementary School, TX

If I Could Give a Gift to You

If I could give a gift to you,
I'd give you a glowing rainbow,
Filled with glistening drops of rain,
I'd wrap it in shimmering sunlight,
To keep the colorful rainbow close to you,
That's what I would give you,
If I could give you a gift.

Thilini Abeywickrema, Grade 3
Daves Avenue Elementary School, CA

The Midnight Mustang

The midnight mustang,
so powerful, wild at heart,
nobody can ever catch him.
In his own herd, he runs, the ground shakes.
The sky parts, the clouds blow away,
and the night sky shines above him.
He flies away into the night sky,
he is magic, he is Zanbar,
The Midnight Mustang!

Jasper Gregory, Grade 3
Writers in the Schools Program, TX

A Family Trip

My favorite family trip was the arches in Utah
Swish, swish,
The wind blew harder and harder,
Boom boom
Crash crash
We almost hit the flash flood,
Flush flush
The toilets are horrible,
Squish squish
The sand is squishy!

Kelcee Wissel, Grade 2
New Emerson School, CO

Lemurs

Black, white, and fluffy —
Quiet, ring-tailed lemurs spring
Strong hind legs and cute

Taylar Eppinger, Grade 3
Lorenzo De Zavala Elementary School, TX

New York

N ice weather in the summer
E verything you wish to see is there
W ant to see the Statue of Liberty?

Y ou will love what you see
O n time for every bus
R ockefeller Center is where ice skating is
K now your street smarts

Carly Montanez, Grade 3
Four Peaks Elementary School, AZ

Fast Cheetah

Running very fast
as fast as a jaguar goes
everything that go.

Jonathan Chen, Grade 1
Highland Park School, MT

I Wish

I wish I were an empress
At Mt. Rainier
Ruling a country
Like a president.

Ellie Hurlbert, Grade 3
Daly Elementary School, MT

Flowers

The flowers bloom,
They smell like perfume
In spring.
The colors show,
Spring is hot,
Spring makes the
Flowers bloom,
Spring makes flowers
Grow.

Megan James, Kindergarten
The Presentation School, CA

Leaf

Leaf, leaf, leaf.
Red leaf.
Brown leaf.
Green leaf.
You'll love, love, love a leaf.
You'll love green leaves.

Shania Doney, Grade 2
Mission Grade School, MT

Mr. Beetle

Weird, interesting
Running, crawling, hiding
An entomologist's dream
Bugs

Robert Naruse, Grade 2
Harbor Day School, CA

Football

If I were a football...
I'd hear cheering,
I'd be thrown to get touchdowns,
I'd get caught,
If I were a football...

Liam Davis, Grade 1
Solana Santa Fe Elementary School, CA

Fall Memories

I sat by my window
seeing all the leaves flow with the wind.
Everything so colorful through the pine trees
landing in my hair, in my mind.

I'm full of excitement
waiting to be discovered
but all the fun always has to go away
until next year...

Alannah Schumaker, Grade 3
Elk Creek Elementary School, CO

The Four Seasons

The winter is the coldest
Snow falls from the sky.
Children like to go sledding
They wave and say good-bye.

Spring brings many lovely flowers
Gardens are filled with growing plants
Birds like to chirp and fly all day
Picnics are great unless you don't like ants.

In the summer you go to the beach
The sun shines all day long
Families take many vacations
And children might sing a song.

The fall brings many colorful leaves
Children make piles to jump in
People take their rakes out
And the leaves go into the garbage bin.

Jacqueline Kester, Grade 3
Woodcrest School, CA

April Fool's Day
You need to have a joke
on April Fool's Day.
I like to tease
my brother every year.
I like to laugh at
him. I have fun.
Libby Wootten, Grade 3
Midland Elementary School, CA

In the Toy Box
Toy box, toy box
Funny, fun, fun.
What's inside the toy box?
Funny, fun, fun.
Cassidy Barrett, Kindergarten
St Paul Preparatory Academy, TX

The Fire of Poems
The fire of poems
burns every worry
in your soul
but not you.
Every ash is a poem
as warm as a blanket.
The heat goes through your body
healing everything that is hurt.
Burning letters make a poem
and from other ashes
new ideas grow.
The fire of poems is going out
when it is not needed.
But when you do
the fire of poems
will appear
again.
Samuel Hill, Grade 3
The Mirman School, CA

Winter
Snow, snow where'd you go
Mud snowmen aren't fun to make
Snow, snow, please come back.
Ridge Rees, Grade 3
Summit Elementary School, UT

Mice
I like mice!
Mice can scare away elephants.
Mice can squeak.
Mice can eat cheese.
Mice can roll outside.
I like mice!
Jordan Masri, Kindergarten
Grace School, TX

Football
Yea! Yea!
The crowd is cheering.
Bam! Bam!
A hard hit.
Oh man, practice
For 2 hours?
Coach is yelling
"Nice job you're ready
To kick some butt!"
Broden Baker, Grade 2
Frontier Valley Elementary School, CO

Doggie Dogs
Brown like chocolate
light as peanut butter
fat as a big watermelon
white as a marshmallow
smaller than a doll
BIG as foals
smaller than a teddy bear
cute and perfect
like my cousins
doggie dogs.
Nathalie Aceves, Grade 1
Lee Richmond Elementary School, CA

Snakes
Snakes
long, slimy
biting, wiggling, rattling
getting ready to hunt
rattle snakes
Kayin Joplin, Kindergarten
Whiteriver Elementary School, AZ

The Sun's Blanket

When continuous snow falls,
the sun pulls up her blanket,
as the blanket becomes thicker and thicker
by the moment, as the snowflakes fall faster
and faster. The wind whistles
when the sun starts sleeping.
But all bundled up, we children
come sledding, skiing and snowboarding
down snowy white hills, until...
the sun wakes up again.

Kate Pippenger, Grade 2
Bridlemile Elementary School, OR

My Dog Likes Cars

My dog loves to ride to school with me.
He jumps around
and acts all funny.
He puts his little nose on the windows.

He loves to rub his nose all over the seats.
He most of all loves to lick my face.
Everyone laughs!
Hee! Hee!
Ha! Ha!

Tanner Doty, Grade 3
Nampa Christian Schools Inc, ID

The Painting

Whik, Whak, Whik, Whak
Slosh! goes the paintbrush
I paint away.

Thwik, Thwak, Thwik, Thwak
Splash! goes the paintbrush
There goes the background.

Tick, Tack, Tick, Tack
On goes the frame with the shiny leather.

Bling, Bling, Bling
Then comes the money!

Caleb Sapp, Grade 3
Briargrove Elementary School, TX

Under the Water

I see over one hundred bubbles under the water.
I see round bubbles.
I see small bubbles.
I see white-colored bubbles under the water.
I hear loud splashes under the water.
They are big splashes.
I hear my own breathing.
My breathing is soft under the water.
I feel warm under the water.
The water waves tickles me a lot.
The water tries to lift me up.
There are painted dolphins under the water.
Water is all around me.
I feel good under the water.

Yui Tantiyavarong, Grade 3
Little Scholars School, CA

The Navajo Nation Fair

Navajo Nation Fair
It is so cool that the fair has returned to Window Rock, Arizona
Bright lights on carnival rides, lights from the rodeo ground and pow-wow ground
While walking on the dusty ground, the dirt covers the dark skies
Dine' Be'kay'yah 'Ahooha'i' (Navajo Nation Fair)
Navajo Nation Fair
Riding the Ferris wheel around in a circle motion
Feet dangling in the air, my heart beats faster while gasping the bar tightly
Sitting on top of the world, people walking around, roaming the fair grounds
Dine' Be' Kay' yah 'Ahooha'i' (Navajo Nation Fair)
Navajo Nation Fair
Cowboys and cowgirls ride under the starry stars
Dust floats in the air when the bulls buck, horses running up and down the arena
The bull rider holding tightly, ropers roping cattle,
barrel racer making a clover leaf pattern
Dine' Be'kay'yah 'Ahooha'i' (Navajo Nation Fair)
Navajo Nation Fair
Grass dancers, jingle dancers, fancy dancers and tiny tots
Dance and singing throughout the night under the full moon
Feathers floating around them, jingles dance gracefully,
colorful feathers create a design
As they dance, singing a whistle through in the night skies
Dine' Be'kay'yah 'Ahooha'i' (Navajo Nation Fair)

Shawn Jones, Grade 2
Ganado Primary School, AZ

The Leaves
The leaves are falling
They dance outside my window
Here comes another

Andrew Wild, Grade 3
Wonderland Avenue Elementary School, CA

Dancing
Ballet dancers twirl also spin.
Jazz dancers shine their dance shoes.
Ballet dancers waltz.
Ballet dancers make their ballet shoes fit.
Tap dancers shine up their tap shoes.
Jazz dancers jazz walk and jazz run.
Also step turn.
Also poubooray.
People in hip-hop have to use hip-hop shoes.
You can use costumes:
 leotards and tights in the Nutcracker.
In Peter and the Wolf
you can wear a tutu.
And I love it.

Mickaela Keiser, Grade 3
Acacia Elementary School, AZ

A New World
A warm feeling came to me
I opened my eyes and I was in a new world
I heard angels singing from joy
I looked into my mother's sparkling eyes
and felt a streak of heaven come to my heart
A golden sun shone through the window pane
I was in a new world

Zoe Muntz, Grade 3
Westwood Charter Elementary School, CA

My Dad
My dad, who was born in Toledo,
Was once seen wearing a Speedo
He thought he looked cute
In that tiny suit
But, I said, "It's definitely not neat-o."

Whitney Raider-Wexler, Grade 3
Wonderland Avenue Elementary School, CA

Colors

On YELLOW days,
I feel warm and quiet in the sun.
On BLACK days,
I feel like a lion
roaring at everyone!
On RED days,
I feel like a clown
laughing with everyone.
On BLUE days,
I feel like a snowflake,
because it is cold.
Alexis Rinaldi, Grade 1
New Emerson School, CO

A Girl from the Bay

There once was a girl from the bay.
Who loved to say hooray!
She played in the sand
With her big band
And she did it all day!
Lindsay Bosio, Grade 3
St Raphael School, CA

I Am Cameron

I am outgoing and kind.
I wonder about my future.
I hear music playing.
I see my best friend.
I want the world to be at peace.
I am outgoing and kind.
I pretend animals could talk.
I feel cheerful.
I touch a book.
I worry about my family.
I cry when I get injured.
I am outgoing and kind.
I understand about Jesus.
I say you are nice.
I try to do my best every day.
I hope I have a lot of friends.
I am outgoing and kind.
I am Cameron.
Cameron Shepherd, Grade 3
River Oaks Baptist School, TX

Butterfly

Butterfly, butterfly
So pretty as can be
Butterfly, butterfly
Why don't you fly away with me
Butterfly, butterfly
You are so special to me.
Emma Sumrow, Grade 2
Criswell Elementary School, TX

The Skunk

Weasel,
Active at night,
Overpowering odor,
The skunk gives out smell odors,
Mammal.
Trevor Howard, Grade 2
Peck Elementary School, ID

Favorite Teacher

Teacher
Nice helpful
Corrects my papers
Always makes me smile
Mrs. Nelson
Dakota Sandoval, Grade 3
Elmira Elementary School, OR

Winter

Winter
Icy, snowy
Snowball fight, drink cocoa, snowmen
Winter is very chilly.
Chilly
Christy Garcia, Grade 3
Zuni Elementary Magnet School, NM

Mermaid in the Sea

Sparkling fin.
Long, colorful hair.
Swimming like a dolphin.
Happy, excited, free, glad.
Making a big splash.
Jenna Eliason, Grade 1
Thomas Edison Charter School, UT

Black Holes

A black hole's gravity is very tight.
Nothing can escape, not even light.

How is a black hole formed?
Does a star go boom, bang, bam?

I wonder what it's like to be a black hole.

Ralph Mendoza, Grade 3
Miller Elementary School, TX

Dog Dream

My small terrier does sleep
In his dream, a cat did creep

Suddenly he wakes and runs outside
Where is that cat and where does he hide

It's all a dream, my "Chopper" boy
Come here, come here! Play with your toy.

Sara Lapen, Grade 3
Adams Elementary School, CO

Sleepover

Last Friday I slept over at my friend's house.
Her name is Rachel like mine.
She has a hamster.
The hamster's name is Sweety.
I like pandas a lot.
I like rabbits a lot too.

Rachel Davis, Grade 2
Orchard Elementary School, UT

Good Dog

I'm on the **G** o!
I'm a go **O** d dog
I like y **O** u
D o you want to play

D o you like to eat bones
O h! I got your couch all muddy
I **G** o far on walks

Liam Freniere, Grade 3
St Raphael School, CA

Outside
I like to climb trees.
I spy honey bees.
Jumping on a trampoline is fun.
I do it a ton!
In the bushes, I will hide.
I will bike ride.
I like to swim.
I swim with Tim.
I like to walk.
I like to talk.
Rosalie Tozer, Grade 2
Froid Elementary School, MT

Sun Blind
Pearl white drifting snow
Blinding my eyes with bright light
Front yard morning scene
Devon Klingman, Grade 3
Midland Elementary School, CO

Cloud
C lean white pillow
L oud with thunder
O val shaped sometimes
U nder the blue sky
D oing nothing but sitting there.
Briana Hernandez, Grade 3
Emerson Elementary School, TX

My Home
When I come home,
I see my kitten playing
With a ball of yarn.
My little brothers are
Chasing each other,
And love is all around the room.
I hear my mom cracking eggs,
And my kitten purring.
I smell cookies and brownies.
They taste gooey and sweet.
I feel my kitten curling
Around my leg.
Kylee Kauffman, Grade 3
Four Peaks Elementary School, AZ

Fox Den
Crystal branches
Over the fox den
Looks like glass.
One of the branches
Looks like a bird
Guarding the door.
Johnny Morgan, Grade 2
Brush Creek Elementary School, CO

So Many Butterflies
They have compound eyes.
Just like mine.
Butterflies tongues are fifty feet long.
I bet they can sing a song.
But I could be wrong.
Morgan Craig, Grade 3
Elmira Elementary School, OR

I Wish
I wish I were Scooby Doo
The crime fighting dog
Solving mysteries in a castle
Finding clues to solve the mystery.
Kyle Scovill, Grade 3
Daly Elementary School, MT

Puppies
Puppies
Sweet cool
They run fast
They make you happy
Dogs
James Hoye, Grade 3
Elmira Elementary School, OR

Things I'm Thankful For
White, cold snow on the ground
Sledding fast as a car down the hills
Waterfalls
Peppers cooking in the oven
The salty taste of bacon
These are what I'm thankful for!
Austin Hulme, Grade 3
Four Peaks Elementary School, AZ

How to Be the American Flag
Wave in the air randomly.
Lower down when someone special dies.
Signal to people this is a free country.
Represent America/U.S.A.
Be an American symbol.
Have thirteen stripes on you.
Get 50 stars on you.
Be red, white, and blue.

Kevin Saenz, Grade 3
Willard Elementary School, CA

School
Roses are red, violets are blue
I like school and I hope you do too!
I like school because of math
Instead of a different path
I like to divide
But sometimes I cannot decide
But I like times more than divide
Because on times there's different kinds.

R. J. Rangel, Grade 3
Robinson Elementary School, TX

February
February is not long.
Valentine's Day is on the 14th of February.
The TAKS test is the 21st.
It takes four weeks and 2 days until
February is over!

Anastasia Almanza, Grade 3
Crestview Elementary School, TX

Rat
This corner of my room is black,
There's a strange noise when I turn my back.
It sounds like a rat,
But I hope it's not fat.
When I found out,
There was no doubt.
It was a cute cuddly rat,
And it's so cute that it wasn't fat.

Sara Chan, Grade 3
Zion Lutheran Church School, CA

I see people in the night sky,
I wish that I were a star.
I wish I lived at the mall,
So I could be in heaven.
I wish I were a famous singer,
So I could have a lot of money.
Julia Tillman, Grade 3
Turner Elementary School, TX

Holidays
When it is a new holiday
You get up, you run down the stairs
And come out.
It is cold!
Chris Clark, Grade 1
Thomas Edison Charter School, UT

Silly
Silly is green like the grass
with flowers, trees, and bushes.
It speeds through my heart
like a race car.
It makes me feel happy
like a smile.
It makes me want to jump.
Brandon Thao, Grade 2
Northridge Elementary School, CO

My Brother
He is my brother who
likes to be called "Curious monkey"
except when he's mad.
Eleanor Small, Grade 3
Our Lady of the Snows School, NV

Slavery
Slavery
is like losing all
your hopes and dreams
to chains.
It is like losing
all your dignity and feelings.
Anthony Bertram, Grade 3
Acacia Elementary School, AZ

Eve
Eve is a fine day
Because
Jesus was born
Tyler Thorn, Grade 1
Thomas Edison Charter School, UT

A Dog
Once there was a dog
walking in the fog.
He saw a flea
which made him say yhee!!!
In fright he tripped over a log.
Aryaman Lamsal, Grade 3
Patton Elementary School, TX

Dear Toy Cars,
Dear Toy Cars,
In the afternoon,
after snack,
I race downstairs
and plug you in.
And you zoom
here and there
on your black track.
Toys cars, you are faster
than a speeding motorcycle.
You are electric zooming rockets.

I got you on Christmas in Ohio.
I couldn't wait to try you out.

Toy cars, you make racing
seem real.
Colton Aubrey, Grade 2
Heatherwood Elementary School, CO

Granite
Granite
Colorful, solid
Aging, shining, changing
Granite is an igneous rock!
Rock
Kyler Barker, Grade 3
Four Peaks Elementary School, AZ

Twilight

Twilight, twilight, in the multicolored sky,
the clouds are purple, and the sky is orange.
The sun is dull, and funny looking,
as I went close to the sun it gets dull.
It seemed to be fading away,
the sky seemed to get darker, and darker,
I saw my shadow on the ground,
as the sun went down.

Ky Wilson, Grade 3
Lincoln Elementary School, CA

Pumice

Pumice
Holey, light
Cooling, bubbling, floating
Pumice is one of the only rocks than can float.
Floating

Quentin Donahue, Grade 3
Four Peaks Elementary School, AZ

Diary and Scrapbook

Diary
Writing, secrets
Lock, key, private
Thoughts, boyfriends, girlfriends, pictures
Collections, awards, events
Life, memories
Scrapbook

Riley Malone, Grade 1
Armstrong Elementary School, TX

Hawaii

When you go to Hawaii
you can go swimming
at beaches like McKenna Beach
you get really really sandy
and you get super super wet
you get pulled over by big big
huge waves that hurt you
you can go out to the ocean and snorkel
and see really neat fish.

Sydney Tanner, Grade 3
Gause Intermediate School, WA

Choose a Color

If I were red I would be a tasty apple that ripened from a tree. If I were orange I would be a round pumpkin that grows in a patch. If I were yellow I would be the hot sun that shines on us in the summertime. If I were green I would be grass that grows in my yard. If I were blue I would be the sky up above. If I were purple I would be a flower that grows. All of these colors put together make the rainbow.

Nicholas Provenzano, Grade 2
St Dorothy School, CA

Where I'm From

I'm from my flower bedroom, school, and Evin.
I'm from Molly and Madi, cinnamon toast.
I'm from Kira, Katy, and Jodi, Zanna.
I'm from Gram and Papa, Thinker Toys, and Hillsdale.
I'm from dancing, books, and beef.
I'm from Harry Potter to Sirius, and "Come on!"
I'm from my world!

Elizabeth Weeks, Grade 2
Bridlemile Elementary School, OR

Magnificent Malachi

When I am lying in my bed, I close my eyes and dream...
I am a basketball swishing in the net.
I am a handball slamming against the wall.
I am a golf ball leveled by a club.
I am a swimmer charging at the waves.
I am a dart shot against the dart board.
I am a tennis ball flying back and forth on the court.
I am a kickball soaring through the air.
I am a hockey puck flying on the ice.
I am a dictionary opening with lots of ideas.
I am a math quiz full of math problems.
I am a cold glass of lemonade in the explosive sun.
I am a cup of hot chocolate on a cold winter day.
I am a bowl full of flaming chicken noodle soup.
I am a cheetah jumping from tree to tree.
I am a falcon gliding in the air.
I am a black panther camouflaged by the jungle.
I am an anaconda wrapping around my prey.
I am a spy investigating criminals.
But when I open my eyes, I am more than I was in my dream.

Malachi Nelson, Grade 3
Open Charter Magnet School, CA

The World

The world is filled
with boys and girls
sugary treats and chocolate swirls
there are beaches and peaches
there are people
there are animals
there are flowers
and there are roses
in the oceans there are fish,
dolphins, sharks
and there are starfish
in the sky the sun comes out in the day time
and the moon comes
out in the night time
food tastes great
if not too late
sweet and sour done by the hour
done hot or cold but
all the same is really good.

Gabby Orozco, Grade 3
Williams Elementary School, CA

My Special Party

I had a party with my Teddy Bears
We had the party and it was rare
Because bears could talk and dance and sing
Then the doorbell went ding-a-ling
The party stopped when my parents came home
The Teddy Bears left and I was alone

Morgan Haefner, Grade 3
Cubberley Elementary School, CA

Joy in the Heart

When I was born
I was full of joy
The November sun with open daisies
Fall leaves crunching and tree branches lonely
Love in the heart spread all around
Open space full of desire for love
Mother, father and sisters bring me joy
Always happiness together.

Amir Enayati, Grade 3
Westwood Charter Elementary School, CA

My Cat Jingles

Grey and black,
Cute and cuddly,
Sneaking in my room to play.
Soft and warm,
Curvy ears,
Jumping on my bed to bounce.
Sleepy, purry,
Playful and nice.
She loves to chase me all around the house.
My cat Jingles would love to find a mouse!
Will Rippeto, Kindergarten
Presbyterian School, TX

Magic Castle

Way up high in the sky
you will see me I'm a castle
a magic castle of your dreams
a magic castle with wooden beams
a magic castle way up high
in the sky
you will see me I'm a castle a magic castle
a magic castle of your dreams
a magic castle with wooden beams
with swirling stairs go up so long
with tall walls that are so strong
a magic castle way up high
in the sky
you will see me I'm a castle
a magic castle of your dreams
a magic castle with wooden beams
with swirling stairs go up so long
with tall walls that are so strong
now we go down on the clouds
on to the ground
and imagine our castle
Natalie Gable, Grade 3
Katherine Delmar Burke School, CA

Red-footed Booby

I like a white bird.
It's a red-footed booby.
It's in the jungle.
Erick Martinez, Grade 3
Lorenzo De Zavala Elementary School, TX

I Wish

I wish I were a pig
In a messy pigpen
Playing in the mud
Running and jumping.
Brianna Huggans, Grade 3
Daly Elementary School, MT

Cows

Cows
Red, soft
Running, laying, eating
Cows have babies
Calves
Brittany Graham, Grade 1
Myatt Elementary School, TX

Winter Snow

W inter
I ce
N ice
T ime
E at hot chocolate
R ed hot fire!

S now
N ew snow is white
O ver land and sea
W et
Ethan Kurz, Grade 2
Carden West School, CA

White

White, white
Hello white.
Welcome to a fluffy cloud.
White, white
Let's cheer for white.
White paper,
White sails,
White snow,
White cotton.
Yeah, let's hear for white!
Porter Bretches, Grade 2
Grace School, TX

I Like Karate

My name is Jared Zarate
and I really like karate.
I have learned self control
even when someone says let's roll!
You have to obey the rule
or you won't be so cool.
My mom says I can't pack my lunch
but I sure can kick and punch!
Karate teaches self respect
and how to defend and protect.
I might be kind of shy
but don't ever spit in my eye!
I may have learned to be rough and tough
but I'm a nice guy and that's enough.

Jared Zarate, Grade 1
Twin Lakes Christian Academy, TX

Grizzly Bears

Strong grizzlies,
A grizzly bear can push over a car!

Huge grizzlies,
When they stand up they are as tall as a tree.

Sneaky grizzlies,
They are hard to find in the forest.

I hope I do not see one
Unless it is Smokey the Bear!

Justin Peterson, Grade 1
Paonia Elementary School, CO

Butterfly in a Field

Butterfly in a field.
With lots of wild flowers.
Lots of color and beauty.
Such a pretty and graceful butterfly.
With trees and birds.
The butterfly loves it here.
There are flowers it can sip like a daisy or lilly.
No wonder the butterfly loves it here.

Taylor Yarges, Grade 3
St Andrews Episcopal School, NM

The Little Black Bunny
There was a little black bunny.
All he liked to do was hop.
He played outside when it was sunny.
It was very hard to get him to stop.
Jason Creighton, Grade 1
St Mark's Day School, TX

Angry Horses
Hungry horses neigh
Pawing hooves on stable floors
No morning hay, Stomp!
Chloe Hannan, Grade 3
Midland Elementary School, CO

April Fool's Day
When it is April Fool's Day
it is a good time to joke around
with people, friends, and Dads.
You laugh and laugh, you have fun.
Chris Lopez, Grade 3
Midland Elementary School, CA

Babies and Adults
Baby
Noisy, quiet
Crying, sucking, falling
Playing, running, nice, tall
Swimming, caring, loving
Sweet, nice
Adult
Arianna Ashton, Grade 3
Turner Elementary School, TX

Love
I love the sun
I like to have fun
In the sun I play
At the beach I lay
The sun is bright
It has a lot of light
The sun is cool
On sunny days I go to school
Angelina Valenzuela, Grade 2
San Jacinto Elementary School, CA

My Kitty
There was a little kitty
And she was very pretty
I love my kitty
My kitty loves me
and I love her, too.
Emma Karpman, Grade 1
Fort Worth Country Day School, TX

Salmon
Oh mighty salmon
Where have you come from?
The fishing boats are out to get you.
Why do you jump so high
when you are sure to die?
Salmon, salmon why die
when there is future in the sky!
Alexandra Agoglia, Grade 3
Katherine Delmar Burke School, CA

Butterflies
butterflies
lovely, gentle
soaring, gliding, dashing
tiny wet wings
gorgeous

butterflies
mother, family
playing, running, chasing
I am a member of
the Apache
Butterfly Clan
Shantel Harris, Grade 2
Whiteriver Elementary School, AZ

Eighth Wonder of the World
Skull Island,
Found humans,
First he was bad,
Met a cute girl,
Then he turned good,
King Kong.
Cameron Voigt, Kindergarten
Jacob Wismer Elementary School, OR

Telephone Poles

Telephone poles are as tall as giraffes,
Sometimes buzzing like bees,
Wires that stretch as long as the Great Wall
of China,
As common as road sings,
Telephone poles help us communicate

Scott Shelton, Grade 3
Daves Avenue Elementary School, CA

An Ode to Spring

Golden poppies and marigolds,
Their colors shining bright.
As the wind tickles my cheek,
There is spring all around me!

The trees are tall.
The bugs are small.
The sky is very blue.
A sparrow sings its song,
For very long.
Its song is oh so true.

Some kids are playing basketball,
Or digging in the dirt,
As I sit here writing,
My second-to-last verse.

I wonder as I lie here
On a bed of grass,
Staring at the tree above,
Am I really the poet I seem
Or only a poet in another poet's dream?

Paige Miller, Grade 3
Fairmont Private School, CA

The Pig with a Wig

There was a boy
Who liked a toy
It was a pig
That wore a wig
That was the boy's joy

Jonathan Lee, Grade 3
Wonderland Avenue Elementary School, CA

Cassandra

C ool
A wesome
S weet
S mart
A lways likes to follow directions
N ice
D ramatic
R eading sweetie
A lways loves dogs.

Cassandra Dimaline, Grade 3
Turner Elementary School, TX

Rosa Parks

R osa Parks was born in Alabama.
O ctober 24, 2005, Rosa Parks died.
S he did not give up to segregation.
A nother law wanted to change.

P risoner in December 1st, 1955.
A rrested in December 1st, 1955.
R osa Parks had to take a test.
K icked off a bus.
S he had to take a test.

Victoria Castellano, Grade 2
Pinnacle Charter School, CO

Roller Blading

Lights
  flashing
    real
    fast.
Roller blading is a lot
of fun.
When I ride my rollerblades
on the street
it's bumpy.
You can roll
  down
    a
  hill
    real fast, too.
Roller blading is a lot of fun.

Makayla Hoesch, Grade 3
Acacia Elementary School, AZ

Parent

Parent
Friendly, nice
Helping, guiding, loving
Always caring for me.
Mother

Lucas Johnson, Grade 3
Four Peaks Elementary School, AZ

Cats and Dogs

A cat and a dog
Went to the park
Together.
They played tag
Together.
A cat and a dog.

Christine Reed, Kindergarten
Jacob Wismer Elementary School, OR

Maggie

Maggie
playful, wild
tears, slides, jumps
she likes to be rubbed on the stomach.
Westie puppy

Lucas Marchiondo, Grade 2
Polk Elementary School, TX

Anger

Anger is red.
It sounds like a volcano erupting.
It smells like smoke.
It tastes like hot chilies.
It looks like fighting swords.
Anger feels like strength.

Sargune Kalsi, Kindergarten
CLASS Academy, OR

Samurai in the Making

I have a special Samurai sword.
It was very hard to afford.
I play with it when I am bored.
When I swing it, I cannot be ignored!

Skyler Wagaman, Grade 3
Sundance Elementary School, WY

The Cat and Mouse
A cat sees a mouse.
What will it do?
Will it climb up or down?
Will it chase it on the ground?
Will it jump in the air?
Will it not even care?
Oops, too late.
The cat just ate
the mouse.

Mason Keefe, Grade 3
Wonderland Avenue Elementary School, CA

Super Mask!
If I put on the mask
I will have the power to run fast as a cheetah
to China and back in 1 minute
and I will have the power to see into the future
and I have one more power
it will be to hear very far away.

Devin Hudson, Grade 3
Briargrove Elementary School, TX

Pirates
People panic in the sea
Inconsiderate people
Robbing them from their treasure chests
Abuse the ships
Threatening other men
Eager to kill and
Shield themselves with cutlasses.

Miguel Valenciano, Grade 3
Emerson Elementary School, TX

Pets
Dog
black, big
eating, running, barking
bone, dog house, mice, claws
purring, scratching, eating
small, orange
Cat

Elise Aguirre, Grade 3
Kathy L Batterman Elementary School, NV

Christmas
Christmas is fun.
I like Christmas.
Santa comes if you are good.
Maybe he will leave a rocket ship,
Or maybe even a chip.
If you're really bad,
He'll leave a bone,
Or a plain old stone,
Or even a cracker if you're a snacker.
Christmas is really great,
Especially in my state!
Austin Higley, Grade 2
New Emerson School, CO

Motocross
Turning, jumping, speed,
Wind and dirt hitting your face,
Motocross is fun!
Reed Koch, Grade 3
Turner Elementary School, TX

Easter Sunday
Sunny morning
Easter Sunday,
And bright light shone everywhere.
Michelle Espinoza, Grade 3
St Raphael School, CA

Spring
Flowers bloom in the spring,
Feel the sun shining on you,
Rain, too.
I love it!
Emily Stelmak-DeWitt, Kindergarten
The Presentation School, CA

Light Jak
Light Jak
Kind, daring, good
Healing, freezing, shielding
Precursor
Light Jak
Samuel C. Lowry, Grade 3
Kootenai Valley Christian School, MT

Rainbows
Rainbow, rainbow so shiny and
colorful every rainbow is.
So every time you know how cool it is
to see a rainbow in the sky.
Matthew Magnison, Grade 2
Frontier Valley Elementary School, CO

I Like Fords
I like Fords.
Any kind of Ford.
Black, blue, green.
Red, purple,
A Ford in a cornfield.
A Ford on a farm.
A Ford in the mud.
A Ford in the dirt.
Ranger to F-350's.
Any kind of Ford.
I like Ford pickups.
John Robert Jackson, Grade 2
Swink Elementary School, CO

Friends Are Fun!!
Friends are fun,
When we run.
We tell jokes,
We get soaked.

We share quarters and dimes,
Sometimes we lose track of time.
Friends have your back,
They keep you on the right track.

Sometimes we fight,
One day she went on a flight.
She didn't tell me where,
But I really did care.

One day my friend came back,
She was carrying a sack.
She came to my house,
With a new, red blouse!!
Jerlin Bustillo, Grade 2
DeQueen Elementary School, TX

A Sweet Soft Sound

A sweet soft sound of birds rang out.
It cut the air like scissors.
Their wings beat hard like knives cutting bread.
As they soared over me
I felt so small and weak
compared to those birds flying high
with all the power I might not have.
Their sweet soft song rang out.

Elena Anamos, Grade 3
Westwood Charter Elementary School, CA

Puppy

Lucky dog Crossman
A very cute and stupid puppy
Anytime day or night
At my grandmother's house and my house
Because he barks and growls
at anything that moves or surprises him.

Kyle Crossman, Grade 3
Daly Elementary School, MT

Dinosaur

Dinosaur, Dinosaur, Dinosaur.
Dinosaurs are so big,
It would take a circus tent to cover them up.
Big, big, big, big.
Dinosaurs are so big.

Damon Castillo, Grade 2
Mission Grade School, MT

Clowns

Clowns,
Clowns
They scare me so much.

Even if they are so funny,
They creep me out.

Sometimes when I see so many,
I wonder if there is a mother
That lays eggs 100 times a day.

Mario De La Cruz, Grade 3
Eduardo Villarreal Elementary School, TX

The World Was Warm and White When I Was Born
the world was warm and white when I was born
the flowers of spring were blooming
the warm blankets wrapped around me
I was held in the cushion of my mother's arms
watching through the window the bright moon
shining on the flowers
I felt like I was blooming
to become my own self

Diane Shabtaie, Grade 3
Westwood Charter Elementary School, CA

Baseball
When I play baseball it is very loud
some people whistle and scream
the ball makes a sound when it hits the bat
everybody yells and screams
and then a player catches it
and they throw it to first base
then I run to first
and then I run to second base
suddenly, the player catches the ball and he drops it
I run to third base and I am safe
it's the next player's turn
and he hits a single
and I run home and I am safe

Tyler Owens, Grade 3
Horn Academy, TX

Love
Love is sweet, but love isn't a picnic.
You may never get another chance at true love.
Once you realize you said, "No" to the person
you love, you feel like it's the end of the world.
You wish you would have said, "Yes," but it might be
too late to say it.
The next day you might feel better or worse, but
who's to know.
You know someday you'll find the one you were
meant to be with.
So…until then, remember,
Someone out there loves you and probably always will.

Gracie Aguirre, Grade 3
Briggsdale Elementary School, CO

Ocean
I am a really beautiful ocean.
I have a bunch of waves.
I am a large body of water
You can swim in me.
I can divide into different parts.
You can sail a boat in me.
If you want to come in me
You have to look out for dangerous creatures

Korie Richardson, Grade 3
Briargrove Elementary School, TX

My Thinking Place
I have a thinking place
Where I'm hidden from the world.
To see the things that others can't
A scream, yeah! The noises of the yard.
As they roll over the hills.
And I think about books I'll write
Or arguments I've had
And I'll sit and watch
And think the day away.

Claire Danna, Grade 3
Wonderland Avenue Elementary School, CA

Butterflies
Butterflies are as graceful as
an ice skater on the ice.
a horse when they run in the field.
a bee flying in the blue sky.
a bird flying around a tree.
a spider making a web.
a bat flying around a tree.
an owl flying in the height looking for food.

Vanessa Perez Patino, Grade 3
Lincoln Elementary School, CA

White
White is the color of soft clouds.
White is the color of bunnies.
White is the color of flowers after they bloom.
White is the color of the birds wings.

Vanessa Andre, Grade 1
Solana Santa Fe Elementary School, CA

A Pot of Gold
I found a pot of gold
It was very old
I don't know what to do
with an old pot of gold.
Nicolette Spriggs, Grade 3
Broderick Montessori School, CA

The Children and Me
I am a playing, running, climbing,
walking, shouting, talking boy.

I am a painting, drawing, learning,
paper gluing, coloring kid.

We are good children bad children.

We are talking children.
We are singing, playing catch,
eating children.
Jonathan Alexander Avila, Grade 3
Briargrove Elementary School, TX

Fruit Bat
Fruit bat sinks her teeth into an apple
And soars through the air with glee
As she hears the whimper of her baby.
Flying fox.
Rebecca Dulaney, Grade 3
Sundance Elementary School, WY

Spring
I like spring because it's almost Easter.
On Easter lots of people find eggs
on a plant, bush or in green grass.
Also you get to fly a kite with a friend.
Raquel Guerra, Grade 3
Midland Elementary School, CA

Coyotes
Meat eaters hunt night
Moving swiftly through the dark
Fur coats protect body
Samantha Kessler, Grade 3
Lanai Road Elementary School, CA

Echo
Echo is a bumpy sound.
It bumps around me even on me.
I cannot see it, but I know it's there.

I think it's in the air?
If I say a word, it plops on the wall.

Well one day I was in a tunnel.
It was dark black.
And I said hat.
And it came back.

I love echoes,
Ec, ec, ec, echoes!!!
Anjali Emsellem, Grade 1
Jefferson Elementary School, CA

Dear Winter Lights,
I want to look
Straight up from my bed,
Unfortunately I can't
Because there is a roof
Above my sleepy head
I know your lights
Dance from tree to tree
Aidan Longhurst, Grade 2
Heatherwood Elementary School, CO

For Mom's 40th Birthday
Something happy something sweet
Something very good to eat
Shall I bake you a lovely cake
It's not just Saturday
It's your 40th Birthday!
Girija Chatufale, Grade 2
Riverbend Montessori School, TX

Frogs
Frogs are green,
With sticky legs,
They need to stay lean,
Frogs lay eggs.
Justin Kenion, Kindergarten
Creekside Early Learning Center, CA

Monkeys
Violets are red
Flowers are blue
Monkeys are cool
What about you?

Monkeys are dumb
Monkeys are fun.
Monkeys are so
Dumb they make
Me want to run.

Monkeys can't run
Monkeys can't walk
Monkeys are so dumb
They can't even talk.

David Hovsepian, Grade 3
Tca Arshag Dickranian Armenian School, CA

Colors
Red is hyper or mad!
Red is burning hot in the fire.
Orange is calm and cool.
Orange is like the juice of an orange.

Yellow is bright or smart.
Yellow is sweet like honey.
Green is young and birth.
Green is light as the grass weights

Blue is sad or depressed.
Blue is calm as the sky in spring or summer.
Violet is light and nice.
Violet is sweet as the flowers smell.

Pink is tired or overwhelmed.
Pink is when you blush.
White is scared and surprised.
White is calm when the wind blows.

Black is evil or murder.
Black is the night.

Kevin Zhang, Grade 3
Lincoln Elementary School, CA

The King Cobra
Quickly,
Fiercely,
Powerfully,
The King Cobra
Was eating a mouse.
— Oh my!
Matthew Bonney, Grade 1
Fir Grove Elementary School, OR

Are We There Yet?
The drive is long
My brother smells
If I could
I would yell
My legs are cramped
My butt is numb
The way is long
This song is dumb
The car is hot
The windows stuck
My head is fried
And I'm fed up
We're almost there
That's what they say
We're almost there
All darn day
Donald McEdward, Kindergarten
Meadow View Elementary School, OR

Sun Shine
It is yellow, red, pink, and gold.
It is very, very, very bold.
It is bright.
It is light.
It is sun shine!
Shelby Rashap, Grade 2
Cottonwood Montessori School, NM

Fireworks
I like to play with fireworks
The fireworks at night
are bright
Kevin Roberts, Grade 1
Fir Grove Elementary School, OR

I Am Divali
I am very fun.
The dancers are doing Indian dances.
The lights are very bright.
The dresses are beautiful.
The feast is very yummy.
The jewelry is sparkly.
The flowers smell better than ever.
Divali is a wonderful holiday.
I am Divali.
Rubika Prasad, Grade 2
CLASS Academy, OR

Soccer
"Kick the ball, Allie!"
Coach Paul screams.
You're almost there!
"Kick it into the goalie box!"
He hollers

SCORE!
WE WIN!
Allie Ciardullo, Grade 2
Frontier Valley Elementary School, CO

Burton
Brother
4 years old
fun
play a lot
very cool
nice
Ricky Reynolds, Grade 2
Cox Bar Elementary School, CA

My Heart
In my heart
I feel joy
and happiness
In my heart
I feel
like my friends
are there too
Sierra Bladorn, Grade 1
Fir Grove Elementary School, OR

Mom

Looks as good as a rose,
Looks nice like a butterfly,
Sounds like a bluebird singing,
Sounds like a pig, oink, oink,
Soft as a bunny running across the road,
Comfy as a pillow,
Tastes like an apple that has been eaten,
And a banana that is very ripe,
My mom smells like a vanilla,
That is like a rose.
She smells like strawberry lotion
That she bought from Wal-Mart.
Rosabelle

Shantelle Kee, Grade 2
Ganado Primary School, AZ

The Dragon

The knight will kill the dragon
But the dragon will succeed.
But the dragon killed the knight
And the knight went up to heaven.

Anthony Glek, Grade 2
St John of San Francisco Orthodox Academy, CA

White

White is the color of the clouds in the sky.
White is the color of the paper I draw on.
White is the color of our uniform shirt.
White is the color of the snow falling down.
White is the color of the teeth in my mouth.
White is the color of the socks that I wear.

Alyssa Aramburu, Grade 1
Grace School, TX

I Dream of Jungles

I dream of jungles where lions don't eat meat.
I dream of jungles where lions let you pet them.
Jungles where animals let you ride them.
Jungles where lions let you ride them.
I dream of jungles where lions don't eat meat.

Franky Burt, Grade 3
Daly Elementary School, MT

Big and Small Animals
Elephants and hippos are big,
frogs and porcupines are small.
It does not matter if you are small or big
you should get treated the same way!

Jesseé Buck, Grade 3
Academy of Charter Schools, CO

Sleepiness
Sleepiness is the color of black.
It sounds like nothing.
It smells like peace.
It tastes like ginger cookies.
It looks like a dream.
Sleepiness feels like a bunny with soft fur.

Ava Young, Grade 2
CLASS Academy, OR

National Parks
National Parks and their wonderful beauty,
Nature has given them lots.
You really should be thankful,
For you can find many cool rocks.

Daniel Jurich, Grade 3
Edmonds Homeschool Resource Center, WA

Spring
Spring reminds me of Easter,
Easter reminds me of Good Friday,
Good Friday reminds me of the Passover,
The Passover reminds me of Jesus,
Jesus reminds me of life,
Life reminds me of spring.

Calli McMurray, Grade 3
Wiederstein Elementary School, TX

Camera
If I were a camera...
I'd see everything,
I'd run out of film,
I'd spend time taking pictures,
If I were a camera...

Rylee Bashkingy, Grade 1
Solana Santa Fe Elementary School, CA

Sugar and Sweets
Sugar and sweets are such wonderful treats.
Sweet, sour, and sugary things that I like to eat.
Lollipops, Snickers, M&Ms, Skittles, and Three Musketeers, too.
We can split them in half, some for me, some for you.
But sometimes these things seem tasteless to me.
So I'll just sit down and have some broccoli.

Natalie Abellera, Grade 3
Hollister SDA School, CA

The Long Walk
The Long Walk
Kit Carson's mission was to gather each Navajos
Sent them on a journey to Bosque Redondo Reservation in 1864
Marched three hundred mile across the hot dirt as two hundred Navajos died
Hweeldi'go Naasdee (the Long Walk)
The Long Walk
Kit Carson invaded through the Four Sacred Mountains
Where sheep roams, cornfield growing and fresh water to drink
Leaving behind die sheep, burnt cornfields and poisons the water
Hweeldi'go Naasdee (the Long Walk)
The Long Walk
A band of Navajo women, men, children and babies
Walk through the hot sand under the night skies and hot sun
Soldiers saunter them eastward toward Fort Summers
Hweeldi'go Naasdee (the Long Walk)
The Long Walk
They were set free to live on the reservation
During the setting sun, people began to cry when they saw Mount Taylor
We were defeated as one, yet we have grown and become rich again as one
Hweeldi'go Naasdee (the Long Walk)

Tred Begay, Grade 3
Ganado Primary School, AZ

What a Mountain Remembers
A mountain remembers the feel of people climbing on it
It remembers how it was made
A mountain remembers the rocks falling off of it
The coldness on it
the weather
It remembers clouds around it
and the river flowing

Alexandra Lee, Grade 3
Westwood Charter Elementary School, CA

Queen Rellaboma, Princess Fellizee

Queen Rellaboma, Princess Fellizee
traveled to London
to have a cup of tea
they met a couple aliens
a couple men from Mars
then got into their space mobile
to explore the stars.
Sophia Sweedler Wyatt, Grade 3
Katherine Delmar Burke School, CA

My Dog Rudy

Black and white,
Cute and cuddly,
Playful and sweet,
Gentle and kind.
She likes to bounce and she likes to pounce,
And beg for doggie treats.
She graduated from school today,
Where she learned to do tricks and play.
She likes to run in the soft, cool sand,
And she runs in the water to catch the waves.
She tries to catch the birds on the beach,
And they fly away out of her reach.
My dog Rudy!
Abigail Williard, Kindergarten
Presbyterian School, TX

Colors

Red is the cover to my bible.
Orange is a carved pumpkin on my porch.
Yellow is the bright stars in the night sky.
Green is a shiny ribbon in my hair.
Blue is the salty water in the ocean.
Purple is beautiful violets in mom's vase.
Emily Gayle, Grade 1
Grace School, TX

The Pig That Flew on the Paper Airplane

Did you hear about the pig that flew?
On the paper airplane the pig turned blue.
He turned blue because he held his breath.
He was afraid of heights and scared to death.
Matthew Luke, Grade 2
Sierra Vista Elementary School, CA

Spider Webs

Webs are jewels that
glitter and sparkle in fog.
Webs are miracles.
Landry Tchamengo, Grade 3
Grace School, TX

My New Baby Brother

His skin was peach.
He was really quiet.
He smelled like fresh air.
He smelled like a baby.
He makes me feel really good.
Kole Tison, Grade 3
Daly Elementary School, MT

What Two Can Do

I like to
play tag
with my dog, Cooper.
He makes me
feel proud
because we play tag
together.
Alex Martinez, Grade 1
Ryan Elementary School, CO

Joy

Joy is sky blue.
It sounds like birds singing.
It smells like a big forest.
It tastes like chocolate cake.
It looks like Christmas.
Joy feels like a teddy bear.
Sean Glackin, Grade 3
CLASS Academy, OR

My Puppy

Puppy
Funny, fluffy
Chases cats, begs for treats
I am so sad when he gets lost.
Peanut
Griffin Simpson, Grade 1
Grace School, TX

The Forest

I hear a stream running through the forest.
I smell wet leaves in the breeze.
I feel wind rushing against my face.
I taste stream water, it is so cold.
I see blue jays flying above the trees!
This is what I see on my way through the forest.

Alabama Scout Rozell-Lewis, Grade 3
CLASS Academy, OR

Silkworm

Silkworms hear through their tummies
Almost like ears of bunnies
Their eyes can see in the night
Like a human in the light
Munches on a mulberry leaf
As a kid would eat a cranberry
A silkworm feels with its back
As cute as a baby in a rack
Silkworms smell though their nose
It is as pretty as a rose

My duty is to spin and spin
As fast as a fishes fin
Slowly and slowly as we fall to the Earth
All I wanted to do is see the Earth
Now I am safe
I will believe in my faith
Now people are screaming at us
They look like they're about to fuss
Now people are cheering
This is what I like to be hearing

Joseph Chamanara, Grade 3
Del Paso Manor Elementary School, CA

Girl from Malibu

There once was a girl from Malibu
She always said cock-a-doodle-do
She slept in the dark
She was always scared of a shark
She always scared people by saying Boo!

Nicole Horner, Grade 3
St Raphael School, CA

Dad

Dear dad I love you,
you are kind,
you are nice.
You love me so much,
so that's why I love you,
you are so sweet to me.

Ateshi Singh, Grade 1
Montessori School of Downtown, TX

Skiing

Can you
feel the
wind when
you are
skiing down
the hill?
It is
fun when
you're skiing
down the
hill! Can
you feel
the bumps
when you
are skiing?
I jump,
slide, and
glide! Soon
zoom I
am down
the hill!

Mirra Gutman, Grade 3
Briargrove Elementary School, TX

Star

Give me a ride.
When I see you fly,
I make a wish.
I go to bed.
I see you in the night,
shining bright.
Give me a ride.

Jessica Love, Grade 2
Acacia Elementary School, AZ

Spider

There once was a spider
who lived all alone
He ate insects
above a puppies bone
One day the spider
went to a hole
and dropped on top
of a little mole!

Albert L. Dedmon, Grade 2
Montessori School of Downtown, TX

Storm

Lightning flashes
Then comes the thundering roar
I am so scared

Ethan Duke, Grade 1
South Shore Montessori School, TX

Places

School
big, rectangular
playing, reading, learning
teachers, kids, mom, dad
sleeping, resting, reading
nice, two-story
Home

Deanna Vinluan, Grade 3
Rogers Elementary School, NV

Turtles

Turtles
green, yellow, cute
shell, sleepy, slow
small, round, adorable, sleeping
looking, moving, quiet, egg

Jennifer Lee, Grade 1
Eton School, WA

My Sister Is Cool

Her eyes glimmer like the moon
She has beautiful teeth
Her face is like the sun

Taylor Larson, Grade 1
Fir Grove Elementary School, OR

Oklahoma
I wish I were
RED
sitting on the sidelines
cheering on O.U.
at the top of my lungs.

P.J. Voorheis, Grade 2
University Park Elementary School, TX

Zoe the Dog
Furry, brown, blue collar, jingle tags,
Licks my mom, jumps when we walk,
Plays ball, chases cats, eats watermelon,
Loves my brothers and me,
We love Zoe!

Emma Kallmeyer, Kindergarten
Presbyterian School, TX

Snowmobiling
The most important thing about
snowmobiling is spinning through the snow.
It is fun and exciting.
It can be hurtful and dangerous.
It is great to climb hills and go over jumps.
But the most important thing about
snowmobiling is it is a blast!

Dustin Springer, Grade 3
Daly Elementary School, MT

Love Is...
Love is hard sometimes
Love is like two doves
Love is funny
Love is mean
Love is when you say, "I love you"
Love is what you feel inside of you
Love is pretty
Love is loving someone and not telling them
Love is two people
Love is sunny sometimes
Love is dark sometimes

Mistydawn Steward, Grade 3
Fort Vannoy Elementary School, OR

Flowers

Flowers, Flowers, Flowers.
Bees get some honey from flowers.
Pretty, Pretty, Pretty flowers.
Flowers are every single color.
Broncette Brown, Grade 2
Mission Grade School, MT

Sparkling Snow

The snow was
Cold as ice
The ice sparkled
Like diamonds
Snow shining
Like sugar
Cold air to breathe
The snow slippery
Like a watery floor
And the wind
Singing around
Leaves falling down
Cold water to drink
Kids voices flying around
Birds dancing and singing
People fishing for food
People wearing warm clothes
I love snow!
Eymi De los Santos, Grade 3
Edison Elementary School, CA

Snow Cones

Snow cones are very good
I like to eat them everywhere
even in the wintertime.
Daniel A. Hoel, Grade 3
Our Lady of the Snows School, NV

Snow

White, glittering,
blinding, floating.
Light as air.
It falls to the wet, damp ground
where you can PLAY!
Ryan Cook, Grade 2
Frontier Valley Elementary School, CO

Volcano and Mountains

Volcano
Shooting, lava
Fire, erupting, smoking
Holes, rocks, hiking, high
Climbing, cold, snow covered
Large, rocky
Mountains
Travis Miller, Grade 1
Armstrong Elementary School, TX

Day and Night

The great big clouds shine over the sun
The grass surrounds the trees
The trees will try to escape
But the wind blows the sun.

The sky turns the world
The stars will be tucked in
Nestled in the telephone wires
In their nightcaps and blankets.
Mackenzie Deacon, Grade 3
Pioneer Primary School, WA

Mermaids and Merman

Mermaids
Bikini, long hair
Beautiful, swimming, Princess
Queen, human, fish, fast
Rocks, shells, crowns
Prince, King
Merman
Valentino Sinacola, Grade 1
Armstrong Elementary School, TX

Dogs and Cats

Dog,
Barks, growls,
Growing, chewing, barking,
Hyper puppy, lazy kitty,
Purring, sitting, laying,
Scratches, meows,
Cat
Breanna Nelson, Grade 3
Turner Elementary School, TX

All Kinds of Cats
Small cats, large cats, cute cats, bad cats,
Skinny cats, fat cats, fluffy cats,

Sand cats, funny cats, messy cats, sad cats,
Snow cats, dry cats, mountain cats, jungle cats,

Tree cats, farm cats, city cats, mean cats,
Sissy cats, shy cats, climbing cats, hungry cats,

Wild cats, silly cats, loud cats, old cats,
black cats, brown cats, white cats.

All kinds of cats!!!

Zachary Horning, Grade 2
Sangre De Cristo Elementary School, CO

Sleeping Puppies
Puppies sleeping
Puppies snoring
Puppies here
Puppies there
Puppies are
everywhere
Some are silent
Some are violent
Dreaming silently

Ebony Stevenson, Grade 3
Wonderland Avenue Elementary School, CA

There's a Puppy in My Doorway
I just woke up, I heard a ruff.
My mom said, "That's enough!"
I said, "What? I didn't ruff."
There's a tiny little mutt.
What?
A tiny little mutt.
I think I'm going to drop my coffee cup.
Shoo, you little mutt!
Actually, my coffee cup is in the shape of a mug.
Hey, little pup, are you a pug?

Cody Clayton, Grade 2
New Emerson School, CO

The Nice Ocean

Ocean rushing like a small grace
it puts a smile upon my face.
Ocean blow me and roll me
and turn me and teach me to fly.
Dance with me ocean like you dance
toss a kite like you dance
toss kites on the hill!

Malik Tapia, Grade 3
Lincoln Elementary School, CA

My Dog Tip

My dog Tip
can drink water in a sip.
He eats like a hound.
He likes to jump around.
He is so cute
and he chews on my old boot.
When he comes in the house
he sits on the couch.
And he loves to play with Rex.

Makenzi Dawson, Grade 3
Robinson Elementary School, TX

My Dad Michael

M usic singer
I ce cream eater
C atches balls with me
H e is a soccer teacher
A ttorney
E xcellent worker
L ikes kids

Kendall Grace Hudgins, Grade 1
Grace School, TX

Monkeys and Gorillas

Monkeys
Climbing, loud
Fast, swinging, jumping
Scratching, laughing, huge, wild
Hairy, fierce, tall
Heavy, black
Gorillas

Madeline Rutledge, Grade 1
Armstrong Elementary School, TX

Moving

We used to be neighbors,
but now we're separated.
We used to be together,
but now we're alone.
Her parents were together,
but now they're divorced.
We used to be together,
but now we're bored...
'Cause she's moving!

Taylor McKnight, Grade 3
Acacia Elementary School, AZ

Harriet

H arriet was born a slave.
A lso escaped.
R isked her life to be free.
R escued lots of slaves.
I learned about her in class.
E scaped in 1849.
T ubman was her last name.

Carrin Barnes, Grade 2
Pinnacle Charter School, CO

Don't Forget

Don't forget to do your homework
Don't forget to brush your teeth
Don't forget to fetch the newspaper
Don't forget to get me candy
Don't forget to read your book
DON'T FORGET ME!!!

Hannah Murphy, Grade 3
Katherine Delmar Burke School, CA

Art

I love art,
It's really not hard.
All you do is,
Take a paintbrush.
They will pay.
All you do is
Make some marks,
And that's ART.

Alanna Williams, Grade 3
Turner Elementary School, TX

Quarter

If I were a quarter...
I'd be dirty,
I'd be in people's pockets,
I'd be in millions of hands,
If I were a quarter...

Luke Ford, Grade 1
Solana Santa Fe Elementary School, CA

Sisters

Rachel
mean, scary
hitting, playing, kicking
girl, sister, female, person
talking, walking, thinking
young, good
Tiffany

Tiffany Ma, Grade 3
Kathy L Batterman Elementary School, NV

The Desert

The desert feels hot and sunny.
The desert tastes like sand.
The desert sounds quiet.

Manuel Gomez-Perez, Grade 1
Robert L Stevens Elementary School, CA

Stars

Stars are bright in the night.
Some stars falling through the night.
Stars are loud when they come crashing down.
Make a wish on a falling star tonight.

Sarissa Lopez, Grade 2
Lincoln Elementary School, CA

Yellow

Yellow is the sour lemon that I bite.
Yellow is the pencil I write with.
Yellow is the sun I see in the sky.
Yellow is the card I pull when I'm in trouble.
Yellow is the sun that shines at me.

Alejandro Puga, Grade 2
Lincoln Elementary School, CA

Travels

When I am hiking up a mountain,
I see wildlife,
Going up the mountain.
But the real thing,
That I imagine is
Going up an ice cream cone.
On the top of the ice cream cone,
I see popsicles which are really trees.

Erin Hing, Grade 2
Brush Creek Elementary School, CO

My Home

The door creaks open.
The dishes clang like a rattle.
My mom humming like birds,
Because she is happy.
The calm breeze
Hitting the chimes softly.
With the smell of hot cookies.
I take a bite.
Yum.
The cookies feel like
Love in my stomach.

Aurora Beans, Grade 3
Four Peaks Elementary School, AZ

School

When you are at school, you learn.
At school, people play at recess.
At school we do work.
At school we go to the bathroom.
At school, we bring in our homework.

Dylan Rivera, Kindergarten
Crestview Elementary School, TX

Fall

It is fall,
The leaves are falling
Me and my mom
the leaves we are raking
Then I jump in the leaves.
Leaves!!!

Micaela Fogle, Grade 1
Montessori School of Downtown, TX

A Depressing Valentine's Day

There is a girl on the block,
And we really like to talk.
I was going to her house,
To ask her to be my valentine.
But on her lawn
There was a moving sign.
I was sad and depressed;
I thought she was the best.
Then a new girl came.
But, she was not the same.
I thought she was pretty and fine.
So, I asked her to be my valentine.

Justin Zumel, Grade 3
St Dorothy School, CA

School

I like school
Because it is cool
We take a long time
To learn how to rhyme
We have a big class
We play in the grass
We love to play in the sun
So we can have fun

Sandy Reyes, Grade 2
San Jacinto Elementary School, CA

The Seasons of Sports

It is spring, yippee yeah!
It is spring, I can play.
Baseball, softball, biking too,
Basketball, soccer, and it's through.

It is summer, very hot.
Swimming really hits the spot.
Diving, racing, running too,
These are things that you can do.

It is fall, there are more sports,
Football, running, and all sorts.
It is winter, more fun, let's play,
Skiing and sledding make our day.

William Whitmer, Grade 2
Montessori Christian Academy, TX

When I Was Born
When I was born
the sunset gleamed upon my face
the heavens called me here to live
my gentle parents kissed me upon my face
soft as the milky way
my little twin brother, Alex, right by my side
made me feel loved
angels clutching my hands
leading me to the life before me
all my happiness fulfilled
the world awaits me
It's my time to live

Shea Copeland, Grade 3
Westwood Charter Elementary School, CA

Bald Eagle
Bald Eagle
White and black,
Soaring through the sky, seriously hunting
Scaring furry field mice.
Carnivore.

Trevor O'Brien, Grade 3
Sundance Elementary School, WY

The Most Important Thing About Bikes
The most important thing about a bike
is the brakes.
It is fun riding and doing wheelies.
It can do a stoppie and a wheelie.
It is really important.
But the most important thing about a bike
is the brakes.

Dodge Hurley, Grade 3
Daly Elementary School, MT

Dance
Dance is fun dance is cool
dance makes me feel so skillful!
We do recitals
and when we are all together we make one.

Miranda Hopkins, Grade 3
Academy of Charter Schools, CO

My 4 Wheeler

My 4-wheeler is cool and blue and kind of fast too
my helmet is blue with stripes too
I get real muddy out in the country, in a wide open space
as I fly down the road in a fast mode across a toad
and I ride all the way home.

Freddy Velazquez, Grade 3
Williams Elementary School, CA

Dusk and Dawn

Dusk appears as dawn meets dusk.
I see dawn just appeared.
I stand perfectly still
I hear rain dribble drop
After that I got out of bed
As my mom said "Come down for dinner."
I looked one last time at the moon
As I came down my mom said "What took so long"
I was watching the moon
I looked at the moon I said to myself
It looks beautiful so magical
Like a sound of a clear sky.
But then after that I went inside
And closed the door behind me.
I call the moon my moon friend
I said to myself good night best friend
I will see you tomorrow
I went to bed
In the morning I saw dawn I said hello friend
Have you met dusk?

Monique Garcia, Grade 3
Lincoln Elementary School, CA

Name Calling Is a Waste of Time

Name-calling is a waste of time.
Don't break the chain,
It's a waste of time.
For if you break the chain of no name-calling rule,
You should know that you've hurt someone's feelings.
Perhaps you have broken the no name-calling rule already
But there is one thing you should know,
Never name-call anymore.

Nancy Valdovinos, Grade 3
Accelerated School, CA

Bearded Dragon

I have a **B** eard
I **E** at crickets
I h **A** ve five toes
I **R** un fast
I sleep upside **D** own
I dislik **E** cats
I am afraid of **D** ogs

I have **D** ull colors
I am almost as long as a **R** uler
I h **A** te snakes
I don't like **G** oats
I'm on the r **O** ad again
I say **N** ope to flies

Justine Peterson, Grade 3
St Raphael School, CA

Halloween Echo

Happy Halloween
Happy Halloween
Happy scary Halloween.
I hope you went trick-or-treating.
How much candy did you get?
How much candy did you get?
I hope you had fun.
I hope you had fun.
Did you eat your candy?
Did you eat your candy?
What are you this Halloween?
What are you this Halloween?
Happy Halloween.

Meena Nanduri, Grade 3
Delphi Academy of San Francisco Bay, CA

Blue Jay

I wish I were
BLUE
I would be sitting on a tree limb
looking for my dinner
flying around houses.

Sadie Shorter, Grade 2
University Park Elementary School, TX

Toucans
Beautiful and soft
tropical and colorful
Toucans fly so high.
Daniela Palomo, Grade 3
Lorenzo De Zavala Elementary School, TX

Pink Panther
There once was a girl named Pink Panther
She liked to sleep in the hamper
She loved to snore
inside her safe door
She loved to skip and scamper
Steven Aasted, Grade 3
St Raphael School, CA

Football Players and Basketball Players
Football Players
Running, passing
Tackling, snapping, receiving
Pitching, punting, shooting, dribbling
Passing, backboard, dunking
Lay up, scoring
Basketball players
Spencer Walker, Grade 1
Armstrong Elementary School, TX

My Cats
My cat, Bruno
And fat, Sulley
Sometimes are real funny!

Sometimes they…
I don't know,
Get into the honey?

I love them
Just so much, you know
It makes me want to cry.

Sometimes I don't notice,
But a tear
Rolls out my eye.
Emmett White, Grade 2
Sangre De Cristo Elementary School, CO

Fairies
Fairies
lovely, fun,
bright, nice, sparkly,
playful, jumpy
fairies
Madelyn Kirsch, Grade 1
Highland Park School, MT

Spring
I love spring!
Spring is here, here,
the wind whistles,
I feel happy!
Sarah Lamp, Kindergarten
The Presentation School, CA

Letters
Letters,
Letters,
I love
letters.
They
spell
a word
every
time
you
put
them
together.
I love
LETTERS!!!
Katerina Geisler, Grade 1
New Emerson School, CO

Sadness
Sadness is dark green.
It sounds like someone crying.
It smells like a wilted rose.
It tastes like sour lemons.
It looks like a dead plant.
Sadness feels like tears.
Abigail Hall, Grade 2
CLASS Academy, OR

Night Bright

In the night I go to bed
and I am a very sleepy head.

In the night it is dark,
but I face it until it is light.

Like a little flower in the day
a little poem is all I have to say.

Clare Fusselman, Grade 1
Prince of Peace Community School, TX

Many Colors

If I were red,
I would be a red dragon that blows fire.
If I were brown,
I would be the bark of a willow tree.
If I were white,
I would be a soccer ball that you kick in a goal.
If I were purple,
I would be a folder with lots of homework in it.
If I were yellow,
I would be the sun that shines very bright.
If I were black,
I would be the night with many stars.

Timmy Ebiner, Grade 3
St Dorothy School, CA

Love

Love is beautiful, love is bad
Love is scary, love is sad.
Love comes with lots of emotions,
Spells, incantations, even potions.
Love is a beautiful thing.
With love, you might hear church bells ring.
Love is bright, love is bold.
Love is found between the told.
Love is cute, love is tough
Love is full of beautiful fluff.
Love is pretty, love is bright
Now you have experienced love at first sight.

Samantha Burton, Grade 3
Goolsby Elementary School, NV

The Class

Happily,
Eagerly,
Excitedly,
The class
Is reading a silly book.
— Fun!

Ashley James, Grade 1
Fir Grove Elementary School, OR

Home

When I come home,
The birds are playing.
They are flying around the cage,
Because they are happy to see me.
My house is big.
It smells clean.
We're having a Cookie Party.
My mom's cookies are good.
It feels good to be home
It feels warm and cozy.

Bryce Kerr, Grade 3
Four Peaks Elementary School, AZ

Accident

One of the hardest things
was that I rode my bike
and I accidentally
ran into my sister on my bike
and she fell and cried.
It was my first time.
Have you ever done that?

Kylie McGinnis, Grade 2
Acacia Elementary School, AZ

Magic Spring

Birds sing songs
Grass grows green
Rain waters the Earth
Sunshine makes me warm
Flowers bloom bright
Butterflies eat nectar
I like spring.

Patrick Miller, Kindergarten
Twin Lakes Christian Academy, TX

Petie

There was once a boy named Petie
They always called him Tweety
He liked to play
His birthday was in May
His mom thought he was a sweetie.

Alexis Catalan, Grade 3
St Raphael School, CA

The First Time

The first time
I played soccer
I lost
The first time
I played soccer
I was nervous
The first time
I played soccer
I fell
The first time
I played soccer
I stayed for soccer practice!!
The first time
I played soccer
I had a competition!
The first time
I played soccer
I made some friends
But the first time
I played soccer
I lost

Diana Rodriguez, Grade 3
Briargrove Elementary School, TX

Summer

Summer is my favorite season
And here is the reason.

To summer camp I like to go
In the lake I like to row.

I also like to swim in the pool.
I think it is pretty cool.

Katelyn Castiglia, Grade 2
Woodcrest School, CA

All Kinds of Cats
Big cats, small cats.
All kinds of cats.

Large cats, little cats.
All kinds of cats.

Gigantic cats, tiny cats.
All kinds of cats.

Dirty cats, clean cats.
All kinds of cats.

Kristin Tiana Decker, Grade 2
Sangre De Cristo Elementary School, CO

Rainbow Colors
If I were red, I would be an apple.
If I were orange, I would be an orange.
If I were yellow, I would be a banana.
If I were green, I would be a Christmas tree.
If I were blue, I would be the ocean.
If I were purple, I would be a grape.
If I were black, I would be the dark, dark sky.
If I were brown, I would be wood.
If I were white, I would be the snow.
If I were tan, I would be tan skin and hair.

Rachel DeMarco, Grade 3
St Dorothy School, CA

My Dog Likes Airplanes
I have a small dog, his nickname is Ed.
He likes to chase planes that fly over his head.

I think it is strange that my little pup
likes to chase things that are so high up.

I have a small dog, he likes to chase planes.
I bet if he could, he'd like to chase trains.

But because he can't, he likes things that fly.
And so do we, because he can't reach the sky!

Madeline A. Squires, Grade 3
Nampa Christian Schools Inc, ID

A Puppy
My dog likes to sleep.
My dog is seven months old.
My dog likes to bark.
Marissa Mariko Suto, Grade 1
Kimball School, WA

What Freedom Means to Me
Freedom is American life.
Freedom is war.

Freedom is the thankfulness
that we give to the poor.

Freedom is love and care.
Freedom is everywhere.
Zachary Nering, Grade 3
Robinson Elementary School, TX

K
K is for the kite you fly on a windy day.
K is for the kiss you get on the cheek.
K is for my name Karina.
K is for the kangaroo that hops all day.
K is for the king that rules the world.
Karina Rodriguez, Grade 2
Lincoln Elementary School, CA

Cars
Cars are fast
Cars are big
Cars are colorful
Cars are cool
Pranesh Singh Jr., Grade 1
Fir Grove Elementary School, OR

Toaster
The first time
I could cook
I used the toaster
to cook
a waffle.
Have you ever done that?
Noah Facemire, Grade 2
Acacia Elementary School, AZ

Learning Oh Learning
The pencil
feels smooth
write write write
on the paper

Finish the test in time
quick quick quick
the clock is ticking

I finish the test on time
Perfect score 100%
Zeeshah Khawar, Grade 3
Briargrove Elementary School, TX

Beautiful Day
The beautiful day
the rainbow shines very bright
on a sunny day.
Sydney Oberhellman, Grade 3
Four Peaks Elementary School, AZ

Something Good to Eat
I wish I had a candy bar.
I want it big as my Daddy's car.
I would share it with my friends
and that would be the end.
Daniel Martinez, Grade 2
Little Scholars School, CA

I Am a Desert
I am a desert
I am a land form
I am covered in dust
Sometimes I have sand storms
I am very hot like a volcano

I am a desert
I am very, very dry
I have sand fairies
Camels walk on me

I am the desert
Brandon Wade, Grade 3
Briargrove Elementary School, TX

Swimming

There once was a boy named Cooper
Who thought swimming was just super
Breaststroke was best
Going east or west
Freestyle's a party pooper

Cooper Ruscio, Grade 3
Wonderland Avenue Elementary School, CA

My Five Senses

I like to see fireworks on the Fourth of July.
I like to hear waves crashing.
I like to smell grape candles burning.
I like to taste a Hershey bar.
I like to touch warm sand at the beach.

Powell Cutts, Grade 1
Grace School, TX

Imagining October

When I think of October
I begin to see yellow leaves and pumpkins.
I Imagine pumpkin pie cooking in the oven.
I hear bears snoring and sleeping.
I smell leaves.
I imagine October.

Tyra Jaramillo, Grade 1
Paonia Elementary School, CO

Glad

Glad
If glad were a color, it would be yellow
Like the sun on a bright, sunny day.
If glad were a taste, it would be a lemon
As sour as a lemon in your mouth.
If glad were a feeling, it would be cool
Like a D.J. on the radio.
If glad were a smell, it would be sweet
As candy I like to eat.
If glad were a sound, it would be screaming
Like fans at a baseball game.
Glad

Tyler Wiesepape, Grade 2
Grace School, TX

Aquamarine Blue
I grew crystals that were aquamarine blue.
I thought about them while I was suffering with the flu.
I'm not sure I followed directions but there are a few.
I hope they grow bigger than my shoe.

Taylor DuPont, Grade 3
Sundance Elementary School, WY

Blooming
As I get older I am slowly blooming into who I am.
I am an ant in the picnic.
I am a sculpture museum in Hollywood.
I am a pencil writing in a notebook happily.
I am a pink rose gently blowing in the wind.
I am a belly-bursting in a joke jar.
I am a foot kicking a soccer ball.
I am a bowl of chocolate ice cream scooped into a mouth.
I am Old Navy bags fully of cute clothes.
I am pink paint covering my bedroom walls.
I am a cake splattered with chocolate syrup.
I continue to bloom from my past and into a beautiful pink flower of my future.

Zandra Clemons, Grade 2
Open Charter Magnet School, CA

Clever Matthew
When I lay on the grass under a tree, I imagine that...
I am a ripe apple under an apple tree.
I am a dinosaur puzzle matching my pieces together.
I am a rocket shooting into space.
I am a cheetah catching its prey.
I am a book page filled with words.
I am a shovel digging up weeds in the dirt.
I am a soccer ball gliding in the goal.
I am a beautiful meadow filled with wonderful flowers.
I am a bin always clean and neat.
I am a handball thwacking against the wall.
I am a math packet filled with problems.
I am a snake slithering through the rain forest.
I am a basketball flying in the hoop.
I am a spy investigating a robbery.
I am a swimmer splashing through the ocean water.
But when I open my eyes, my dream is still there in the sky.

Matthew Lee, Grade 2
Open Charter Magnet School, CA

The Hobbit

There once was a boy from the shire
But he knew he wouldn't grow higher
He went to Mount Doom
The volcano went BOOM!
And then out came some fire!

Seth Paydar, Grade 3
Wonderland Avenue Elementary School, CA

The Colors of My Feelings

Red is anger,
when someone kicks me down in soccer.

Orange is confused,
when I'm taking a test that's too hard for me.

Yellow is gladness,
when I have hot cocoa on a very cold day.

Green is cheerfulness,
when I am well rested, and refreshed.

Blue is sleepy,
when I stay up way too late at night.

Brown is sad,
when someone special dies.

Pink is love,
when my parents give me their bear hugs.

Gold is proud,
when I work hard, and my work pays off.

Michelle Lentfer, Grade 3
Lincoln Elementary School, CA

Blue

Blue as the sky when I look up.
Blue are the flowers that grow in my garden.
Blue as the sea when I jump in for a swim.
Blue as the moon in the night as I look up.

Elio Sanchez, Grade 2
Lincoln Elementary School, CA

Kyle in the Nile

There once was a boy named Kyle.
He loved to swim in the Nile.
But one sunny day
While he was out to play,
He was eaten by a crocodile.

Daniel Miner, Grade 3
CLASS Academy, OR

Getting a Horse

I might get a horse in September.
If I get a horse, I will
name it Starlight.
It will be a
bay color.
I will ride
Starlight every day.
But, on
Sunday I will give
riding lessons.
If I get a horse
I will be lucky.

Rachel Boyko, Grade 3
Acacia Elementary School, AZ

Rocky Point

I went to Rocky Point
in the summer with my dog
named Lummis.
We went to the ocean
and he was swimming
and I got on his back
and he was swimming
with me on his back.
It felt cold and fun.
I rode on his back
for about six minutes.
He was going fast.
I got scared.
It felt crazy, but fun.
When I fell off,
I was cold.
Have you ever done that?

Ryan Fox, Grade 2
Acacia Elementary School, AZ

America's Sport

Baseball
fun, colorful
running, hitting, fielding
get a snack at the 7th inning stretch
catching, throwing, sliding
competitive, league
America's Sport

Douglas Simpson, Grade 2
Grace School, TX

Whales

Splashing with his tail.
Scaring fish away, and shrimp.
Ruling the ocean at the bottom.
Making bubbles all day long.

Dylan Cosgray, Grade 2
Acacia Elementary School, AZ

Bouncy Ball

Black and gray house cat
Playing with her bouncy ball
When I try to sleep.

Gracie VanHorn, Grade 3
Sundance Elementary School, WY

My Baby

I have a baby brother.
I was really excited!
I thought it would be a girl.
But it was a boy.
I like boys.
I like babies too!
I have lots of brothers.

Lily Wyatt, Grade 1
Thomas Edison Charter School, UT

Baseball

Baseball
Fun! Run!
I'm running and jumping!
Red, White, and Blue.
Homerun!!!

Collin Johnson, Grade 2
C C Hardy Elementary School, TX

Waterfall

The water coming down into the darkness.
The waterfall so black in the darkness.
The rocks and the water together.
So pristine in the morning.
When the sun is out,
The waterfall gleaming.
But darkness closes over it

Jason Sanderlin, Grade 3
Spring Creek Elementary School, WY

My Friends

My favorite thing to do each day
Is to go outside and play
My friends are the best bunch
To meet at the park for lunch
At the park we run, jump, and play
We always look forward to the next day.

McCall Jimenez, Grade 2
Jackson Elementary School, CA

Alone Is...

Being in your room with the power off
Being out in a dark scary cave
Being the only one in the cold, dark street
When you can't find anyone in the mist
Being the only fish in the ocean
Being the only dragon in the sky
Being the only house on the street.

Christian Palmer, Grade 3
Fort Vannoy Elementary School, OR

I Am Not

I am not a polar bear all cold and wet.
I am a polar bear all soft and dry.
I am not a fly squashed on a window.
I am a fly free in the air.
I am not a buttercup all brown and dead.
I am a buttercup all yellow and bright.
I am not a boy all sad and dull.
I am a boy all happy and bright.

Akhil Mulpuru, Grade 3
CLASS Academy, OR

The Pig
The pig
Rolling in the brown mud
On a chilly day
In the muddy puddle
To get dirty
Shaalin Days-Hawkins, Grade 3
San Onofre Elementary School, CA

Best Friends
She makes me smile
She makes me laugh so hard
She is so funny.
Emily Gore, Grade 3
Our Lady of the Snows School, NV

Christmas
Snowflakes dance in the wind
Hot chocolate tastes good
Presents come from under the tree
Gabriel Michel, Grade 3
St Raphael School, CA

The Mystery
A noisy bark
Comes into my ear
I feel happy and scared
A noisy bark
Comes out of a room
What is it?
What does it look like?
A black, black dog
Comes out of the room
Daniel Jimenez, Grade 3
Edison Elementary School, CA

Easter
E njoying the season
A ngels watching over us
S tarting a new life
T omb opening
E veryone wondering where He went
R isen for us
Christopher Wray, Grade 2
Grace School, TX

Grandparents
G reat fun!
R eally fun to be with
A re really great people
N ever tells a lie
D oes fun things
P erfect for me
A lways there for me
R espectful to me
E xperts at sewing and glass
N ever gets mad at me
T errific!
Valarie Varanese, Grade 3
Four Peaks Elementary School, AZ

Flowers
I love flowers
They are pretty friends.
Dressed in spring color.
Dancing in the sun.
Elizabeth Chen, Kindergarten
Twin Lakes Christian Academy, TX

Dance Until the End
Smile
Move your feet
Move your head side to side
Listen to the beat
Start to dance
Clap clap clap
Snap snap snap
Stomp stomp stomp
That is the way to dance until the end.
Georgia Spears, Grade 3
Katherine Delmar Burke School, CA

Plants
The plants grow from seeds.
The plants are nature,
They are flowers.
Flowers are pretty.
Plants give air like trees.
Trees help us live.
Andrew Kwak, Grade 3
Cahuenga Elementary School, CA

Brothers

My very favorite living thing is my brother.
He always likes to spit and then he throws a fit!
So he always gets what he wants,
And it is really hard to deal with this living thing
I call my brother.
I love my brother a lot,
But living things can really be a fuss!

Mark Laborde, Kindergarten
Presbyterian School, TX

Window

Through my window I see a bird.
I see its nest and its eggs.
I see the mother coming home.
Through my window I see a family of birds.
I see a mother and father bird.
I see the mother going to get worms.
Through my window I see the eggs hatch.

Tess Gallagher Clancy, Grade 3
Daly Elementary School, MT

A Snowball Fight

The children are having a snowball fight
They hide behind their walls of snow
They are having fun

Patrick Konkol, Grade 3
St Raphael School, CA

My Cat Fluffy

My cat always chases bats.
I say "Get back here!"

But,
He does not get back here!
Then I call my mom.

But, mom can't catch him either!
So, I have to call the cops.

The cops catch him, hurray!

Brooke Slane, Grade 2
Sangre De Cristo Elementary School, CO

Puppies

They are cute and nice.
They play ball.
They eat and sleep.
They are happy, sad, mad, excited.
They are dogs.
Zayhetzi Nunez, Grade 1
Thomas Edison Charter School, UT

Swing

The person
Went
On the swing.
His shoe
Fell off.
He was
Having fun.
Solomon Thomas, Kindergarten
Jacob Wismer Elementary School, OR

The Four Seasons

Winter is almost over,
Spring is almost here.
Summer is coming after that,
Fall with then appear.

Winter is freezing.
Sometimes it hails I'm told.
Spring is a very happy time.
It's still a little cold.

Summer is very sunny.
It feels like you're boiling in a pot.
Fall is very windy.
It's too windy to be in a cot.

Winter is cold,
Spring is calm.
Summer is hot,
Fall is when I catch leaves in my palm.

Winter, spring, summer, and fall,
Spring is my favorite one of all.
Clare Chou, Grade 3
Woodcrest School, CA

Who Am I?

Ben Franklin's birthday bash,
I am going to crash!
Singing "Yankee Doodle Dandy,"
My musket comes in handy.
Oh yes, my Brown Bess will be there.
Hope it isn't a scare!

Minuteman Nick
Nicholas O. A. Engle, Grade 1
NorthCreek Academy, CA

The River Monster

The monster
Lives in the river
It drinks and it sinks
It slurps and it burps
All day long
All day long
Ben Zuckerman, Grade 2
Brush Creek Elementary School, CO

Christmas

Christmas
Family tradition
Singing, peaceful
Celebrating
Putting up our tree
Holiday
Austin Reynolds, Grade 3
Canyon Rim Elementary School, CA

Costa Rica

C amouflaged monkey
O range sunset
S plashing turquoise waterfalls
T hick deep, dark, rainforest
A mazing hummingbirds

R ainbow-beaked toucans
I nteresting iguanas
C olorful macaws
A mazing Costa Rica!
Lydia Thompson, Grade 1
Paonia Elementary School, CO

Kaylee

Brown hair all over her head.
Brown eyes are small.
Playing outside she rides her little bike.
Small. She is small.
Going for a walk outside the park.
Sister.

Ashley Price, Grade 3
Sundance Elementary School, WY

Beds

Beds are big.
Beds are little.
Beds can be squared,
rectangles, or circles.
Beds can be red, orange, purple,
green, or brown.
Some are made of mud, straw, or rock.

Michael Deyo, Grade 3
Crestview Elementary School, TX

Invisible Fairy

Invisible Fairy Invisible Fairy
Please talk to me Please talk to me
You are the light that might shine tonight
That may be a star in the night
You will watch over me tonight
As if I can see you which I may
If I stay up very late tonight.

Kelty H., Grade 3
Katherine Delmar Burke School, CA

All Kinds of Cats

Big cats, little cats,
All kinds of cats.
Good cats, bad cats,
All kinds of cats.
Fat cats, skinny cats,
All kinds of cats.
Nice cats, mean cats,
All kinds of cats!

Sara Berlinger, Grade 2
Sangre De Cristo Elementary School, CO

Wedding

There was a guy singing.
There were some of my friends.
It was Seth and Chilton.
My grandmother was there,
And my granddaddy, too.
My great-granddaddy was there,
My great-grandmother was there, too.
My uncle Aric was there and
His girlfriend, Danielle.
They got married.
I was there watching.
Aunt Eema was there.
I was a photographer and took lots of pictures.
There were people playing in a band and people dancing.

Alex Beach, Kindergarten
Twin Lakes Christian Academy, TX

Red

"Hello, Minnie," stammers Mickey,
"This is just for you —
A pretty yellow daffodil,
To match your yellow shoes."
Minnie bats her lashes;
Mickey ducks his head.
And as they blush, this yellow verse,
Turns slowly into "red!"

Lusineh Bedikian, Grade 3
C & E Merdinian Armenian Evangelical School, CA

Thanksgiving

T hinking of others
H elping people out
A nd eating the turkey with other people
N othing better than Thanksgiving feast
K eeping promise and prayer
S ide dishes that taste great
G ood pumpkin pies
I like Thanksgiving and family and friends get together
V egetables and warm bread are part of Thanksgiving
I love when my mom bakes pumpkin pie
N obody looks better than my mom
G ravy and potatoes are good for Thanksgiving

Jason Sahr, Grade 3
Four Peaks Elementary School, AZ

My Closet Is…a Wizard's Magical House
The mysterious wizard's house is filled with spells,
The magical, mystical mirror tells your fortune and makes your wishes come true,
Read a spell and put it in the bubbling brew,
Chant and repeat the word to make something new!

Bubble, bubble, boil and trouble,
I hear the peaceful spirits whisper in my ear,
The spirits play weave in and out of the tapestries stitched with stars and moons.

No one dares to come into my closet because the magic is far too strong,
My running shoes are the spell books,
The coats are the colorful tapestries all around,

Don't you see the color blend into sound?
The shelf is the wizard's chair,
See the brew mix,
My hats are the wizard's hats,
Look at them grow taller and taller every time that they are worn,
Everyone wants to know the secret that is hidden up the wizard's sleeve.

My hats blended into one special hat,
Everyone gathers around to see the powerful wizard,
That wizard is me!!

Sydney Banner, Grade 3
The Mirman School, CA

My Life and Me
When I'm dreaming in my head, I think of my life.
I am a beautiful star twinkling in the sky.
I am a tennis ball soaring over the net.
I am a Mancala piece speeding into every hole on the board.
I am a fun game played by two loving sisters.
I am a psychic telling people about the future.
I am a genius working on an invention.
I am a beautiful sunset fading away to moonlight.
I am a computer completely filled with excitement and brains.
I am a steaming hot pizza frying in the oven.
I am a funny clown happier than ever.
I am a beautiful sun shining in the sky.
I can be anything that I want to be in my life.

Maya Matthews, Grade 2
Open Charter Magnet School, CA

My Home
When I come home,
I hear birds chirping and singing.
I know it is my home.
I smell my dad's and brothers' sweat.
I know that is my home.
I smell my mom's sugar cookies.
I know it is my home.
I see my bed and my room waiting for me.
I know it is my home.
I look out my window.
I see trees that grow every second.
I know it is my home.
I smell dinner, that sour, sweet smell.
It feels so good not to be on the road.
It feels so good to be home.
Jenny Fisher, Grade 3
Four Peaks Elementary School, AZ

Snowball War
With our parents we have a snowball war
We threw so many they begged, "NO MORE!"
We were cold so we changed our clothes
We sat by a fire and warmed our toes
Sean Sehlhorst, Grade 3
Cubberley Elementary School, CA

DeBrazza's Quenon
Colorful monkey
DeBrazza's Quenon is big —
a strange animal
Rogelio Garcia, Grade 3
Lorenzo De Zavala Elementary School, TX

Happy
Happy is yellow
like a sun.
It jumps through my mind
like a bouncing ball.
It makes me feel cheerful
like a cheerleader cheering for the Broncos.
It makes me want to play
on the playground.
Nicole Feldman, Grade 2
Northridge Elementary School, CO

Geckos
Large mouth
Flat head
Thick tail
Climb glass
Eat eggs
Yellowish eyes
Reddish-tan spots
Class reptilian
Kate Steelman, Grade 1
Grace School, TX

Nature
Leaves are green.
Snow flakes are white.
Trees are brown.
Clouds are white.
Sky is blue.
Grass is green.
Zach Shald, Grade 1
Ryan Elementary School, CO

Kang
I am 6 years old
I like to play with my mom
My mom is so nice
Kang Li, Grade 1
Kimball School, WA

The Snake
Fastly,
Coolly,
Sadly,
The snake
Was eating a mouse.
— Wicked!
Marcus Dabbs, Grade 1
Rose Elementary School, OR

Kiu
I like to read books.
My mom likes to eat a lot.
I like to wear shoes.
Kiu Vong, Grade 1
Kimball School, WA

A Water Fountain

A water fountain sounds like rain dripping in a bowl of water
Like a little waterfall on a creek
Like moving a stick through a puddle
Like water going up and down a rock

Jericko Goolsby, Grade 3
Fort Vannoy Elementary School, OR

The Dream

On a hot summer day
joyous and happy
I was nearly asleep
when the thought of a meadow
came to my mind
I saw the colors rushing through
what seemed as a garden
I simply realized it was all a dream
It proved dreams can take me beyond where I imagined
I plan to visit that place again someday

Shannon Lemke, Grade 3
Westwood Charter Elementary School, CA

Jesus

During the season that we call Lent,
We are reminded of Jesus and how His body was bent.

He died on the cross so that we could be saved.
The road to Heaven with His blood was paved.

Easter eggs and chocolate bunnies may be fun.
Just always remember that Jesus is the ONE.

Logan Blow, Grade 2
Twin Lakes Christian Academy, TX

Christmas

Christmas lights glistening, just like the night sky
Think about the magic of Christmas

The snow is like glittering Christmas diamond jewels
Think about the magic of Christmas

Colorful presents just like mixed up rainbows
Now do you know about Christmas?

Sage Dougherty, Grade 3
Lyons Elementary School, CO

Bulldog

B est dog in the
U niverse
L arge enough but still
L ittle
D oing stuff
O r
G nashing his teeth on a bone.

Kevin Arambula, Grade 3
Emerson Elementary School, TX

Mom Loves Me

Mom loves me
With all her might.
Mom loves me
Dancing in the night.
Mom loves me
Putting me in the light.
Mom hugs me
Through the night.

Zoe Parker, Grade 2
Central Elementary School, CA

Yellow

Yellow as the sun shining so bright.
Yellow as the people passing by.
Yellow as the book that I just read.
Yellow as the children passing by.

Lizbeth Godinez, Grade 2
Lincoln Elementary School, CA

My Best Friend

He is really nice.
He makes me laugh all the time.
He is my best friend.

Nicholas Davis Turner, Grade 3
Our Lady of the Snows School, NV

Stars

Beautiful stars, twinkling bright,
Spinning away with delight.
Up upon the rainbow they fly,
Floating away, never to die.

Henry Lange, Grade 2
Cottonwood Montessori School, NM

My Pet

I had a pet
I cannot see.
I cannot see
because it was
in back of me!

Abigail Hutchinson, Grade 1
Kathryn Senor Elementary School, CO

It's My Life

My life is a bundle of fun
I like to eat hot dog buns!
Whenever I get bored
I read books galore
Whenever it is raining
I'm never never complaining!

Miranda Puppo, Grade 3
Daves Avenue Elementary School, CA

Shaggy Dog

Shaggy Dog can run as fast
as fast as a light,
he is very bright
and intelligent.
He can find his way to any state,
and memorize any license plate!

Cassie Olguin, Grade 3
Parker Elementary School, TX

Saguaro

Home
for birds and the food for bugs.
Die
when they don't get enough water.
More bugs move in.
Saguaros
been on earth for a long time.
Dangerous and gorgeous.
Can get up to twenty arms.
Green
with very sharp spines.
You
cannot kill or hurt saguaros.

Sydney Kratzert, Grade 2
Acacia Elementary School, AZ

The Trip to the Inn

Once upon a time there lived a woman,
The woman felt crowded in her house and at the sea there were so many dolphins.
The woman wanted to go out exploring and going into an inn.
She planned to tomorrow night,
If it wouldn't be too light.
And there wouldn't be any war fights.
So the next morning, the woman gathered up her things and got ready to go,
And so the woman walked to the train and along the way, she saw a doe,
The woman paid and went inside and dropped her things and said, "Oh!"
What she saw was an unfamiliar sight,
Everything was so nice and, oh! She might cry! Might!!!
There was nothing but gold, gold, GOLD!!! NO fights or no heights!
And the woman wanted to live in here no matter what,
And a sign said on a couch, "NO other things but your butt."
Finally the train reached it,
So the woman took out her suitcase but it didn't fit.
But the suitcase slid and fell into a pit.
Then the suitcase came out and the woman was on her way,
When the woman went in the manager did say,
"Remember to wipe your shoes, and do not delay!"
And the woman lived happily ever, after.

Hannah Pham, Grade 3
Northwood Elementary School, CA

My Beautiful Eyes

When I wake up in the morning they open
they are brown like the color of my skin
they move like hair when the wind blows

You control them like the rest of your body
but sometimes they close and open smooth and softly
sometimes when you touch them you will cause them to burn

When the day disappears into the pitch-dark night
and you get tired you close them slowly
if you leave them open for a long time they'll turn red

They are white and brown for some people
But others have blue, green, hazel, or brown just like me.

What are they?
Why, they are my beautiful eyes

Nicole Oduche, Grade 3
Horn Academy, TX

Flowers and Butterflies

Flowers bloom
Butterflies flying
It's very peaceful.
Beautiful butterflies
On top of flowers,
With the colors of the
Rainbow. Butterflies
And flowers are
Perfect mates
Sunflowers, roses, daisies,
Blossoms, and more kinds
Of flowers.
Orange butterflies,
Blue butterflies,
And more kinds
Of butterflies.
Butterflies and flowers
Are my favorite
Living things of nature.
Nancy Garcia, Grade 3
Edison Elementary School, CA

Love

Love is a dove
that comes from above.
If you love,
you might even be a dove!
When you're happy, love is there
to show you care.

If you share love,
you do come from above.
Jonothon Durodola, Grade 3
Montessori Learning Institute, TX

Happiness

Happiness is neon blue.
It smells like s'mores.
It sounds like camping out.
It tastes like lemon cakes.
It looks like a forest.
Happiness feels like fluffy fur.
Orion Mayers-White, Grade 2
CLASS Academy, OR

My Dog

My dog Chief lives in the house
He goes crazy if he sees a mouse.

He cheers me up when I'm sad
He makes me calm when I'm mad.

I play with him night and day
His birthday is right after May.

He jumps on me and licks me a lot
I'm not getting rid of him, no I'm not!

I won't let him run away
If he does, I'd search night and day.
David Amar, Grade 3
Woodcrest School, CA

I Am A

I am a
soccer playing,
tired sleeping,
friend talking,
kid.

I am a
shape tracing,
movie watching,
paper coloring,
child.

I am a
soup making,
paper cutting,
book painting,
third grader.

I am a
baseball playing,
Rebelde singing,
hip hop dancing,
cocoa drinking,
sister.
Jasmine Jimenez, Grade 3
Briargrove Elementary School, TX

Page 171

How to Draw William LeVay's Face
Sketch my face as round as a smooth pebble
Shape my neck as straight as a perfect line
Color my hair as yellow as the bright sun
Trace my eyes as a huge rain drop
Make my eyebrows as brown as the dirt
Illustrate my nose as straight as a piece of paper
Outline my short lips as pink as a pink flower
Design my teeth as white as sparkling piano keys
Curve my mouth as a ripe banana
Paint my skin as white as play sand

William LeVay, Grade 3
Briargrove Elementary School, TX

Months
January is the first.
But the season winter is the worst.
February is when we have Valentine's Day.
When I get a date I like to shout hooray!
March 29 is my b-day.
I want to go to Skate City that day.
April is when we have April Fool's Day.
When a prank is a success I like to shout hooray!

Jesse Torres, Grade 2
Pinnacle Charter School, CO

About Me
On the outside I'm a unique girl,
but when I close my eyes, I feel like I can be anything,
I am a joke book full of laughter.
I am kind hands helping other sad kids.
I am an angry fist balled up.
I am a leather box full of money.
I am a restaurant full of delicious food.
I am a mall full of clothes.
I am a cookbook full of delicious recipes.
I am a Junie B. Jones book full of funny pages.
I'm computer files with lots of problems.
I am rainbow-colored paints splattered on art paper.
I'm a gymnastics mat that people land on.
I'm a softball flying in the air.
I'm a golf ball curving into the hole.
When I open my brown eyes, I'm a unique girl.

Taylor Selfridge, Grade 3
Open Charter Magnet School, CA

Bengal Tiger

B reeds in spring
E xcellent night vision
N otable swimmer
G rips prey with claws
A stonishes prey before killing
L eaps to kill

T eeth like scissors
I ndia — where most live
G ood at camouflage
E ats deer, buffalo, pigs, and monkey
R eally big cat!

Andrew Mattly, Grade 3
Camptonville Academy, CA

My Senses

I like to taste warm cookies.
I like to see little gray Riley.
I like to hear my rat run in the wheel.
I like to smell sweet oranges.
I like to touch my fluffy cats.

Logan Childs, Grade 1
Grace School, TX

Dragon

I have a pet dragon.
It has a toy wagon.
My flame throwing dragon,
burns up his toy wagon.
Now my pet dragon,
has no toy wagon.

Alex Williams, Grade 2
Montessori Learning Institute, TX

The Page All About Harriet

H arriet was a slave
A lso did not like being it
R ailroad she used
R ebels used her
I t probably was hard
E mpty stomach so still hungry
T ubman was nicknamed Moses

Renee Martin, Grade 2
Pinnacle Charter School, CO

Bats

Bats
Scary, crazy
Mean, cookoo, nuts
Bats are annoying.
Flying mammals

Sarah Valdez, Grade 2
Swink Elementary School, CO

My Hermit Crab

My crab is my crab
all reddish blue and yellow
he pinches my nose

Braden Matthews, Grade 3
Our Lady of the Snows School, NV

Chinatown

The bright colors of Chinatown
The good smelling tea
The scent of the cookie factory
The beautiful sights
Mostly sunny, but sometimes windy
All in one small place

Mary, Grade 3
Katherine Delmar Burke School, CA

The Rain Forest

Come and explore the rain forest.
Can you hear the monkeys howling?
Can you see the plants being still?
Can you taste the water sweet?
Can you smell the steam rising?
Can you feel the showers dripping?

Colton Godwin, Grade 1
Paonia Elementary School, CO

Love Doves

Love, love, love doves,
a love dove is a sign of peace.
Love, love, love doves,
a love dove brings us joy.
To be a love dove,
spread peace and joy.

Samantha Russell, Grade 3
Montessori Learning Institute, TX

Pink

Pink tastes like sweet cotton candy
Melting in my mouth on a hot summer day

Pink looks like long, pretty, sparkling dresses
Hanging in a closet

Pink smells like a wet, first picked rose
Handed to me on a spring day

Pink sounds like a spotted baby butterfly
Flying in the cold breeze on an autumn day

Pink feels like a soft cottonball
Being squished in between my fingers at my house

Brianna Barrailler, Grade 3
Miller Elementary School, CA

Leprechauns

Leprechauns Leprechauns here and there
Leprechauns Leprechauns in my hair
Leprechauns Leprechauns here and there there and here
Leprechauns Leprechauns everywhere
I can't escape them because I told you
They're here and they're there
And here over here over here over there
They're just everywhere

Kainen Gonzales, Grade 3
Robinson Elementary School, TX

Summer Fun

Summer is very hot
Children run a lot
Kids play all day long
People ring the doorbell "Ding-Dong"
Everyone swims in the summer
If they don't it's such a bummer
Some kids have to go to school next summer
That's so sad, I would rather sleep and slumber
Teenagers like to tan
One hot day I met a boy named Dan
That's what people do in summer
Without summer it would be a long hot bummer

Allison Foster, Grade 3
Finley Oates Elementary School, TX

A Waterfall You Will Remember
You look out on the foggy mist.
You watch it sneak out over the waterfall.
The rapids feel icy cold,
You feel the cold trickle through your body.
The rapids crawl out on to the river.
You look up at the waterfall shimmering in the sunlight.
Embroidered with boulders with foggy green moss,
Every detail is a picture you will remember forever.

Niamh Doyle, Grade 3
Daves Avenue Elementary School, CA

Army Man
An army guy is going to fight enemies
Ahhhh help me pppppbbbbb

I have been shot
BOOM!

"One of our cannons has been destroyed," he said

Randy Clark, Grade 1
New Emerson School, CO

My Closet Is a Planet
When you go inside my closet,
Things may not be what they seem,
My pants are the bizarre alien men,
My socks are the alien's busy feet walking all day,
My skirts are the alien girls going to the mall,
My shoes are little alien dolls,
My hair ties are the alien bracelets,
They are the laser beams the aliens use for light travel.

The little hangers are little light sabers,
My closet lights are the stars shining brightly,
The drawers are the flying cars,
"Swish, boom, zoom, swish!"
As I jump into my little flying car,
I wonder how far up in the sky I will be dancing,
When I step out of my closet,
I step out of my planetary world of fantasy.

Ariel Fishman, Grade 3
The Mirman School, CA

Jupiter
Jupiter is the fourth brightest object in the sky
And brightest planet of them all.
The ring around it makes a rainbow.
Jupiter is the biggest planet of all
It is next to the belt of rocks that fall.
A planet Jupiter has a big red spot.
A constant storm is on the dot.
It is the fifth planet from the sun.
It is out of gas so you can't go on the planet to run.

Aleq Queja, Grade 3
Little Scholars School, CA

Excitement
Excitement is the color emerald green.
It sounds like the sound of an athlete playing sports.
It smells like marshmallows.
It tastes like Mac and Cheese.
Excitement feels like race cars.

Harish Palani, Grade 1
CLASS Academy, OR

Native Jewelry
Jewelry
Looks pretty on people
Shiny silver turquoise, coral
People want to buy turquoise, silver, coral bracelet to wear
Native Jewelry
Necklace
Short or long strands
Numerous rows of glossy smooth polished sophisticated beads
Mixture of color or sizes for their style
Native Jewelry
Earring
Equivalent to people's necklace
Ladies look elegant showing off their earring
Fashionable style to look attractive to buy and sell
Native Jewelry
Bracelet
It looks stunning on people's wrist
Men say the bangle looks fastidious
There are remarkable turquoises on all big and small bracelets
Native Jewelry

Jarrod Toadecheenie, Grade 2
Ganado Primary School, AZ

South Dakota

I went on a trip to South Dakota
on an airplane,
It was so fun.
We saw roofs of cars
and went through the clouds.
Have you ever done that?

Bethany Stewart, Grade 2
Acacia Elementary School, AZ

The Spider Web

There was an abandoned spider web,
Glistening in the morning light,
Just a fragile sheer strand of web,
From the gate to the tree,
A spider's masterpiece.

August Bergh, Grade 3
Daves Avenue Elementary School, CA

Books

Books
Words and pictures
Looking, reading, and flipping pages
Sad, crying, happy, giggling
Story

Cambry Durand, Grade 1
Thomas Edison Charter School, UT

Omar

O range is my favorite color
M ango is my favorite fruit
A rabic is my favorite subject
R unning is my favorite thing to do

Omar Haymour, Grade 2
Phoenix Metro Islamic School, AZ

Happiness

Happiness is spicy red.
It sounds like fireworks.
It smells like ice cream.
It tastes like an orange.
It looks like a smile.
Happiness feels like Christmas.

Rachel Ha, Grade 2
CLASS Academy, OR

Sheep

The sheep is cool.
It gives us wool.
A sheep is a big fool.
It does not go to school.

Jullian Valadez, Grade 1
Montessori Learning Institute, TX

Ponies

Ponies are so cute.
They are for sale.
I want to buy a pony.
I will brush my pony's fur.
I will take good care of her!

Vanessa Delgado, Grade 3
Honey Hollow Elementary School, CA

Hanna I Like

Hanna I like.
she's cool and funny
she likes to dance.
and has cool pants.
she likes pink
and always blinks
I like her a lot
she acts like a robot

Sami Hafez, Grade 3
Phoenix Metro Islamic School, AZ

Moms

Moms take care of you.
Moms help you.
They make you laugh.
They make you smile.

Maison Zboril, Grade 3
Robinson Elementary School, TX

Apples*

Apples are sweet,
Apples are nice,
If you don't like apples
You better think twice!!

Nirali Rahul, Grade 3
CB Eaton Elementary School, CA
*Dedicated to Anoosha Boxi

Colors All Around Us

If I were red.
I would be hot lave, steaming in a volcano.
If I were green.
I would be a leaf, floating in the air.

If I were blue.
I would be the sky in the air. Or the deep blue sea floating in the water.
If I were tan.
I would be the skin but might bet sun burnt!

If I were pink.
I would be a pink balloon, but I might pop!
If I were black.
I would be the sky at night.

If I were orange.
I would be a tasty bungee.
If I were purple.
I would be a juicy grape.

If I were a mix up color.
I would be the rainbow in the sky.

Which color would you like to be.

Michael Enabi, Grade 3
St Dorothy School, CA

White Wonder

The air is cool and crisp. Snow is gleaming in the sky.
The ground is fluffy and white.
I take a step.
The snow makes a crunching sound and my foot sinks in deep.
My friend and I have snowball fights and my brother and I make snowmen.

Owen Kominiak, Grade 3
Cottonwood Montessori School, NM

The Grand Canyon

Grand Canyon
Long, rocky
Falling, flowing, silent
The Grand Canyon is one of the Wonders of the World.
Ditch!

Tarik Ross, Grade 3
Four Peaks Elementary School, AZ

Baseball

If I were a baseball...
I'd fly in the sky like a bird,
I'd get hit by a bat,
I'd get caught by a lot of gloves,
If I were a baseball...
Connor Barry, Grade 1
Solana Santa Fe Elementary School, CA

Pink Tulip

I wish I were
PINK.
I would be a tulip
getting fresh air
and decorating the garden.
Annie He, Grade 2
University Park Elementary School, TX

Gorilla

Big, black gorilla
Oh, how you bang your chest hard.
How you scream loudly.
Alex Scott-Avalos, Grade 3
Lorenzo De Zavala Elementary School, TX

My Animal

My animal is a dog
It doesn't live in a log.
It lives in a doghouse
It's nothing like a mouse.

Some dogs are pretty,
Some dogs are not,
Some dogs can be crazy
And some dogs are hot.

Some dogs are messy
Some dogs are lazy
And of course crazy.

I love dogs very much
They're very smart and clever
And I'll keep one forever.
Anais Nahapetyan, Grade 3
Tca Arshag Dickranian Armenian School, CA

Deer

Deer
Quiet, fast
Hiding, eating, sleeping
Deer hide from people
Buck
Alexis Lopez, Grade 1
Myatt Elementary School, TX

Snow

Snow is a very cold thing
It brings hot chocolate
And a fire
Nice and warm
Let it snow!
Nicole Powers, Grade 2
Carden West School, CA

Alice

I like to read books.
I like to play with my doll.
I am 6 years old.
Alice Huang, Grade 1
Kimball School, WA

A Secret Stage

A secret stage
Sparkly and bright
It only shines
At dawn midnight
For those who stay
Only know
How the Secret
Stage can glow.
Riley Meere, Grade 1
Ryan Elementary School, CO

Elephants

Elephants
Gray, huge
Eating, stomping, splashing
Elephants can run
Pachyderms
Keasia Greely, Grade 1
Myatt Elementary School, TX

Horse Love

H orses are our friends.
O ats are their desserts.
R aces in the fields.
S ome are strong and some are weak.
E ven though they're not mine, I love them so.

L ove for horses is great!
O ats and grains they love too.
V ery lonely all night long, well they're there for you.
E ven though they're not all ours, we can still love them.

Cameron Doran, Grade 3
Daly Elementary School, MT

Myself

When I am alone and close my eyes,
I'm a plane flying to America,
I am a *Baby Sitter* book full of pages,
I'm a red rose watered in the garden,
I'm a rocket, racing into space,
I'm a pencil writing on a paper
I'm a pile of laundry swirling around in a washing machine.
I'm a letter sent all the way to Korea.
I'm a telephone ringing loudly,
I'm a piano playing a Beethoven song.
I'm a joyful puppy loved by a little girl,
I'm a wind blowing the tree's leaves,
I'm an ugly duckling transforming into a swan,
I'm a puppy taking a nap on a bed,
I'm a wild horse running away from hunters,
When I open my eyes, all that I am is inside of me!

Sharon Jung, Grade 3
Open Charter Magnet School, CA

Superpowers

If I had a mask that gave me superpowers
It would give me the powers to…

Blow fire out of my hands
I would have super strength so I could rip phone books in half
I would use super fast powers to run around the sun.
I would have the power to make force fields
I would have to power to fly as high as a rocket.

Trevor Allison, Grade 3
Briargrove Elementary School, TX

All About Me
I am a
school learning,
math adding,
problem subtracting boy.

I am a
kickball playing,
two square gaming,
soccer kicking, active person.

I am a
fast running,
kangaroo jumping,
land tagging person.

I am a
cheese pizza chewer,
meat chewing,
chocolate crunching kid.
Kevin Vo, Grade 3
Briargrove Elementary School, TX

Flowers
F loating over the ground
L ilies, roses, and daisies
O ver the grass
W ith colored petals
E specially nice in summer
R ising in the spring
S melly little sprouts.
Maddie Solis, Grade 3
Emerson Elementary School, TX

Love
I love my nice mother a lot
She has never fought
My cute mother is nice
She doesn't like mice
My mother likes to play
But not with clay
My mother is mine
She looks fine
Stephanie Villalpando, Grade 2
San Jacinto Elementary School, CA

Tigers
Big, black tiger stripes
hidden in the grassy lands
looking for some food.
Rina Feldman, Grade 2
Northridge Elementary School, CO

Black
Darkness in my room is black.
I feel alone.
I cannot wait for daylight.
Michael Woodson, Grade 3
Shasta Elementary School, CA

My Family
My family loves me.
I love my dad and he loves me.
My mom she is a good mom.
I love my family.
Aberly Winn, Grade 2
Montessori Learning Institute, TX

Spring Is in the Flowers
Spring is in the flowers
spring is in the air
flowers are blooming
flowers are changing
poems are changing in every way
spring is always here
spring is always coming
spring is in the flowers
spring is in the air
spring is pretty
flowers became joyful
joy became flowers
spring is in the trees
spring is in the sun
spring is spring
spring rises up like the sun
the sun rises up like spring
the birds are awakening
from the winter's sleep
and the wind stopped weeping
Sabrina Johnson, Grade 3
Los Padillas Elementary School, NM

My Past

Before I start my journey into my past, I have to remember I am really present.
I am from my ancestors, who I am extremely proud of.
I am from a diverse country of troublesome activities.
I am from many boxes stuffed and overflowing with wrapping paper.
I am from feet moving on the Kwanzaa dance floor.
I am from encouraging phrases and life lessons of
"You can do anything if you practice."
I am from baby's first lovely day.
I am from siblings squirming in their naming blankets.
I am from chocolate chip cookies rising in the oven.
When my journey is over, I am from my past, looking towards my future.

Asha Wafer, Grade 3
Open Charter Magnet School, CA

The Haunted House

The haunted house
Was a creepy house
There were spiders in it
And skeletons in it
And no one wanted to go in it
Ever again.

Alexis Iwaszewicz, Grade 2
St John of San Francisco Orthodox Academy, CA

Owl

Owl, oh owl, you king of the sky
I gaze at you as you fly by
Your feathers glisten black, gray, and white.
Oh, you look so beautiful tonight.
How I wish I could fly with you, you midnight hunter,
Whoo, whoo whoo!

Daria Drenker, Grade 3
Writers in the Schools Program, TX

What I'm Thankful For

The sound of a soft, beating waterfall,
The feel of a daisy, soft like clouds,
The refreshing water that comes from mountain streams,
Imagining I'm on a full moon
Whenever I see one,
Kids playing and riding their bikes in the morning,
That's what I'm thankful for!

Francesca Kiel, Grade 3
Four Peaks Elementary School, AZ

School

School is cool,
School is fun.
Everybody's work
Is done!
Tatiana DeSopo, Grade 3
Robinson Elementary School, TX

Vampire Bat

V ery long wings
A ngled upper teeth used to pierce skin
M ammals are common hosts
P redators of bats are owls
I nhabit caves in daylight
R oost alone or in small groups
E cholocation is used to find their prey

B lood feeders
A t birth pups are well developed
T humb used to cling to host
Jordan Koons, Grade 3
Camptonville Academy, CA

Sled Dog

Whoosh off I go
hours in the hurling snow,
wind in my face
fur freezing on my legs
wet cold nose
feet racing through soft snow
wet eyes wagging tail
racing through the freezing gale.
Madeleine Jones, Grade 3
Grattan Elementary School, CA

Crocodile

Crocodiles are fierce.
Eats anything.
Has a tail and big teeth.
Lives in water.
Can see underwater.
Crocodiles are fierce.
Cody Owen, Grade 2
Acacia Elementary School, AZ

Flowers

Some flowers smell good.
Some flowers smell bad.
Most of them are pretty.
Some of them are not.
They are good to grow.
Put in your backyard.
But they will die out.
They are so fun to look at.
They have so many colors.
I just can't name them all.
Flowers!
Erin Freker, Grade 3
Acacia Elementary School, AZ

My Dog

My dog is
funny,
silly,
weird,
and crazy.
She does a lot
of stupid stuff, and
she is
scared of everything!
She will run
from
a lot
of stuff.
Ashley slobbers on everything!
Ew,
Gross!
Too bad when I was
six, she passed away.
I miss her a lot.
Rachel Fitzpatrick, Grade 3
Acacia Elementary School, AZ

My Dog Zeke

I like my dog Zeke
He has big brown eyes like me
My dog Zeke is meek
Kelly Croasdell, Grade 3
Our Lady of the Snows School, NV

My Name
Anna, it's like a summer breeze on the meadow.
Anna, it's like a newly hatched chick in the nest with its mother.
Anna, it's like a lemon getting squeezed in a yummy mixture.
Anna, it's like the ocean waves crashing against me.
Anna, it's like a horse running quietly in the trees.
Anna, it's like a colorful balloon getting popped at a party.
Anna, it's like a coyote howling at night.
Anna, it's like cat meowing and meowing for dinner.
Anna, it's my name.
Anna, it fits me perfectly.

Anna Rebscher, Grade 2
San Geronimo Valley Elementary School, CA

I Wonder What It Is Like to Be a Tree
I wonder what it is like to be a tree?
And grow from a seed.
I wonder what it is like to be as small as a seed?
I wonder what it is like to have blossoms growing
out of my branches?

Ariel Devenport, Grade 2
Creslane Elementary School, OR

Running
When the air blows in my face
Some noise, some whistle, sometimes they're high, low.
Leaves blow, crickets buzz.
Trash rolls and trashed the street.
Fast heartbeats, long breaths
People pass
Cars honk
When my legs stop
Suddenly
Life goes back to quiet.

Kassandra Diaz, Grade 3
Horn Academy, TX

My Five Senses
I like to see the Thanksgiving parade.
I like to hear my friends laugh when we play.
I like to smell hot pepperoni pizza.
I like to taste hamburgers with mustard and ketchup.
I like to touch a rabbit's soft, warm fur.

Braedon Schneider, Grade 1
Grace School, TX

I Am Lauren

I am caring and kind.
I wonder what grade I got on the test.
I hear the sound of music.
I see my adorable cats when I come home from school.
I want to make lots of friends.
I am caring and kind.
I pretend to sky dive.
I feel happy with my brother.
I touch my cat's soft fur.
I worry if my dad will get better.
I cry when I get in trouble.
I am caring and kind.
I understand when my friend says something.
I dream I can soar.
I try to do my best on tests.
I hope my wishes come true.
I am caring and kind.
I am Lauren.

Lauren Reppert, Grade 3
River Oaks Baptist School, TX

My Closet Is…a Restaurant

My closet is a restaurant,
My closet is tasty filled chili-hot shirts,
My closet is tangy filled with watered down hangers,
My closet is as sweet as my chocolate colored sweater,

My building blocks are platters of delicious food, "Yum, yum,"
My socks are the spaghetti and scrumptious meatballs topped with gravy,
My green pants are the waiters,
My white shirts are the table clothes white and shiny as snow,
My closet is so much fun!

My closet has all the food in the world,
My T-shirt is the bread, with scrumptious butter on top,
My shoes are the salty, buttery, tasty potatoes,
My big chessboard is the pizza,
One of my games is the delicious steak with gravy and grilled onions on top,
My shoe laces are the stringy spaghetti,
My closet is the most delicious restaurant ever!

Aaron Marks, Grade 3
The Mirman School, CA

What I See

Through my window I see a big field.
I see a unicorn and a bird.
I see the dragons sleeping.
Through my window I see a castle.
I see a lake and a mermaid in it.
I see the dragons wake up.
Through my window I see the field is behind me.

Emily Bremer, Grade 3
Daly Elementary School, MT

How to Make Felix's Face

Make my face as round as the shining sun.
Draw my hair as brown as the freshly grown coconut.
Illustrate my eyebrows as brown as the brown walls in my house.
Color my eyelashes as black as the dark panther.
Form my eyes as green as the dark tree leaves.
Make my ears as a broken heart in half.
Sketch my nose as a sharp pointed triangle.
Design my mouth as wide as a fat watermelon.
Complete my teeth as a white marshmallow.
Shade my skin as the beach sand.
Outline my portrait as good as it can become.

Felix Schigel, Grade 3
Briargrove Elementary School, TX

Springtime Animals!

Baby calves are alive.
The four-wheeler I drive.
The fawns are with their mother deer.
The baby deer stay with their mother for one year.
The geese are starting to come back.
We can climb on the haystack.
In springtime the seagulls fly.
The grass turns green, but I don't know why?

Ryah Young, Grade 2
Froid Elementary School, MT

My Mom

Today is sunny.
Today I am going to play basketball and go to my mom's.
Andrea, that is my mom's name.
I will go to the skate park with her.

Morgan Uytenbogaardt, Grade 2
Orchard Elementary School, UT

Fireworks

Fireworks, they *boom,*
crackle, pop and *bam.*
They're colorful
and a beauty to see.
Some have fogs
of different colors.
Some are all different
shapes and sizes.
Some big and some small.
Anyway, I love fireworks!

Lara Klaus, Grade 2
Frontier Valley Elementary School, CO

Things I Like and Do

I am a slow swimming
fast running
tennis playing
ball hitting
hula hooping
kid

I am a cat enjoying
bunny loving
dog walking
pizza liking
rock climbing
girl

I am a hardworking
good writing
cooking
student

Katlyn Sanders, Grade 3
Briargrove Elementary School, TX

Family

Family
Fun, exciting
Loving, caring, helping
My family supports me.
Relatives

David Grifo, Grade 3
Four Peaks Elementary School, AZ

Star

S hining brightly
T ill dawn
A fterwards
R elaxing in the sky

DesiRae Mendez, Grade 3
Emerson Elementary School, TX

Pizza Ingredients

Cheese
Pepperoni
Sauce and salt
That's all!

Kellan Pinson, Kindergarten
Jacob Wismer Elementary School, OR

The Ocean

ocean, crashing gnashing hitting rocks,
roaring through the waves
through the night, and through the day,
I can hear the water crash
I can hear it, thunder, clap.

See Yang, Grade 3
Lincoln Elementary School, CA

Horses

H orses are big and strong
O n the plains
R unning free
S tanding in pastures
E ating green grass
S urviving in nature

Casey Crane, Grade 3
Montessori School of Ojai, CA

Love

Love is red.
Love sounds like wind in the trees.
Love tastes like chocolate donuts.
Love smells like a baking cake.
Love looks like hearts.
Love makes me feel happy.

Kianna Miller, Grade 1
Highland Elementary School, CO

My Feelings

When I go to the fair!
I tell my mom to buy me this and that,
this this and that.
And she says "I can't be buying you every single thing you want!"
And then I am sad
and after that I get very mad!!!
So I look over my head.
I see a beautiful sun shining just like a sunflower.
And I look around me and there's boys all around me
and I feel so shy.

Maribel Sanchez, Grade 3
Lincoln Elementary School, CA

When I Was Born

The world was full of love when I was born
with sunlight streaming in colors of brown orange
and red leaves falling off trees
I felt the warmness of my mother's arms
me looking at her looking down at me
she wrapped me in a pink cloth
with ducks on it
Something on my chest was bouncing like a big drum
My mother's face was sweet and wet with tears
Birds were chirping like a lullaby
voices in the distance cried
what is her name
a familiar voice replied
Cheyenne
that is her name
Then I fell asleep

Cheyenne Sullivan, Grade 3
Westwood Charter Elementary School, CA

Space?

I don't understand what space is.
Is the moon made of cheese?
Are there aliens that say please?
I don't understand what space is.
I thought the Milky Way was a candy bar.
What does the Milky Way taste like?
Is there a galaxy called Reeses or Three Musketeers?
What's in that big black place…Space?

Susan Dembny, Grade 3
Miller Elementary School, TX

The Snake

Madly,
Grouchily,
Crabbily,
The snake
Is slithering through the woods.
— Watch out!

Shaun Konig, Grade 1
Fir Grove Elementary School, OR

College

I was sad because I didn't
know if I was able to go to college.

One day I thought
I could save my
money so I can
go to college.

Yes! So far I got
14 dollars. I'm going to
get my allowance. About
5 or 10 dollars.

A little bit more money!
I have 30 or 40 dollars.

Yeah! I'm sure
I'm going to college!

I'm getting good grades
and if I keep getting good grades
I get to go to college for free!

Elizabeth Martinez, Grade 3
Acacia Elementary School, AZ

Clouds

Clouds
are fluffy
like sweet cotton candy
clouds are powdery
like this girl named Mandy

Aileen Lee, Grade 3
Cahuenga Elementary School, CA

Magic Stuff

A special wand,
A cape and a bad guy,
Some old magic books,
A broom that reaches the sky!
A spell, a charm
An old witch's hat,
Through all this stuff I cannot find
My little black cat!

Clara Rosenberg, Grade 2
Broderick Montessori School, CA

My Dog

I have a dog
That likes to chase frogs
My dog's name is Noodle
He is a poodle
My dog eats his food
He's usually in a good mood
He has a lot of stuff
And he is very tough

Jose Gutierrez, Grade 2
San Jacinto Elementary School, CA

Braces

Braces, braces,
They make me sick.
Braces, braces,
Are made of sticks.
When you get them,
You want them off.
If you get them,
They may never come off.

Jordan Wallis, Grade 3
Criswell Elementary School, TX

Spring Fever

Spring
Elegance, sweet
Charming, breezing, flourishing
Plant covered hill
New time of year!

Austin Scott, Grade 3
Morningside School, MT

My Sister Virginia
Virginia is a baby.
She is my favorite sister,
Because she is so playful.
She plays with Charlotte and me and likes many things.
Virginia's favorite thing is to play peak-a-boo.
I say peak and then go boo, she laughs,
And I do too!
That is my sister, Virginia.

Emma Fairfield, Kindergarten
Presbyterian School, TX

All About Me
When I look in the mirror, I can see two of me:
The inside and the outside.
It's hard to tell which is which.
I am a dolphin soaring through the waves.
I am a caveman shouting for dinner.
I am a paper exploding with ideas.
I am a sharpened pencil.
I am a crystal sharpening a pencil.
I am a football flying to a player.
I am an apple all bitten.
I am a couple of hairs pulled off.
I am a condor flying through the wind.
I am a cookie that is orange.
I am a scroll searching to find an artifact.
I am a juicy apple pie.
I am a map searching.
I am a surfboard.
I am a dog starting to fight.
You can see me on the outside, but you can't see me in the inside.

Shane Williams, Grade 2
Open Charter Magnet School, CA

Window
Through my window I see water splashing against the rocks.
I see a palm tree waving in the air and coconuts dropping onto the sand.
I see the soft smooth sand.
Through my window I see dolphins jumping into the sea.
I see a boat sailing and air floating through my window.
I see a bunch of birds flying.
Through my window I see Hawaii.

McKayl Rothie, Grade 3
Daly Elementary School, MT

Where I'm From

I am from a house where 5 (soon 6!) live
and I feel safe and warm.

I am from climbing the plum tree
while playing hide and seek,

from my front porch where I see the lawn, the sidewalk,
my neighbor's house, my friends and my brother.

I am from my dad, BoPa and having fun,
from Swedish pancakes and Sunday morning breakfast,
from the apartment where I used to live.

Ethan Roberts, Grade 3
Fox Elementary School, CA

The Moving Place

Long, wavy spiraling lines whipping and crashing together;
Large colorful spaces forming complicated shapes;
Hard, detailed puzzle waiting to be solved.

Andy Gross, Grade 3
Fox Elementary School, CA

Everything I Am

Call me Arlan.
As a child I am anything and everything I want to be.
I am a rose growing with care all around me:
helping me, hugging me, and talking too!
I am a someone never separated from my other twin.
I am a tree filled with bright red leaves that never fall from my family.
I am a friend of loyalty and kindness.
We share special secrets (I cannot tell).
I stand up if you are teasing (you better not).
I hold the friendship rainbow in my hands.
I am a portrait filled with the purring of 956 cats meowing wildly and happily.
I am a winged, green-eyed dragon exploring the magical world of imagination
    around the castle.
I am one curious kitten looking at tiny things and making too much of a mess.
I am a witch and wizard mixing unicorn potions. (Which one do you like?
    Princesses or kittens?)
I may always be anything and everything I want to be, and there's one thing I will
    be for sure…
Arlan and always Arlan.

Arlan Engin, Grade 3
Open Charter Magnet School, CA

When I Am 100!

When I am 100, I will walk in my walker lazily. When I am in public, I will use my cane, that my grandmother used to own. I will look old and wrinkly, but beauty is on the inside. I would mostly be grumpy, but I don't care. The world will be different than when I was young. There'll be fancier things than before, I'll have new friends that will soon go away from when I die. But I'll be fine, I'll be in Heaven, next to God, and be in a new world.

Max Van Gelder, Grade 3
Hollister SDA School, CA

Choose a Good Color

If I were pink I would be a butterfly.
If I were orange I would be an orange that you eat.
If I were green I would be a dollar.
If I were yellow I would be a sun.
If I were blue I would be a shark.
If I were gray I would be a dime.
If I were red I would be a rose.
If I were purple I would be paint.
If I were black I would be a crow.

Samantha Ledezma, Grade 2
St Dorothy School, CA

A Rocket

A rocket gets blasted into space
It has left without any trace!
And off to the stars so far away,
So bright and shiny in outer space.
Seeing black holes and lots of super novas,
The rocket travels so far that you can't spot the Earth's auroras!
Suddenly the rocket breaks up and BANG!
Like magic a shuttle appears.
It starts its engines and BOOM
Goes the exhaust and the rocket comes back to Earth,
Just in time to see a star's birth!
Soon, the rocket gets close to Earth,
Suddenly: WAM!
The rocket collides with the Earth's atmosphere!
Whoosh! The rocket releases a large parachute and touches aground.
Then the astronauts step out to hear everyone cheer.
"What great astronauts!" that's what they hear.

Andrew Guo, Grade 3
Miller Elementary School, TX

BMX

Tumbling, turning, sliding, and twisting
I go for the ramp
I slide and I zoom
I feel the wind gushing through my face
I land it!
I do it again
The handle bars feel hard and jagged
I land it again!
Next I want to jump over something...
What about a skateboard
I put it at the end of the ramp
It's time, I get ready
I go as fast as a car
I jump, I feel like I am flying...
I close my eyes
Uh oh I'm falling
Finally my wheels touch the ground
I land it!
I feel really shocked
I get off of my bike
I wonder what I'm going to do tomorrow!

Dylan Proctor, Grade 3
Briargrove Elementary School, TX

Horses

Brown and black and spotted
Big horses small horses and medium horses

Eating carrots all day long
Galloping on the dusty roads

Running races and jumping stands
Horses are beautiful animals.

Elaine Helen Ahola, Grade 3
Gause Intermediate School, WA

My Five Senses

I like to see a tidy house.
I like to hear rock music.
I like to smell cookies baking.
I like to taste chewy watermelon Starburst.
I like to touch the strings of a guitar.

Nicholas Okerlund, Grade 1
Grace School, TX

I Dream

I dream to be a teacher.
I dream to teach well.
A teacher that is nice.
A teacher that is swell.
I dream to be a teacher.

Carlie Jessop, Grade 3
Daly Elementary School, MT

A House Is a House

A house is
a home for
a person.
A blanket
is a house
for a
ribbon and
a bow.
And all those
beautiful
things.

Elise Cuevas, Grade 1
Ryan Elementary School, CO

Lizard

Lizard
Fast, quiet
Crawls on walls in my house
A fun exciting pet to watch
Reptile

Ashford Hastings, Grade 1
Grace School, TX

Star

Stars are hot.
Stars twinkle.
Sometimes it's fun to watch.
Stars are suns.
They are bright.
They are up in the sky.
Stars live in space.
They are big.
Some stars move, some don't.

Marcus Story, Grade 1
Kimball School, WA

The United States of America

The United States of America is my favorite country
it has fifty states
it's home to the world's healthiest city
and five great lakes

Mississippi and Missouri are its rivers
Blue Ridge Mountains and Grand Canyons are so great

It had 43 presidents
who served us in many ways
they all worked hard for days and days

I am proud to be a citizen of a country
with so many landmarks

I will always want to live
in the Golden State

Zaki Siddiqui, Grade 3
Little Scholars School, CA

Colors I like

If I were brown I would be a cross.
If I were orange I would be a beautiful sunset or a juicy fruit.
If I were yellow I would be the sun that lights up our world.
If I were pink I would be a flower.
If I were blue I would be a dress.
If I were silver I would be strong metal.
If I were green I would be a hundred dollars!

John Tengco, Grade 2
St Dorothy's School, CA

The White House

The White House is a beautiful mansion in Washington D.C.
It is the official residence of the President.

I can see a giant White House with huge porticos.
I hear phones ringing all over the place as the President tries to grab them.
I smell the wonderful aroma drifting from the kitchen.
I feel soft grass at the annual Easter Egg Roll.
I taste insanely good entrées, appetizers and desserts steaming hot
just pulled out of the giant ovens in the kitchen
and brought to the State Dining Room.

Jonah Dipoto, Grade 3
Four Peaks Elementary School, AZ

Summer

The flowers are blooming
the sun is shining
Oh! How I love summer.
The birds are singing
the children are playing
Oh! How I love summer.

Emily Bennigsdorf, Grade 3
Academy of Charter Schools, CO

Snails

Shell hard
Skin soft
No teeth
Curly shell

Jacob Smith, Grade 1
Fir Grove Elementary School, OR

My Cat

M essy
Y ellow

C ourage
A dventurous
T alented

Skylar Davis, Grade 2
Criswell Elementary School, TX

Parrot

Parrot
Colorful bird
Talks loud, makes funny noises
I really like to hear him talk.
Good pet

Alden Suttle, Grade 1
Grace School, TX

Spring Break

Spring break starts on Monday,
oh will I be filled with joy!
Spring break will be so fun.
I just can't wait another day!

Melody Vigil, Grade 3
Academy of Charter Schools, CO

The Weather Report

The wind is blowing
I wish it was snowing.
The rain is dropping
I wish it was stopping.
A tornado is coming
Oh no! Start running.
A hurricane came
and things weren't the same.
A blizzard came through
people are sick and say achoo.
The flood came to town
and people started to drown.
Buildings came falling down
when an earthquake hit downtown.
The sun is shining, it's so hot.
We feel like we're dying.
The volcano blew its top
and the lava didn't stop.
Whether it's hot, cold, rainy or sunny
The weather's always changing.
And that's the weather report.

Marley Jones, Grade 3
Turner Elementary School, TX

Bear

You can love them.
Teddy bears are cuddly.
Sleep with them.
They are fun.
They can be any color.
Teddy bears.

Kristen Faltz, Grade 2
Acacia Elementary School, AZ

The Penguin

Cheerfully,
Wobbily,
Coolly,
The penguin
Waddles on the ice.
— Wow!

Trenten Dukes, Grade 1
Fir Grove Elementary School, OR

My Yellow Hummer

I like yellow hummers,
My dream is to have a hummer,
My favorite one is yellow with black,
I know I have to get good grades for my hummer.

I will have a TV in my hummer,
My hummer will have a big engine,
I will drive fast and slow,
I will enjoy every mile of the ride.

I want to have the H3 one,
It is the best one for me.
I know I have to work hard for it,
But I know I will get it.

My yellow hummer,
It will be high and bright,
That's what I am working at,
To be high and bright.

Jonathan Bakchellian, Grade 3
Tca Arshag Dickranian Armenian School, CA

My Thoughts

When I look in the mirror, I see my face.
When I look in my eyes, I see my thoughts.
I am a ladybug sharing my food.
I am a pair of sunglasses that are cool and beautiful.
I am a kiss on a boy's cheek.
I am pretty clothes on a fashionable girl.
I am a funny clown that makes people laugh.
I am a crazy baby-sitter who is sitting on a baby.
I am a math book full of homework.
I am a chess player planning a win.
I am a kick and punch inside a mom's tummy.
I am a heart that pumps a lot.
I am a screaming cousin at the front door.
I am a monkey that eats fish but not bananas.
I am a ball that jumps around.
I am a name that is weird.
I am a shoe that has a butterfly on it.
In my eyes, I am a friend.
Can you be in my thoughts?

Elizabeth Seo, Grade 2
Open Charter Magnet School, CA

Leaf

Leaves are brown
Leaves are crunchy
Leaves are an umbrella
for
ants
Sam Tibbetts, Grade 1
Fir Grove Elementary School, OR

Red

Red is the color of the Valentine hearts.
Red is the color of the nice rose.
Red is the first color of the rainbow.
Red is the color of Santa's suit.
Red is the color of love in your heart.
Abigail Hepburn, Grade 1
Grace School, TX

Pizza

Take a big bite
get some cheese
when the time's right
eat with ease
MMM MMM Good!

Make the crust thick
or maybe thin
thick or thin
eat it then
MMM MMM Good!

Get a big piece
eat it all
If you can't
get a small
MMM MMM Good!

When you're done
get some more
If there's none
fall on the floor
MMM MMM Good!
Will Gaus, Grade 3
Briargrove Elementary School, TX

Things

Fantastic things,
Excellent things,
Bright and beautiful things,
Red and white things,
Unbelievable things,
Awesome things,
Rock'n things,
You things.
Brittney Franklin, Grade 3
Turner Elementary School, TX

Stars

Stars shine in the sky.
Stars shine brighter than the moon.
Stars are the shiniest
thing in the world.
Ernie Pesce, Grade 2
Acacia Elementary School, AZ

Look at Me

I am a pool swimming,
fast running, school learning,
writer.
I am a friend helping,
fantastic writing, snack eating,
friend.
I am an art drawing,
paper gluing, color mixing,
learner.
I am a freeze tag playing,
dolphin feeding, joke laughing,
math super star.
I am a math working,
paper writing, smart thinking,
girl.
I am a music listening,
contest creating, book reading,
fun kid.
I am a tennis hitting,
trampoline jumping, magic believing,
reader.
Carlotta Paone, Grade 3
Briargrove Elementary School, TX

My Brother's Rocket Car
My brother has a rocket car. He got it from our grandma.
It was fun to use and to build.
What you do is, you take some baking powder and vinegar. You put it in the
rocket car, pull off the lid and…Pow!!
It glides across the ground.

Andrew Dron, Grade 2
Orchard Elementary School, UT

If I Were
If I were red, I would be a rose growing,
If I were orange, I would be an orange growing from a tree.
If I were yellow, I would be a pineapple.
If I were green, I would be a caterpillar.
If I were blue, I would be the sky shining.
If I were purple, I would be grapes on a vine.
If I were pink, I would be an eraser, erasing mistakes.
If I were gray, I would be shiny nickels.
If I were black I would be paint.

Aubrey DeMarco, Grade 2
St Dorothy School, CA

I Am
I am a kind, little girl
I wonder if mermaids are real
I hear the devil laughing meanly
I see fairies dancing gracefully
I want peace in the world
I am a kind, little girl

I pretend I am a beautiful fairy soaring through the moonlight
I feel my mother's gentle hand at school
I touch a mermaid's scaly fin in the deep blue sea
I worry about my mother when she is home alone
I cry when my parents fight
I am a kind, little girl

I understand some things aren't easy
I say mermaids are real
I dream of having wings
I try to be anything I can be
I hope I will see my dad's hand coming back to me
I am a kind, little girl

Chanele Waldvogel, Grade 3
San Onofre Elementary School, CA

Winter

It's snowing in the air
the way it was yesterday
it's not snowing anymore

Today the winter is so cool
you can throw snowballs
you can make a snow angel

You can make an ice sculpture
of yourself in the snow
you can make a snowman

The snow can land on your tongue
but don't forget
to wear your jacket, gloves, beanie

You can stay in your house
in the winter if you want,
you can even eat the snow,
The crystal in the snow,
lights up the night.

Angelo Jake, Grade 2
Los Padillas Elementary School, NM

Dear Snow Bird,

You are a beautiful shade of blue
With a lot of fluffy feathers.
I love to see you
Cuddling up in your
Warm cozy nest.
It is almost like
You are sitting by
A warm inviting fire.
Your song sings about
Beautiful snowflakes
That are falling gently
Down
  Down
To the freezing
Powdery
Snow.

Elly Beyer, Grade 2
Heatherwood Elementary School, CO

My Kitten

On a Saturday,
October first to be exact,
My mom, my sister, and good old me,
Went to the pet store
And what did we see???
Two dozen adorable kittens!
Which one should I pick?
I could only pick one.
I wondered,
I wondered,
WHO?
At last I found it!
The perfect match!
I named her Glory,
And we took her home.
I love her,
I care for her, so she loves me!

Aidan J. Adams-Campeau, Grade 3
Daves Avenue Elementary School, CA

Black Holes

Do black holes really exist?
Can they swallow a scientist?
What if he has a rocket?
And the gravity. Can he block it?
Will he die?
If yes, why?
Do black holes exist???

Nirmal Madhavapeddi, Grade 3
Miller Elementary School, TX

All About Me

I am nine years old.
I wear a jacket when I'm cold.
I have brothers who are fun.
They play with me in the sun.
I eat pizza, macaroni, and soup.
I play basketball with a hoop.
I play tag with a bag.
I will be a teacher.
A teacher is a wonderful creature.

Claudia Gutierrez, Grade 3
Honey Hollow Elementary School, CA

When I Dream

When I dream about my life…
I am from a page full of math problems.
I am from a thunderstorm full of rain in Texas.
I am from a boogie board on a vacation catching a wave.
I am from a cold ocean full of swimming fish.
I am from a library full of books.
I am from a television entertaining someone.
I am from roller blades riding on the world.
I am from a spoon full of chocolate fudge sliding down a throat.
I am from a paper full of drawings.
I am from a story overflowing with ideas.
I am from trees and grass in the mountains.
I am from a soccer ball smashed into the goal.
I am from a beautiful pink horizon over the sea.
I am from the earth itself.
But most of all I am from my family.

Cormac Gleeson, Grade 3
Open Charter Magnet School, CA

What Do Leaves Remember

Leaves remember the chirping and whistling of birds
Falling off its tree in fall
Getting stepped on by a huge foot
Leaves remember swaying in the cool gentle breeze
Staring at the long rough branches
The squirrels running on their ends
Leaves remember the joyful and unhappy things of life

Jade Ashley Cook, Grade 3
Westwood Charter Elementary School, CA

Kaiser

Kaiser is my great big German Shepherd Dog.
Sometimes he plays in the thick white fog.

Kaiser also plays catch with his yellow tennis ball.
He is the best dog of them all.

One day he ate the ear of his tiger toy.
He then became a really sick boy.

Next day we had to take him to the vet.
The doctor said, "Kaiser would soon be a well pet."

Tanner Workman, Grade 2
Grace School, TX

Talking About Tubman
T ubman made 19 trips.
U nderground Railroad.
B orn in 1820.
M oses was her nickname.
A fter the war she was free.
N ight time she went to the north.
Erica Rios, Grade 2
Pinnacle Charter School, CO

Harriet Tubman
H arriet Tubman took 19 trips
A n iron hit her head
R escued 300 people
R ailroad only slaves knew
I njured
E scaping is what she did
T ubman was nicknamed "Moses"
Oswaldo Menchaca, Grade 2
Pinnacle Charter School, CO

Dear Fuzzy Hat,
Thank you
For keeping
Me warm
Especially
My head

Thank you
Thank you
Your person,
Audrey
Audrey Lieb, Grade 2
Heatherwood Elementary School, CO

Spring
S pring is green and light,
P ristine and beautiful
R abbits hopping
I n the morning calm,
N ow do you see that spring is
G reen?
Sierra Bienz, Grade 3
Spring Creek Elementary School, WY

Thanksgiving
T hankful for everything
H ooray for Thanksgiving
A pples were at the feast
N ice pleasant food
K indness is being generous
S hip full of sailors
G rateful for freedom
I ce cream on our pie
V ery long voyage from England
I ncredible feast
N ew found land
G athering with family and friends
Rachel Brouzes, Grade 3
Four Peaks Elementary School, AZ

Bees
Bees
yellow, stings
buzzing, flying, working
making honey
honey bees
Tony Crocker, Kindergarten
Whiteriver Elementary School, AZ

Dear Hot Chocolate,
You're hot, not cold
You look like
Some chocolate
But you are
Just too hot!
You might burn me,
but I know
You taste delicious.
So, I'll drink
You now and now.
You taste like
A cup full
Of magic
So now
Can I have
More?
Avery Anderson, Grade 2
Heatherwood Elementary School, CO

Playing the Piano

When playing the piano I feel the rhythm through my fingers.
The sound is lulling sometimes hard.
The keys make those vibrating noises.
Sounds go higher and lower higher and lower.
Sometimes playing hard sometimes soft.
Sounds vibrate.
Sounds beat.
The air carries the sound.
Finally
The music stops and the music is done.

Nazir Middleton, Grade 3
Horn Academy, TX

Rainbow Colors

If I were red, I would be a very juicy apple.
If I were orange, I would be an orange.
If I were yellow, I would be a fresh banana on a tree.
If I were green, I would be a very big oak tree.
If I were blue, I would be the deep blue sea.
If I were purple, I would be a big valentine heart for you.

Joseph Kelly, Grade 3
St Dorothy School, CA

My Brother

My brother is very annoying.
He always bothers me when I really don't need it.
It never works out when I try to calm him,
but he never stops doing it.

Alyssa Frye, Grade 3
Academy of Charter Schools, CO

Baby Dogs

Baby dogs are fun.
Little dogs will play with anyone.
Little dogs are so lazy.
They are so lazy they drive me crazy.
Little dogs sometimes are hyper.
To get him calmed down, I put him to sleep by petting his fur.
Little dogs are so hyper and they love to run.
After they take a bath they like to nap in the hot sun.
When he wakes up we play a game of catch and he brings me the ball and I say,
"Well done!"

Jordan Smith, Grade 3
Froid Elementary School, MT

Friend?

Friendship is good but sometimes friendship is hard.
Friends are the people who are fun to be with.
If someone is unfriendly,
They are difficult to be with.
If someone is funny, playful, good and interesting,
They are a good friend.
But if someone is uninteresting, not polite, and mean,
They are a bad friend.
If someone does something nice
You will remember for a while,
But if someone is mean to you,
THAT you will NEVER forget.

Abbie R., Grade 3
Katherine Delmar Burke School, CA

The Night Is So Scary

The night is so scary,
It was made by Larry.
He first spreads a blanket across the sky,
(While eating a chicken thigh!)
He grabs some things from out of his pocket like the stars,
Also Pluto, Venus, Neptune, and Mars.
Then he tosses them up in the air,
And Larry does it with good care.

Since the night is so dark,
It scares little children and makes their dogs bark.
I was told all this by a fairy,
The fairy's name is Mary.
Mary didn't like Larry,
Because Larry made the night so scary.

Madison Moe, Grade 3
Hidden Hills Elementary School, AZ

Black

Black is the color of the night and he likes to play with you.
You might be afraid of my friend night
but there is no reason for you to be afraid of him.
He's just around the block.
Black is my favorite color.

Justus Arthur, Grade 1
Solana Santa Fe Elementary School, CA

Spring

When the bunnies come out in spring,
they come out to play.
I also love the beautiful smell of flowers.
Smell the fresh air of spring.
This is the time to plant seeds so flowers could grow.

Monica Cervantes, Grade 3
Midland Elementary School, CA

The Most Important Thing About Dogs

The most important thing about a dog is they don't get hurt.
It is fun and amazing to play with a dog.
It can be racing in the backyard and playing fetch.
It would be fun to be a dog.
But the most important thing about a dog is love.

Dream Underwood, Grade 3
Daly Elementary School, MT

Love

Love is great
Love is everything to be
Everything you want
You can make it with love
And you can make it in your heart
And that will be forever

Everybody can come and love

Love is heart
Love is kind to be
In every family
I love to be in my family
And my family really loves me
Because I am so loving
When I am loving, I am kind
When I am kind, I feel like magic
And when I feel like magic, I have lots of space in this world

When I feel good
I always feel good
When I feel bad
I think about my family
And go to my heart

Jamie Dorst, Kindergarten
Ohlone Elementary School, CA

My Dog

The dog is very cute it is very fluffy.
I like fluffy dogs.
The dog is white. I like dogs.
Dogs have legs. Dogs have fluffy ears.
The dog has four legs.

Yusra Serhan, Grade 1
Phoenix Metro Islamic School, AZ

Riley

She is a fun dog
She loves the green tennis ball
She whines a lot too

Jake Feldt, Grade 3
Paloma Elementary School, CA

Horses

Flies!
Apples!
Bite!
Hay!
Sweet!
Brown!
Bucking!
Kicking!
Shoes!
Bridle!
Saddle!
Run!
Fun!

Makayla Burgess, Grade 2
C C Hardy Elementary School, TX

Running

I like running,
it's really, really fun.
Once I entered a race,
and I won!
Running is a good exercise,
you will see;
you'll like it too,
Whoopee!!!

Suvansh Dutta, Grade 3
CB Eaton Elementary School, CA

The Cat

There was a cat
He was very fat
He laid on a mat
He chased a rat
He wore a hat
He sat and sat
Till he could catch the rat

Rebecca Kloos, Grade 2
Community Children's Center, CA

My Home

My dog barking
As I walk through the door,
And birds chirping loudly.
Apples being dipped in hot fudge.
Cookies coming out of the oven.
My backyard sparkling like diamonds.
In the evening, the windows
Look like the sun burning out.

Cameron Ribail, Grade 3
Four Peaks Elementary School, AZ

Shells

Shells are white
And they fight
Right?
When they see
They freeze
From fright —
The hermit crab
Is in sight.

Zac Lawrence, Grade 2
Brush Creek Elementary School, CO

Mother's Day

On Mother's Day you will give
a lot of thanks.
Be sure to give your
mom flowers. There's a lot of
love on Mother's Day. Then you
will give your mom a card and a kiss.

Elissa Marin-Garcia, Grade 3
Midland Elementary School, CA

How I See the Ocean

The swishing ocean,
See how the water crashes onto the beach,
how it steals the sand.
See a rainbow exploding in a wave,
like an artist's dream.
Feel damp sand under my feet.
See a silvery wave, and think of the moist mist.
I merge with the waves and as the seagulls cry,
I become something else.
As I glide through the chilly waves, I think about life.

Hannah Tyler, Grade 3
Writers in the Schools Program, TX

Joey

My dog Joey loves to run and play.
He wakes up early and bites my toes,
And gets in my bed to play.
My mom yells, "Down or out you will go to live with the toads!"
Poor little Joey he is just a puppy.
He is always jumping and getting into trouble,
Right under my mommy's nose!

Georgia Drager, Kindergarten
Presbyterian School, TX

Happiness

Happiness is yellow.
It sounds like a boy having fun.
It smells like beautiful flowers.
It tastes like good hot cocoa.
It looks like a sunny day.
Happiness feels like a dad saying prayers with you.

Alex Miller, Grade 3
Grace School, TX

Campfire

Campfires can be very handy and warm.
I like to roast marshmallow s'mores.
I like camping and sometimes I like to go swimming.
I like to go with my friends.
I've been camping a lot of places.
You have to be careful.
Good-bye.

Emery Hirschfeld-Smith, Grade 1
Kimball School, WA

I Wish I Was a Bat

Bats are like rats except they have wings.
I wish I was one of these winged things.
Bats are not birds
And they don't have much fur.
I wish I was a bat.

Madison Kernaghan, Grade 3
St Mark's Day School, TX

Nature Is

Nature sounds
like rain.
Nature is
green grass,
a wet grass.
Nature is spring.
Nature is yellow
flowers that smell
like lemons.
Nature tastes
like sweet dirt.

Monica Loza, Grade 1
Robert L Stevens Elementary School, CA

Owl

An owl is like the creature of the night,
Swooping down with its powerful wings,
Hoots travel across the forest,
The creatures below shiver,
As it sits in a tree hooting,
Staring, Waiting,
It takes flight once more.
Run little mice below, run!
The owl turns as the sun rises,
He goes to sleep once more.

Olivia Woodford-Berry, Grade 3
Daves Avenue Elementary School, CA

Winter!

I wake up and see snow!
I eat my breakfast and play in the snow.
Snowball fights, frostbite, hot cocoa and more.
That's what I like about winter!

Ellen Zylstra, Grade 3
Academy of Charter Schools, CO

Cats

Cats
jumping, purring
scratching, furry, lovable
soft, cute
fun!

Ade Halter, Grade 1
Highland Park School, MT

Ghost Houses

There are some
Ghost houses
Everywhere.
So...
Beware of them,
Be tough,
Don't be scared.

Hayden Martz, Grade 3
Daly Elementary School, MT

My Dad Jack

J oins me in basketball
A thletic coach at home
C an mow the lawn
K isses me good night

Josh Pian, Grade 1
Grace School, TX

I Wish

I wish I were an ocelot
In the jungle
Hunting animals
Running sleekly in the trees.

Marie Morin, Grade 3
Daly Elementary School, MT

Dogs

Dogs like to run,
Dogs are so fun,
They REALLY
like playing
in the summer,
when it's raining.

Conner Coleman, Grade 1
New Emerson School, CO

My Cat Louise
Black and gray,
Always sneaky,
Getting ready to pounce!
She is up to no good when she sits in the window seal.
She watches for animals playing outside,
Hoping someone will come inside.
Oh! Are they in for a surprise,
When Louise gives them a squeeze,
And brings them down to their knees!

Lucy Jane Herbert, Kindergarten
Presbyterian School, TX

Colors of the Rainbow
Red is anger, red is flush.
Red is happiness, red is blush.

Orange is sadness, orange is sun down,
Orange is beauty, but orange also means brown.

Yellow is bright on almost anything.
Yellow brightens the dark dull days.

Green is sour. Sweet and sour.
Green is young, and green is power.

Blue is sad, or blue is light.
Dark blue is rough, but in it's lightest form, it is bright.

Purple means lonely thinking time,
When summer went on vacation and long sad winter is here.
Spring will never come and it's all dark purple
But light purple is cheerful.

When all the colors meet together,
It forms a feeling new rainbow!

Bella Zhang, Grade 3
Lincoln Elementary School, CA

My Neighborhood
A friend is good to be in my neighborhood.
He got some wood because he should.
In that wood was a buzzing bee, and that wasn't good!

Cole Levine, Grade 1
St Mark's Day School, TX

Hades

In Hades the shade of night
Covers all things in sight.
With no joy of life
For the dead who want to live.
LuAnn Townley, Grade 3
Carnation Elementary School, WA

Peaceful Morning

It's all calm
out here
That I only hear
The sound of
People whispering
It's a beautiful
Morning
But it's
a little
windy though.
The trees
look bald
with a few
leaves
and have about 1,000
Branches. It's really
safe to be out
here.
Sarina Rodriguez, Grade 3
Edison Elementary School, CA

I Like Moms

I like moms.
Any kind of moms.
Fat moms, skinny moms, round moms.
Cool moms, sleepy moms,
A mom in a car.
A mom on a couch.
A mom in the house.
A mom in the classroom.
Nice moms, sweet moms.
Any kind of moms.
I like moms.
Taiylor Holland, Grade 2
Swink Elementary School, CO

Night Sky

A dark cave with
Flashing
It's all around
Twinkling in the
Pitch black sky
A glowing ball shining
On the Earth
Dana Holtzen, Grade 2
Heatherwood Elementary School, CO

Soda and Water

Soda
Caffeine, fat
Sticky, delicious, bubbles
Burping, flavors, clear, healthy
Lakes, rivers, seas
Wet, running
Water
Grey Giddens, Grade 1
Armstrong Elementary School, TX

Unicorn and Horses

Unicorn
Horn, flies
Magical, valleys, imaginative
Beautiful, graceful, powerful, smelly
Fast, neighing, racing
Galloping, riding
Horses
Athena Davidson, Grade 1
Armstrong Elementary School, TX

Saguaros

Saguaro.
Birds, snakes, bugs live in it.
Tallest cactus.
Lives in Arizona.
Can live about 500 years.
Can weigh as much
as five automobiles.
Saguaro
Nathan Peterson, Grade 2
Acacia Elementary School, AZ

Monument Valley

Monument Valley
An isolated red mesa and butte
Surrounded by hot sandy desert of countless silent
The natural art of mother natures was created by four scared elements
Sedimentary rock
Monument Valley
A remarkable, beautiful, famous landscape
On the Navajo Reservation connecting Utah and Arizona
The widespread landscape consists of colorful red buttes and high raisin spires
Sedimentary rock
Monument Valley
Layers of sandstone, siltstones and shale
Eroded by the wind and rain produce buttes and pinnacles
A place where my grandparents once roamed as free can be
Sedimentary Rock

Isaac Bia, Grade 2
Ganado Primary School, AZ

Indian Rodeo

Indian Rodeo
Fine, hot dirt in the arena
Bulls standing tough, strong and proudly
Wild horses kicking in the air, calves in the chute ready to be roped
A hoo hai' (Indian Rodeo)
Indian Rodeo
Cowboys young and old, ropers and riders
Papa wearing Wrangler, pants tuck inside his boots,
hat crease together in the middle
A bull rider and a roper telling his stories back in the rodeo days he once placed
A hoo hai' (Indian Rodeo)
Indian Rodeo
Cowgirls young and old, ropers and racers
Sister traveling to the next IJRA rodeo to compete in barrel racing and pole bending
Each day she practices swinging her rope, getting ready for the next rodeo drive
A hoo hai' (Indian Rodeo)
Indian Rodeo
As time goes by, I hope to ride and rope
Such as my papa back in his days and sister who is looking for her next
champion buckle
As I practice to be the next steer rider champion and tells others about my
rodeo dreams
A hoo hai' (Indian Rodeo)

Julian Lee, Grade 3
Ganado Primary School, AZ

My Closet Is...ToyLand!
Welcome to ToyLand,
When you step into my closet, it's a magical world,
My pants are the model trains carrying the toys around,
My shirts are the humorous video games,
My socks are the tiny sports cars,
My sweatshirts are helping robots,
My shoes are the chocolate candies that the robots eat,
My underwear is the slingshot.

The toy soldiers are the kids in ToyLand playing,
The children are like little gods,
Playing and working with Legos,
With no parents to control them,
The royal shin guards are the funny king and queen,
Creating the funny laws,
This is the best closet anybody could have!

Ryan Bergman, Grade 3
The Mirman School, CA

I Am
I am a crazy, cuckoo girl who loves Donald Duck
I wonder what it is going to be like in the future
I hear the whistling of the man on the moon
I see the rainbow with a pot of gold at the end
I want equal rights for all people in the world
I am a crazy, cuckoo girl who loves Donald Duck

I pretend I'm an astronaut flying off to space in 5, 4, 3, 2, 1
I feel someone trying to be my new best friend
I touch the velvet leprechaun hat
I worry about my dad's health
I cry about all the people who passed away from cancer
I am a crazy, cuckoo girl who loves Donald Duck

I understand that there are people who need help
I say we should take care of the homeless
I dream of a land far, far away that is always happy
I try to invent something new
I hope the world will be a drug free world someday
I am a crazy, cuckoo girl who loves Donald Duck

Olivia Bango, Grade 3
San Onofre Elementary School, CA

Fighting

I am emotional.
I am physical.
I destroy friendship and respect.
Love is my enemy and Chaos is my brother.
I love screaming, shouting, pushing and shoving.
I am hated by some and loved by others.
I am wars.
I am the worst of your fears.

Camden McMillan, Grade 3
Katherine Delmar Burke School, CA

A Bear Goes to School

A bear named Freddy walked to school on Fun Friday.
He had to sit in a special chair because he was too big to sit in a desk
like the other children.
He got stuck in the chair so he growled and scared the teacher and the children.
The teacher sent Freddy to the principal's office.

Kaitlyn Solomon, Kindergarten
Twin Lakes Christian Academy, TX

Colors All Around

If I were green,
I'd be a big tree in the forest or grass in the yard.
If I were blue,
I'd be the sky, clouds floating or the ocean waves crashing.
If I were red,
I'd be a stripe on the American flag or a yummy cherry.
If I were purple,
I'd be a flower blooming in spring or juicy grapes.
If I were pink,
I'd be an eraser that erases all mistakes or a tall flamingo.
If I were yellow,
I'd be the sun shining on us or a dirty sponge.
If I were orange,
I'd be an orange you eat or a basketball you play with.
If I were gray,
I'd be a shark who we fear or a sidewalk you walk on.
If I were black,
I'd be a crow who glides in the sky or a pen writing a message.
If I were white,
I'd be paper you write on or a wall you hang pictures on.
If I could be all the colors in the world, I'd be a rainbow that goes across the sky.

Briana Rios, Grade 2
St Dorothy School, CA

The Bear Hike

The bears are going on a hike,
they're going to hike on the pike.
They're using bikes to go on the hike.
A hike to the top of the pike.
Ty Stines, Grade 3
Academy of Charter Schools, CO

My Mom

My Mom
My #1 Mom
She's nice
To other people
She's sweet
Like an angel
To me
She's really kind
To people
She never
Hurts people
And I love
My Mom
With my
Heart
Matthew Alvarado, Grade 3
Edison Elementary School, CA

Sounds of Traffic

Verroom-verrooming
HONK-HONKing
Beep-beeping
Cheering
Whooshing
Screeching
Crashing
BANGing
Clucking
Pssst (flat-tire)ing
Tic-tic-tic-tic (turn signal)ing
Slam (trunk close)ing
Pop (trunk open)ing
Click (seat belt)ing
Julia Padilla, Grade 3
Cubberley Elementary School, CA

Fairy from Neverland

Fairy from Neverland
what is it like in a beauty
so fine and rare?
It is like living in a land of
light and beauty.
Jasmine Lee, Grade 3
Katherine Delmar Burke School, CA

Harriet and Abe

T ubman was good
U nderground Railroad
B eing a helper
M en weren't nice
A te nothing
N ice person

L incoln was good
I n good mood
N icknamed "Honest Abe"
C ould be a soldier
O n task
L incoln was president
N o slavery
Robert Thomas, Grade 2
Pinnacle Charter School, CO

Earth

Earth
Round, big
Turning, orbiting, shining
The only planet with air
World
Chris Varanese, Grade 3
Four Peaks Elementary School, AZ

My Snail Caroline

My snail Caroline,
Slithering, slimy, cute and climby,
Leaving a trail wherever she goes.
With a hard shell and antennae eyes,
She travels very slow.
Mollie Hanna, Kindergarten
Presbyterian School, TX

My Dogs

Oscar is small with brown and black stripes.
He barks when someone knocks on the door.
Lambchop is big, white, and soft.
She likes to chase me when I run.
They like to play catch with a ball,
And chew on some bones.
They like to lie down in the cool, cool grass.
And of course, they like to chase cats all day long.
These are my dogs.

William Hoekel, Kindergarten
Presbyterian School, TX

Pink

Pink feels like my baby sister's hand in my hand.
Pink looks like a pink rose in a garden.
Pink tastes like a pink lemonade lollipop.
Pink sounds like a pink eraser erasing my pencil marks.
Pink smells like a pink Foxglove flower in a flower bed.
Pink.

Sophia Fraser, Grade 2
Bridlemile Elementary School, OR

That's Me

My name is Eli.
I like to think about myself when I am in bed at night.
I think about things that I'm going to do in the morning.
But I also have more things on my mind.
I am a soccer ball dashing into the goal.
I am a spoonful of ice cream rolling down someone's throat.
I am an artifact waiting in the sand.
I am a classroom roaring with kids.
I am a chair collapsing.
I am a pencil running away from the sharpener.
I am a book screaming to be read.
I am a car crashing into everything.
I am a dolphin soaring in the air.
I am a map showing all the countries, states, and cities.
I am a camera taking pictures of the Pink Panther.
I am a paper towel swiping across the table making everything clean.
I am a fish swimming all around a small ocean.
I enjoy thinking about all of these things.
They are all part of who I am.

Eli Remba, Grade 2
Open Charter Magnet School, CA

Lamb

White and fluffy lamb
They're sweet asleep in the field
Little baby sheep.
Kaitlin Stromberg, Grade 3
Daly Elementary School, MT

My Brothers

Little,
Naughty,
Some days I play,
Some days I not play,
My brothers.
Don Nguyen, Kindergarten
Jacob Wismer Elementary School, OR

The Frog

Colorful speckles,
Leaping over lily pads,
Through a summer day.
Rebecca Alch, Grade 3
Lanai Road Elementary School, CA

My Family

My dad is fun.
He plays video games with me
And we watch TV.
He plays with my dog
As I do, too.
Her name is Tahni
And her cousin is Bonnie.

My mom is nice
Because she fixes supper
For us every night.
But sometimes she's mean
Because she doesn't let me
Have Cokes before supper.

That's my family
All except Two Fizzy and
Sophie doo dee doo doo.
Tyler Graves, Grade 2
Liberty Ranch Christian School, NM

Playing Piano

I love playing piano,
It is fun.
It makes me happy!
Why does it make me happy?
It makes me feel good.
Cydney Bradford, Kindergarten
Twin Lakes Christian Academy, TX

Abe Lincoln

A nice person
B orn in Kentucky
E lected 16th president

L ead the Civil War
I ntelligent
N ot mean to others
C aptain of his company
O beys rules and people
L awyer in Illinois
N ation's president
Christopher Young, Grade 3
Canyon Rim Elementary School, CA

The Flower

I have a flower
It is a sunflower
It is cute and pretty
It resembles other flowers
I like my flower
I wish it grows well.
Si-yeon Park, Grade 3
Cahuenga Elementary School, CA

Writing

You can write any kind of way.
You can write in hieroglyphs.
You can write in cursive.
You can write in Spanish.
Or you can write in Japanese.
Or Chinese will do.
You can write any way you want.
Grammacy Howard, Grade 3
Crestview Elementary School, TX

When I Close My Eyes
My days are usually busy and filled with action.
But when I am in bed and I close my eyes I am calm and I think about myself.
I am a speeding ball dashing around the world into a goal!
I am a waterfall sliding down a rock, whirling around.
I am cookies, cake, and ice cream falling down a throat.
I am a mouse jumping around, soaring into a cat's mouth!
I am fairy tales finding my way out of my problems.
I am a smooth red ball hitting a wall, sometimes very slowly.
I am a bed putting myself to sleep.
I am a spy helping imaginary friends.
I am a small, fluffy dog jumping up and putting slobber on faces.
I am a red car speeding across the finish line.
I am colors smoothly making a beautiful picture on a paper.
I am fingers coming on and off keys.
I am a light coming on and off, on and off.
I am a mouth opening every second with ideas.
I am big red shoes making everybody explode with laughter.
I am trains going up and down tracks.
I am a plane hopping from place to place.
When I open my eyes I will wake up remember all the things I am.
I begin another action-packed day!

Danielle Koenig, Grade 2
Open Charter Magnet School, CA

Penguins
The important thing about penguins is that they waddle.
They are black,
And white,
And they make sounds,
And they jump out of the water.
But the important thing about penguins is that they waddle.

Brayden Meza, Kindergarten
River HomeLink Program, WA

Where I'm From
I am from a house coated with white
and from flowers, trees, wildlife, people, cars and animals.
I am from Tim, Sarah, Grampa, my mom and dad and my Nana
and from "I love you."
I'm from pasta, bread, salad, pizza, chicken, steak, rice,
beans, eggs, Mexican and Indian food.
I am from a scrapbook of memories.

Tommaso Ferme, Grade 3
Fox Elementary School, CA

Wind
Blowing from the sky
Hiding from the stars
I'm the wind
Casey Tuin, Grade 1
Fir Grove Elementary School, OR

Cardinal
Chirp! Chirp! Chirp!
Pecking worms.
Flying through the sky.
Cardinal.
Andrea O'Bert, Grade 2
Acacia Elementary School, AZ

Blueberries
There once was a pig named Mary
She loved to eat blueberries
She got tired at a store
Then she started to snore
To get home she got carried.
Isaac Calderon, Grade 3
St Raphael School, CA

Welcome to My World
I am a
fast writing,
cool dancing,
awesome sport playing,
kind of girl.

I am a
great runner,
good reading,
Coke drinking,
awesome person.

I am a
math learning,
cool drawing,
Egyptian traveling,
child.
Alaa Aly, Grade 3
Briargrove Elementary School, TX

I Like Kittens
I like kittens
Because they're cute!
I love kittens for a reason,
Because they are so, so, little!
Jacey Elkjer, Kindergarten
Jacob Wismer Elementary School, OR

The Duck
Happily,
Loudly,
Fantastically,
The duck
Is quacking in the pond.
— Listen!
Jayden Dukes, Grade 1
Fir Grove Elementary School, OR

The Puppy
Happily,
Beautifully,
Nicely,
The puppy
Is resting in the house.
— Ahhh!
Sean Ely, Grade 1
Fir Grove Elementary School, OR

The Sun and Moon
The sun shines.
The moon lights up the night.
The stars are beautiful,
and you are, too!
Bailey Kisiel, Grade 2
Acacia Elementary School, AZ

A Boy's Wish
I wish I was a boy,
I wish I had a toy,
I wish I could annoy
All my girls, and they can
Annoy me back.
Brandon Franklin, Grade 3
Turner Elementary School, TX

Biking the Bumpy Road!

Bumpy, bumpy. bumpy
The bumpy road is lumpy.
I want to go home!
I can't believe I am in a bumpy bumpy lumpy lumpy road.
The winds keep blowing me swoosh swish!
It's a windy day!
I am miles away.
5 miles, 3 miles.
What a nightmare with an oily road.
If I'm home I'll say hip hip hooray!!!!

Jacob Siahaan, Grade 3
Briargrove Elementary School, TX

Colors

If I were blue I would be a beautiful sky.
If I were yellow I would be a juicy lemon.
If I were gray I would be in the sky.
If I were pink I would be a beautiful flower in the ground.

Elizabeth Timko, Grade 2
St Dorothy School, CA

My Closet Is…an Enchanted Forest

My closet is an enchanted forest
My shoes are the lions
My socks are the lion cubs
My belts are the snakes
The baby snakes climb up to the ceiling
My umbrellas are the trees
The rattlesnakes are the shirts moving around on the floor.

I love the enchanted forest that is my closet
Snow falls in the enchanted forest
The snow is as soft as a white blanket
The sky is as blue as a rainbow
There is a mountain in my closet
It is the pile of pants folded neatly on the shelves.

My hardwood floor is a murky swamp with fish in it
The fish, which are my pajamas, are yellow, blue and orange
When you open a suitcase in my closet
A castle magically appears
I love my enchanted forest.

Morgan Wallace, Grade 3
The Mirman School, CA

Theater Acting!
Theater acting singing, singing my lines.
What about my lines? Do I get any lines?

Yes you get some lines, but most of it is singing, singing.
Now let's try to do it.
First can I have a snack?

Yes you can have a snack.
And then you start singing, singing.

Now it's all through.
Tomorrow we perform.
I know you will do good singing and singing.

Bailey Kogut, Grade 3
Briargrove Elementary School, TX

Senses of Russia
I see the colorful domes of St. Basil Cathedral right in front of me.
I see the people rushing from one place to another
on the snowy paths of St. Petersburg.
I see miles of snow in Siberia.
I see the skiers skiing down Mt. Elbrus in the Caucasus Mountains.
I see a Russian man harvesting his mushrooms.

I hear the exotic chatter of two Russians in the middle of a conversation.
I hear cars rushing by on the busy streets of Moscow.
I hear the fluttering of a flag nearby.
I hear the waves of the Arctic Ocean.
I hear a gush of wind in a snowstorm.

I feel the cold air hitting my face.
I feel the freezing snow settling on the palm of my hand.
I feel the cold ground under my feet.
I feel the warm breeze on a summer day in western Russia.
I feel the chilly water in Lake Baikal.

I smell Russian blintzes baking.
I smell the wild flowers in Siberia.
I smell salt water in the distance.

I taste the Russian salads in a Russian restaurant.
I taste the juicy raw smoked salmon.

Andy Szwiec, Grade 3
Four Peaks Elementary School, AZ

Nature

Nature is full of multicolored green,
Tree frogs and sharp-eyed eagles that I have seen,
Bugs under leaves for camouflage,
Butterfly wings like a collage,
Throughout the forest the wildlife spread,
A green-eyed deer with antlers on its head,
Grass-eating rabbits hopping to and fro,
Hungry foxes in slender grass crouching low,
Moss growing on tree stumps,
Olive toads with lumpy bumps,
Green is here and emerald is there,
Forest green is everywhere.

Demi Chang, Grade 3
Daves Avenue Elementary School, CA

The Grocery Store

Clean fresh fruits shine
in the boxes and smell like a flower.
Voices were all around me
as I passed through the fruit aisle.
The fresh foods make me hungry.
It also makes me want to eat them and buy them.
A kind of candy smells good and fruity
because it's made of peaches.
Kinds of bread give out their fresh smell
and make me want to go close to it and breathe that fresh air.
Mmmmmm I love it.
When I got home I rested from that fun excellent time.

Cristina Martinez, Grade 3
Lincoln Elementary School, CA

How to Be Mimi

Reads 2 chapters of *Fairy Dust*.
Combs hair and loves it.
Talks too much and talks too fast.
Lives in a crowded small house with two other people.
Changes sister's diapers.
Studies math facts at every lunch recess.
Tutors 1st graders in reading.
Goes to Coral every day after school.

Mimi Orellana, Grade 3
Willard Elementary School, CA

Danger Island

A shower of arrows is coming,
Shooting up like fireworks,
Coming down hard.
Your heart is throbbing,
You're digging holes,
Looking for tunnels,
Any shelter will work.
Time is running out.
A boat is coming ashore,
You call to it but it's too late.
The arrows are here!
They aim, they miss!
You see the man wielding the dozen arrows.
He has a dozen more.
You fall on the ground, playing dead.
Spider webs are everywhere.
The man is getting closer and closer...
A shower of arrows is coming.

Joseph Guerra, Grade 3
Writers in the Schools Program, TX

I Like the US Army

I like the US Army.
Any kind of US Army.
The Navy, the Air force, the Confederate army.
Marines, Delta Force,
The US Army in a wave.
The US Army on a tank.
The US Army in the revolution.
The US Army in the battle.
US Army, US Army.
Any kind of US Army.
I like the US Army.

Dominic Mondragon, Grade 2
Swink Elementary School, CO

My Five Senses

I like to see the blue sky on a sunny day.
I like to hear my cats meowing.
I like to smell blueberry shampoo.
I like to taste vanilla cake with chocolate icing.
I like to touch my dog's soft fur.

Cate Dunne, Grade 1
Grace School, TX

Math!

Math is fun.
Math is cool.
Math is awesome.
Math is tremendous.
Math is huge.
Math is big.
Math is humongous.
Math!

Tyler Sweet, Grade 1
New Emerson School, CO

Spring

Spring is here —
Soft rain pours down quietly,
Colorful flowers bloom,
The sunny sun is bright,
Butterflies fly
And fill the longer day.
Spring is beautiful!

Kindergarten Class
The Presentation School, CA

Chaos

Everybody going wild,
foot kicking,
arm throwing,
food flinging,
roaring people,
cat scratching,
people pouncing,
dog barking.
It's pandemonium!
It's chaos!

Anna Bruce, Grade 2
New Emerson School, CO

My Dog

Sophie
Apricot fur
Likes to jump on people
I like to hold her in my arms.
Great dog

Audrey Keenan, Grade 1
Grace School, TX

I Am A…

My name is Rudy Omar Escobar Sandoval.
My name remind me of my family.
My family helps me to be many things.
I am a new game of Monopoly with my sister.
I am a pencil squirming all around a paper.
I am a basketball swishing in a hoop.
I am a sky watching over the people.
I am a monster roaring at people.
I am a ball jumping all around.
I am a TV that has cable.
I am a song in people's ears.
I am a book filled with a lot of secrets.
I am a folder that has a lot of homework.
I am a soccer ball in the air.
I am a skateboard dashing across the floor.
I am a ball bouncing around.
I am a pencil scribbling around the paper.
I am a drip of water when someone cries.
When I am awake I don't have dreams.
But when I am asleep I have dreams and they are about my family and me.
My family helps me to be many things.

Rudy Omar Escobar Sandoval, Grade 2
Open Charter Magnet School, CA

Rain

Drip
    drop
drip
    drop
says the rain when it
hits the ground
making a flood
across the cool
green carpet of mother earth
The pitter patter
of the rain
like the beat
of
a
drum
The rain's diamond drops fall from the cloudy gray sky.
Rain

Georgia Brown, Grade 2
Horizons K-8 Alternative Charter School, CO

Eels

I don't mind eels
Except their meals
And the way they feel
Elsi Flores, Grade 3
Clarence Ruth Elementary School, CA

The Pumpkin Patch

Pumpkins pumpkins
Everywhere there's pumpkins
Pumpkins at night
What a great sight
Round pumpkins
Smooth pumpkins
Orange pumpkins
Green pumpkins
Pumpkins ripe
Pumpkins unripe
Bright pumpkins
Light pumpkins
Pumpkins pumpkins
Everywhere pumpkins
Hannah Burgess, Grade 3
Williams Elementary School, CA

My Dog Snowball

My dog named Snowball,
Had a dangerous fall,
For we put him in a cast,
And as time went past,
It came for him to die,
So say goodbye,
As he died by my side.
Joshua Chedsey, Grade 3
Academy of Charter Schools, CO

America

America
Proud, brave
Helping, defending, leading
A country of freedom
Country
Michael Appel, Grade 3
Four Peaks Elementary School, AZ

A Girl from Brazil

There once was a girl from Brazil
She wanted to go to the mill
She gathered some grain
it started to rain
and so she felt quite ill!
Anna Mooy, Grade 3
St Raphael School, CA

Parakeet

Ch-ch-ch-ch-ch!
Pecking on seeds.
Plays in his cage.
Parakeet.
Sanne Casello, Grade 2
Acacia Elementary School, AZ

Happiness

Happiness is brown.
It sounds like a bark from a dog.
It smells like fresh grass.
It tastes like roast beef.
It looks like a dog.
Happiness feels like fur.
Kennedy Wirfs, Grade 3
CLASS Academy, OR

Fall

Fall is when leaves change.
Swirling, dancing, colored leaves.
All of them different.
Linsey Peterson, Grade 3
Summit Elementary School, UT

Day and Night

Day
Dawn, light
Morning, waking, stretching
Bright, sun, dark, night
Darkening, sleeping, dreaming
Creepy, scary
Night
Dylan Bason, Grade 3
Turner Elementary School, TX

I'm A...

I'm a lot of things in the inside that people can't see.
I'm a brown piece of pie.
I'm a refrigerator filled with food making a tummy and head go wild!
I'm a clock ticking really loudly.
I'm a cookbook filled with recipes making a mouth water.
I'm a ridiculous looking bear with a black nose.
I'm a strong and fast scooter speeding to the classroom.
I'm a soccer ball screaming into the goal.
I'm a book read by two teachers' big imaginations.
I'm a sweet tasty milk shake sliding down a big throat.
I'm a huge heart filled with kindness, respect and responsibility.
I'm the laughter in a joke.
I'm a mouthwatering steaming hot pizza soaring into a wet mouth.
I'm important because I'm special on the inside and the outside.

Kennedi Simmons, Grade 3
Open Charter Magnet School, CA

My Closet Is...Never Land

My closet is not the same anymore!
What happened?
The pretty shoes are the fairies,
The flying free dress is Peter Pan,
The different little socks are the Lost Boys,
I am going to see Peter Pan.

I take the fairy dust that he gave me to go to Never Land,
I fly up to the cloudy, night sky,
The colors of the night are like a rainbow,
It's pretty like all the enchanting fairies.

I look at my watch, it's time to go,
"Whoosh, whoosh,"
I'm flying back home, out of my closet,
Good-bye fairies,

When I step out of my closet,
My room is the same as when I left it,
The magical fairies turn back into the pretty shoes,
Peter Pan turns back into my beautiful green dress,
The Lost Boys turn back into all the different socks,
I better not tell anybody what happened in my closet,
It's my magical, mystical, marvelous secret!

Samantha Paul, Grade 3
The Mirman School, CA

The Pool

The scariest thing I ever did
was I fell in a pool.
I almost went to the bottom
but I grabbed the side
and pushed up.
When I got up
I was soaking wet.
My grandma dried me off.
Have you ever done that?

Joshua Blecha, Grade 2
Acacia Elementary School, AZ

Christmas

I like Christmas. It is fun,
Yellow, green, red!
Santa, Jesus? Ho! Ho! Ho!

Jordan Porter, Grade 1
Thomas Edison Charter School, UT

Just Like Martin

I want to be like Martin,
Martin Luther King.
I want to have a dream,
just like Martin Luther King.
I want to turn the world upside down,
just like Martin Luther King.
I want to lead a march,
just like Martin Luther King.
I want black and whites to join hands,
just like Martin Luther King.
I want to do what Martin did,
Martin Luther King.

Paige Harris, Grade 3
Redwood Christian School, CA

Zorro

Z orro is my best friend.
O n this day until the end.
R ibbons are his favorite toy.
R unning around all day.
O n the stairs he likes to play.

Hadi Naseredden, Grade 3
Phoenix Metro Islamic School, AZ

Grandparents

G ood at making me happy
R eally fun to play with
A mazing to me
N ice to me when I don't feel good
D oing lots of things
P erfect at dressing up
A nd never let me down
R espectful always
E very day you smile
N ever mean
T errific!

Sydney Pauly, Grade 3
Four Peaks Elementary School, AZ

Niagara Falls

I went all the way to Canada.
I went on a boat
in Niagara Falls.
It was amazing.
I had to wear a jacket.
I got wet.
It was a little bit scary
getting on the boat.
Have you ever done that?

Jayme Beall, Grade 2
Acacia Elementary School, AZ

I Can't Write My Poem!!

I can't write my poem
Why my pencil broke
I have a headache
My neck hurts
Can I go home?

Marshay Wilson, Grade 3
Patton Elementary School, TX

Lion

Roar!
Hiding from their prey.
Sleep all day.
Lion.

Eldon Fielding, Grade 2
Acacia Elementary School, AZ

It Was a Rainy Day

As light drops fell on the ground making a little puddle the rain got harder
the thunder made a pounding sound on the ground
like an elephant playing jump rope.
When the rain got harder and harder there was a big black puffy cloud in the sky
looking like a poodle dog floating in the sky.
While I stood outside by the door
I saw big drops from the sky like it was raining cats and dogs.
It sounded like a drum playing music.
I felt drops on my face like if I was in the shower
and the water was wetting my face.
I thought to myself is there going to be a flood?

Karen Almaraz, Grade 3
Lincoln Elementary School, CA

Orange

Orange is the fish that swims through the stream.
Orange is the orange I eat from the tree.
Orange is the ball that I play with at the park.
Orange are my pants that I wear in the dark.

Christina Malogi, Grade 2
Lincoln Elementary School, CA

Where's My Ice Cream?

Have you seen my ice cream?
Where can it be, can you show me?
It's chocolate, it's vanilla, it's strawberry too.
If you help me find it, I will share some with you.
So if you find my ice cream, you will be the girl of my dream.

Ceiveon Munoz, Grade 2
C C Hardy Elementary School, TX

My Teddy Bear

My teddy bear is pink
And I made a picture of it with ink, I think.
It smells so good that I almost ate it for lunch.
And when I go to school I feel sad because I missed my teddy bear a bunch.

I want to sleep with it but I have too much asthma
So I cannot sleep with her.
I love it because it is so cute and fluffy,
If you hug it very silly, both eyes will become very puffy,
Just like my friends Muffy and Snuffy.

Viczel Victoria Z. Suguitan, Grade 2
Little Scholars School, CA

Blue Balloon

I once had a balloon of blue.
The wind came and away it flew.
I yelled...
STOP!
STOP!
STOP!
And then I heard...
POP!
Now my blue balloon is no more.
I will have to buy another at the store.
Karla Aguilar, Grade 2
Grace School, TX

Summer

On one summer day,
Snow is melting away.
Goodbye cold winter!

The snow is gone,
the day is bright and happy.
Hello summer day!

The leaves are falling,
plants are dying today,
Goodbye summer day!
Jonathan Trautman, Grade 3
Four Peaks Elementary School, AZ

I Love Allah

I love Allah

L ook at Allah's creations
O h I love you
V ery forgiving
E verything is Allah's creations

A llah is very nice.
L earn about Allah
L isten to Him
A llah sent lots of prophets
H is things are beautiful
Shafie Serhan, Grade 3
Phoenix Metro Islamic School, AZ

Dog

Lick!
Slobber!
Bite!
Bark!
Fleas!
Chase!
Digs!
Drools!
Run!
Poop!
Oops!
Scoop!
Ernesto Vega, Grade 2
C C Hardy Elementary School, TX

My Home

When I come home,
It feels new.
It smells like sweet flowers.
I see birds chirping.
I am happy and excited.
It feels good.
I hear, "Welcome home."
Reagan Chalmers, Grade 3
Four Peaks Elementary School, AZ

Wheelie

I have done a
front wheelie on my bike
and I almost fell off because
I turned my front wheel
and then the front wheel
came down.
Have you ever done that?
Nathaniel Spiller, Grade 2
Acacia Elementary School, AZ

Snowman

Snowmen melt a lot
And when it is cold they stay
And it is so fun.
Canyon Nix, Grade 3
Summit Elementary School, UT

My Shooting Star

I
see
the stars
at night
they're really
bright. When
it's day I cannot see them
when it is night I see them again. They have five points. I really
like them. I wish they were out. When it's day. They're
really pretty. I know they are those beautiful stars.
They are really bright yellow they shine
in the sky just like the sun.
Stars are out all night —
just like the moon. Stars don't
last that long.　　My star is not
just a regular　　star. My star is
a shooting　　star. I wish
I were　　　　a star.

Madeline Swanborn, Grade 1
Kimball School, WA

Sounds

Today is like every other day.
As I drop another flake into the fish tank.

One by one it disappears by the fish.
Glittering scales show on the fish.

Very quiet to the wind outside.
Listening to the sound from plants and tree leaves
That comes from the outside.

Like hissing snakes hissed by.
In the distance watched as the trees were still rustling.
But in a soft way.

Angela Fan, Grade 3
Horn Academy, TX

Ocean

I see fish and animals in the calm clear sea.
I see the sun shining on small scaly blue fish.
I hear the roar of waves rushing across the peaceful ocean.

Albert Swingler, Grade 3
Grattan Elementary School, CA

I Dream

I dream of a world of peace.
I dream that there is no more war.
In the future, I dream of love through the world.
I want love through the world, not hatred.
I dream of a world of peace.

Mason Ziegler, Grade 3
Daly Elementary School, MT

My Pets

Today is like any other Saturday on the computer with my sister at basketball.

My family is away at my sister's game and my dog and cat are playing together
and I'm listening for whatever comes up.

Suddenly

I hear a hiss and a jingle from my dog's collar.
Then my dog is barking my cat meowing and hissing.

It's bad and so I go and I get my dog by her collar and I stop the fight
and the house is quiet again.

Ben Cooper, Grade 3
Horn Academy, TX

I Am Different Things

I am a sister, a daughter, a cousin and much more.
I am some other things inside.
I am a pencil on a paper.
I am a "peek-a-boo" to get a giggle.
I am a pizza soaring into a mouth.
I am a red ball on a nose that makes people laugh.
I am a pair of cleats zooming around the bases.
I am a band aid on a knee.
I am a mouth saying the truth.
I am a ball captured in the goal.
I am a pair of flippers swishing in the water.
I am a line to be studied.
I am skates gliding on ice.
I am all these things, but I am also a sister,
a daughter, a cousin and so much more.

Ariel Mengistu, Grade 2
Open Charter Magnet School, CA

The Coral Reef
When I'm in the ocean,
I feel like I'm weightless,
surrounded with little sea horses.

I see coral swaying back and forth
through the ocean water.

I taste all the salty water
in the ocean.

I hear the waves crash around me.

When I reach the surface,
I smell the fishy air.

I know that the coral reef is a great place to live,
and now I understand that anyone who lives here is
very lucky to have a home like a coral reef.

Melissa Ervin, Grade 3
Four Peaks Elementary School, AZ

Why Am I in Jail?
Why am I in jail?
I didn't even steal a pail.
I didn't kidnap, steal or rob.
I didn't make someone sob.
I'm not a criminal or a bad guy;
I didn't even make someone sigh.
I didn't use a gun and I didn't even hurt a thumb.
I didn't pop a ball and...
Oh...
I'm just in Time Out...that's all!

Reagan Call, Grade 3
Crater Elementary School, OR

My Lucky Cat
My cat Lucky, she loves me a lot.
She is soft and cuddles with you.
She has a sister that loves to play with her.
She loves to be with you and get in your face.
Her and her sister will never let me sleep.
My love for Lucky and Frisky is beyond a million miles.

Kimmy Davis, Grade 3
St Andrews Episcopal School, NM

My Dad Rhett

R ests a lot
H obby of woodworking
E njoys golf
T eaches me about baseball
T ells me how to throw

Davis Jackson, Grade 1
Grace School, TX

Dad

Tucks us in
Takes us places
To the movies
To the stores
To Walmart
To Hollywood Video
To the zoo
He tickles me.
He loves me.
He hugs me.
He feeds me.
He likes me.
He kisses me.
He reads to me.
He says good night.
He takes care of me.

Israel Pena, Grade 1
Lee Richmond Elementary School, CA

The Bus Driver

All hail to the driver
(he has a good knack!)
Everyone loves him
and he loves them back.

Augustine Larsen, Grade 3
Summit Elementary School, UT

I Wish for Everything

I wish I was a king,
To rule the world.
I wish I could ride a dirt bike,
I wish I was Spiderman.

Alyx Thibodeaux, Grade 3
Turner Elementary School, TX

Bright Blue Sky

I love the bright blue sky.
I wish I could fly
In the bright blue sky.

Rachel Giron, Grade 3
Academy of Charter Schools, CO

Magical Minerals

Minerals
Colorful, useful
Transforming, melting, hardening
Minerals make glass
Gems

Brandon Barth, Grade 3
Four Peaks Elementary School, AZ

Mountain Boy

Mountain Boy lives up high in the sky
and on Mountain Peak.
It's cold where he lives.

Because he can't feel his ribs,
people call him a freak.
He's only six years old.
But he's big and bold.
That's what I was told.

Brenndan Johnson, Grade 3
Crestview Elementary School, TX

Gameboy

My Gameboy has games
My Gameboy makes me very happy
I love my Gameboy

Lauren Mazurowski, Grade 3
Our Lady of the Snows School, NV

Valentine's Day

I see lots of hearts.
I hear love all over.
I taste sweet heart candy.
I smell roses.
I feel a pretty heart on a valentine card.

Emma Brown, Grade 2
Swink Elementary School, CO

Let Us Play

Today is like any other day
But, not just any other day
As the yellow fellows pop out of their rocks

Fluffy yarn jumping above the ground
Like raindrops refusing to come down

As the painted clouds play with each other
You would not want to miss it chirp chirp in the air

Everyone follows each other's path
Like tiny bugs over the ground
Follow the leader follow the sound

Let us run let us play
Let us chirp every day
Let the sky be full of wind
Let us play on a perfect day

Hijab Nomani, Grade 3
Horn Academy, TX

Jewel

Jewel is like a round fuzzy ball sitting on the couch.
When it is springtime bloom, my little Jewel can pounce on thick, sharp, solid pieces of grass.
When it is white-ice wintertime, my fuzzy little Jewel will sit by the fire in a round fuzzy ball, soft asleep.
In summer, my little Jewel will walk on the brick tone red walk to the garden where the beds of roses are.
In the summer, my little Jewel will climb trees and will smell the honeybees.
In the colors of fall, my little Jewel will watch the squirrels eat their nuts that are dark nut brown.
My little Jewel will roll up in a fuzzy ball and go to sleep.

Kathleen Yuskewich, Grade 3
Horizons K-8 Alternative Charter School, CO

Socks!

Socks are very, very stinky!
They come in all shapes and sizes!
They are different colors too!
When it's time to buy a new pair you will really know.
Pee! Yew!

Trevor Bender, Grade 2
C C Hardy Elementary School, TX

Weather
Loud crashing thunder
Windy and gloomy dark sky
Then a rainbow appears
Alexis Manzo, Grade 3
Willard Elementary School, CA

I Can't Write a Poem
I keep nagging myself.
I can't think of a poem.
I lost my ideas.
Someone took my poem.
Someone took my pencil
You will laugh
If you look at my poem.
Meagan Musgrave, Grade 3
Patton Elementary School, TX

Poinsettia
Poinsettias are growing
Dirt, flowers, green, red
Poinsettias
Max Benson, Grade 1
Thomas Edison Charter School, UT

My Dog
My dog is nice
it won't harm a mice.
My dog is brave
he saves the day.
My dog is fast
he won't be last.
My dog is trustful
he is friendful.
My dog is smart
he could dodge a dart.
My dog is tame
I teach him how to say my name.
My dog is funny
as a bunny.
My dog is enthusiastic
he is fantastic!
Priscilla Phua, Grade 3
CB Eaton Elementary School, CA

Pumpkin
Pumpkin
Orange, cool
Scary, sad, quiet
I like pumpkins because they light up!
Jack-o'-lanterns
Hope Lyn Holder, Grade 2
Swink Elementary School, CO

Bears
Bears are cute,
Bears are kind,
I like bears 'cause they are mine.
Pick one out,
Show it to me,
I will have so much care for thee.
Dezáray Lowery, Grade 3
Katherine Delmar Burke School, CA

Seal
I love seals because
they swim and they eat fish
and they play ball
and they are brown
and they have babies
and they take care of their babies.
Mosab Haymour, Grade 1
Phoenix Metro Islamic School, AZ

Strawberries
S weet, sweet tasting
T errific looks
R ipe as can be
A wesome juicy goodness
W onderful sourness and sweetness
B erryriffic
E xcellent nutrition
R ipe redness
R osy red
I ncredible
E njoyable
S o, so yummy!
Cameron Cates, Grade 3
Cottonwood Montessori School, NM

The Civil War President

L incoln was a man that didn't want slavery.
I n February 12 in Kentucky he was born and died in 1865.
N orth was the side that he was on.
C ivil War began two weeks after he became president.
O ur 16th president was nicknamed Honest Abe.
L incoln was a man that didn't let the southern states separate.
N ot president now because John shot him in the head.

Ivan Aguirre-Olivas, Grade 2
Pinnacle Charter School, CO

Hurricane Rita

Hurricane Rita you tore up our town
You left a big mess and families with frowns

You pounded our barn and kicked down our trees
Then you left leaving us lots of debris

When we got home they said "There's no school!"
We ran outside cheering "This is so cool!"

Two weeks have passed, now we have lights
We play our Game Cube and stay up at night

Three weeks have passed it's time to go back
The principal wants us all to pass TAKS

Hurricane Rita I just want to say
"Never come back and PLEASE stay away!"

Michael Scott, Grade 3
China Elementary School, TX

Yellow

Yellow the color of the sun that is shining
and the color of a duck swimming through a pond.
Yellow is a lemon that makes your mouth feel funny
and the color of a beautiful butterfly flying through the air.
Yellow are the flowers growing in our garden.
Yellow is the color of the sunset
and the card that we pull when we are in trouble.
Yellow are the fish that I see in the rushing river.

YELLOW!!

Everlyn Castaneda, Grade 2
Lincoln Elementary School, CA

My Home

When I come home,
I taste nice fresh air,
And steam from dinner.
I hear dogs barking loudly,
Kids running quickly,
Birds chirping quietly,
TV on high.
It is very loud.
I see a black dog,
A grayish cat,
Very green trees outside,
TV inside and computers turned off,
And benches outside on my porch.
I smell Febreeze getting sprayed,
Dinner getting cooked,
And strawberry vanilla candles getting burnt.
I love my house.

Madison Conner, Grade 3
Four Peaks Elementary School, AZ

My Guinea Pig

F at as a tire
L oves to have carrots
U nhappy when we got my dog
F ussy when I take him out
F eels soft
Y ucky when he kicks poop out of his cage

Cassandra Burt, Grade 2
Frontier Valley Elementary School, CO

My Cat, Tiger

I named him Tiger.
He looks like a tiger.

He's just so, oh no!
He got into my honey!

Love it when he purrs at night.
Ouch! What a sight he scratched me.

I wonder if I have a cat
Or a tiger sometimes.

James Casados, Grade 2
Sangre De Cristo Elementary School, CO

Spring

Spring
Tepid water, flowers
Cool winds blowing
Light and breezy whispers
Season

Theo Nicholson, Grade 3
Morningside School, MT

Roses

Roses are red
And violets are blue.
I think you are lovely
And pretty, too.

Gabby Ahumada, Grade 2
St Mark's Day School, TX

Spring

S wimming
P lanting plants
R ain
I nsects
N ests in trees
G rowing animals

Mateo Sandi, Grade 2
Polk Elementary School, TX

The Sky

The sky
is blue
the world
is too.
Except for
you
are not
blue.
I have a bow
that I am
going to
put on.
No, no, no
that bow
is mine.

Alexandra Guthrie, Grade 1
Ryan Elementary School, CO

Valentine's Day

I see friends, family, mailmen, red and pink hearts.
I hear people say "I love you. Be mine."
And "You're cute!"
I smell chocolate cookies, chocolate kisses.
I taste food, candy, chocolate and drinks.
I feel a kiss, a hug, a stomachache and someone's hand.
Valentine's Day

Hayley Stephenson, Grade 2
Swink Elementary School, CO

My Wonderful Friend

I have a best friend named Jocelyn.
She is funny and interesting to write about.
She is also a wonderful friend to me.
'Cause sometimes she helps me with my homework
and I help her too.
Oh, and she is also pretty
Like a sunflower.
She has soft skin.
We are like sisters except we don't come from the same mom.
Jocelyn and I have tons of friends
that say so many crazy and funny things.
Jocelyn has a great family.
Jocelyn likes to play tetherball.
She gets better each time she plays.
When she plays she looks funny.
I will never forget how much fun we had.

Priscilla Barrera, Grade 3
Edison Elementary School, CA

Day Bright, Day Light

This morning it is bright.
This morning it is light.
But still there is no hope that the sun will come out.

Elaine Townley, Kindergarten
Carnation Elementary School, WA

Petrified Fossils

Fragile, sedimentary
Covered, imprinted, solving
Fossils can be tracks or bones covered by sediment.
Preserved objects.

Mashad Arora, Grade 3
Four Peaks Elementary School, AZ

Snow

Snow, you drift down,
Covering the world
with you.
You sparkle,
mysterious and bright.
And O Snow,
Wonderful Snow,
You let us make
Hot cocoa.
Sophie Wolfe, Grade 2
Bridlemile Elementary School, OR

I Can't Write a Poem

I can't write a poem,
I am a bad writer,
This is my best writing,
It is too hard.
I am allergic to poems.
Hey I just wrote a poem.
Cough, cough!
Wyatt Burkhalter, Grade 3
Patton Elementary School, TX

Ocean

I have cute fish
That was my wish
The ocean is big and blue
That's where my fish grew
My fish are cute and terrific
They came from the Pacific
I feed my fish every day
I made them a house out of clay
Qilieun Watson, Grade 2
San Jacinto Elementary School, CA

Football

Tackles, touchdowns, playing hard,
Jumping and chasing the ball,
Everyone screaming and yelling,
Players get dirty, whistles blow,
So cool!
Abigail Cohan, Kindergarten
Presbyterian School, TX

Grouchy

Grouchy is the color gray.
It sounds like funny talk.
It smells like bath time.
It tastes like chalk.
It looks like broken dishes.
Grouchy feels like little pinches.
Rohan Zade, Grade 2
CLASS Academy, OR

Disneyland

I visited Disneyland.
The scariest ride I went on
was the Matterhorn.
I waited and waited
for thirty minutes total.
It was a fast roller coaster.
In Disneyland
on that big of a ride
I was a brave person.
Have you ever done that?
Marquis Jacobson, Grade 2
Acacia Elementary School, AZ

Anger

Anger is like the sun burning.
It sounds like somebody falling.
It smells like burning steak.
It tastes like hot salsa.
It looks like fire.
Anger feels like a volcano.
Benjamin Davidson, Grade 2
CLASS Academy, OR

My Good and Bad Pencil

I have a pencil that writes perfect dust.
Whenever I think about it,
It makes me want to bust.
It writes so well,
I want to take it to school.
And when I try it,
It won't write anything cool.
Brook Weber, Grade 3
Criswell Elementary School, TX

Horses

There are horses,
Running through the snow,
Slipping on the ice,
Going crazy like Brittney Franklin,
Then they had a snowball fight for five hours,
Then they all stopped...
And saw something strange,
It was a seal,
So they played with her,
They played snow tag for three hours,
Then they slid on the ice,
And going crazy like Katelynn Scott,
Then they had a sleepover at the seals house,
They played snow and ice games until 2:00 in the morning,
Then they went to sleep,
They woke up at 8:00,
And they were friends forever.

Katelynn Scott, Grade 3
Turner Elementary School, TX

How to Draw My Face

Draw my head as round as a basketball.
Paint my neck like an upside-down bowl.
Design my hair straight like a line.
Illustrate my eyes as brown as a fresh coconut.
Shape my eyelashes as pointy as a unicorn's horn.
Make my eyebrows as black as a witch's hat.
Create my nose as round as a peanut butter cookie.
Curve my mouth like an upside-down frown.
Color my skin as tan as sand at a beach.
Sketch my teeth as white as chalk.
Please don't outline my ears!
Trace my background with a lot of flowers.

Ashley Tran, Grade 3
Briargrove Elementary School, TX

The Deep and Dark Lake

A deep and dark lined lake
That is sometimes calm and beautiful,
Sometimes it is harsh and dizzy.
My reflection inside the calm, deep, and dark water is clear.
A giant creature is slowly rising from the dark, black lake.

Jade Klingler, Grade 3
Writers in the Schools Program, TX

What I Remember
I remember the sweet smell of my mother's dinner
and the rich soft creamy ice cream
that melted in my mouth
right after I finished it

I wish I could enjoy both moments one more time
Callan Moor, Grade 3
Westwood Charter Elementary School, CA

Window
Through my window I see a maple tree.
I see a squirrel sitting on a branch.
I see the wide open spaces.
Through my window I see a squirrel.
I see a dog playing and a squirrel cracking a nut.
I see the happy things of summer.
Through my window I see a maple tree.
Alicia Culbertson, Grade 3
Daly Elementary School, MT

What to Write?
I don't know what to write.
It's killing me in my brain.
My pencil just can't write the words I want it to say.
I think my pencil's out of lead,
But I know it isn't.
It's like my brain is not smart enough
For the simple task of
Writing poems day and night.
Arielle Schoen, Grade 3
Wonderland Avenue Elementary School, CA

Treasures
There's something called "heavenly treasure" and "earthly treasure."
"Earthly treasure" is gold, clothes, toys and your house.
"Heavenly treasure" is helping, caring, loving, giving and obeying.
They are both good, but "heavenly treasure" is better
because you're obeying your God.
That is best because you can have money, but you might get greedy.
I learned that you might not want money more than "heavenly treasure."
Martin Hackett, Grade 3
Delphi Academy of San Francisco Bay, CA

Nature Walk
On my nature walk I can hear a stream and I can see animals.
The stream sounds like a soft hum.
The animals I see, a frog and a bird, look like an alien and an airplane.
I can feel a breeze in my face and hair and the breeze feels refreshing.
I can smell some beautiful smelling flowers.
The last thing I did was take a drink of the stream's grape tasting water.

Fallon Freed, Grade 3
Williams Elementary School, CA

Mogul

Playful

     likes fetch

  puppy

      handsome

 energetic

    in trouble

      can't stop moving

   huge

     fast runner

    chews balls

in

 bed

  taking

  a

   nap

after a long day.

Jesse Andringa, Grade 2
Horizons K-8 Alternative Charter School, CO

Alive!
Wildlife with bugs and animals
Camping in the forest,
With deer trotting by my tent,
Climbing trees to find exotic bugs,
And hearing the lovely cardinals and other birds
Singing their songs high up in the trees,
Quail fast-walking across the street,
Lizards climbing the walls,
Wildcats being really lazy,
Just like my cat.
That's why I'm thankful
To be alive!

Jay Nichols, Grade 3
Four Peaks Elementary School, AZ

Winter Sickishness

When winter comes
sickishness is here!
It's the worst time of the year
because it hurts.
As soon as it comes
you'd better be in bed
with a blanket over your head.
Or you're going to feel not real!!!
You start getting kind of woozy!
Then your brain hurts
so, stay away from WINTER!!!

Rosanna Roberts, Grade 2
Mount Stuart Elementary School, WA

Science Park

10 beetles, 15 plants, 5 seeds,
and many, many growing plants.
Of course, blooming!
Many, many, many flowers blooming
because it's spring.
Spring, spring, spring,
Spring!
Spring is so wonderful,
So, so wonderful.
Running in the grass.
Water to go in little sail boat.
Put a sail boat race in the pond.
Many, many, many wonderful things
everywhere you go!

Ashley Howell, Grade 2
New Emerson School, CO

A Lost Dog

I found a dog who looked lost.
He was very sad.
I took him home and gave him food,
Which put him in a happy mood.
I checked him over
And found his collar
And learned that his name was Rover.

Anuj Davé, Grade 2
Little Scholars School, CA

Flowers

Flowers
red, pretty
growing, bending, moving
smells very good
roses

Tristan Nosie, Kindergarten
Whiteriver Elementary School, AZ

The Cookie Ballerina

Making chocolate chip cookies
It's my job now to turn on the mixer.
I look into the bowl
I see a ballerina
Twirling around and around
In a brown tutu.
The mixer goes off.
The ballerina stops twirling
And her brown tutu
Gets poured onto a cookie sheet.

Avery Miller, Grade 2
Sabine Elementary School, TX

I'm Dirty

I'm dirty,
I'm lucky.
I can't get out of the muddy
It's drying,
I have to,
I want to
Get out of here now!
I'm not so lucky now!

Devin Peterson, Grade 3
Parker Elementary School, TX

All About Me

I'm eight years old.
I go to school.
I think school is cool.
When I go to school
I have lots of fun.
I play and run.

Elaunte Irvin, Grade 3
Honey Hollow Elementary School, CA

The Flowers

As I walked across the shore
I fell upon a patch of tulips
red as drops of blood glimmering
in a silver glow
like the stars glowing blue
in a lovely light
I stand looking at the flowers as they swayed gently
in the wind
Their petals showered down upon me
wrapping me in a velvet red blanket
shielding me from the cold
The flowers whispered in excitement
throwing up their hands in a deep deep bow
a golden butterfly landed on a lovely flower
as it skipped in delight
The flowers spun around with joy

Ben Greenberg, Grade 3
Westwood Charter Elementary School, CA

My Dog

I asked my dog if she could do my homework
She barked at me I didn't understand
But I gave her my homework
When she gave it back to me
I saw a bunch of ripping marks
I learned not to give my homework to my dog again

Ronnie Breaux, Grade 3
Hood Case Elementary School, TX

If I Were...

If I were brown I would be dirt in the ground.
If I were green I would be a stem on a flower that I found on the ground.
If I were blue I would be the sky.
If I were red I would be a heart on Valentine's Day.
If I were tan I would be the sand on the beach.

Toni Wood, Grade 3
St Dorothy School, CA

Alone Is...

Alone is when you are lost in a very large forest in the middle of the night.
Alone is being the only question mark on the whole paper.
Alone is when one of your pets dies and you are alone crying.

Luke Valle, Grade 3
Fort Vannoy Elementary School, OR

Austin

A T M
U niversity of Houston
S mart guy
T exas A&M
I like school
N ative American

Austin Merritt, Grade 3
Hood Case Elementary School, TX

My Family

My mother is very pretty
She keeps her classroom neat
She is very funny
And she can sing very sweet

My dad is very smart
He is very nice to me
He can be funny sometimes.
Sometimes he can be very neat

Mary Ellen DiGiovanni, Grade 2
Woodcrest School, CA

Courtney

C upid shot an arrow at
O ur teddy bear
U sing a lot of love
R uined! It was ruined!
T he turtle bit the arrow
N ow they cannot love
E ach other
Y uck! It had spit on it.

Courtney Shannon, Grade 3
Turner Elementary School, TX

The Princess

Enthusiastically,
Hungrily,
Happily,
The princess
Is eating pickles.
— Yum!

Caelynn Griggs, Grade 1
Fir Grove Elementary School, OR

Pain

Pain is purple.
It sounds like an exploding toaster.
It smells like seven-day-old garlic.
It tastes like cat fur.
It looks like a popped ball.
Pain feels like turning into Iron Man.

Dominic Betts, Grade 1
CLASS Academy, OR

Dumb Cupid

Love is here to wake us up
It sends us out the door
It takes us to an early walk
I do not walk anymore

There is a cupid on my feet
I don't find it very smart
It took out a bow and arrow
And shot it in my heart!

Jeremy Choe, Grade 3
Parker Elementary School, TX

The Blue Sky

The sky is very blue
And very beautiful.
The clouds are very white.
I like the sky and clouds.
The clouds are very beautiful.
Do you like the sky and clouds?
They are pretty?

Leslie Brooke Holland, Grade 1
Thomas Edison Charter School, UT

Birds

Birds have wings. Birds have beaks.
Some are big. Some are small.
Birds like to chirp. They play a lot.
They fly so gracefully up in the sky.
I, too, wish I could fly.
Although, when I close my eyes
I feel like I am flying.

Nida Hasan, Grade 3
Acacia Elementary School, AZ

Skiing in Mammoth

In Mammoth, to get up a mountain you need to ride a lift,
I was not scared because they were not very swift.

Skiing is very fun,
It is just like when you run.

I miss my instructors because they taught me how to ski and stop,
And now I am not afraid to go to the top.

I had a helmet on my head,
The one I wore was red.

Skiing is the best thing I have done,
If I had to pick a favorite sport, skiing would be the one.

Tristan Lee, Grade 1
The Pegasus School, CA

The Forest

Forests smell like flowers.
Many animals live in the forest.
I wish that I will go to the forest.
Some animals hurt other animals.
It is so bad because we will not have those animals.

Ana Gonzalez-Cardenas, Grade 1
Robert L Stevens Elementary School, CA

Rose in Winter

I'm Ankofa.
I have met no other.
I'm a unique rose in winter.
I'm a cummerbund around a waist.
I'm a southern pecan pie with homemade ice cream on Granny's bed.
I'm a geometry puzzle dying to get put together.
I'm a gingerbread house smothered in icing on Nanna's desk.
I'm a pan that is covered in Crisco.
I'm a heel-toe dance move on a hardwood floor.
I'm a brain bursting with ideas.
I'm a friendship necklace swinging back and forth.
I'm a paintbrush swimming across the paper.
I'm a violin bow screeching sounds across its bridge.
In spring, I'm going to burst, but you have not seen all of me.
I will be back next winter.

Ankofa Billips, Grade 3
Open Charter Magnet School, CA

What's Best About Europe
What's best about Europe?
Is it the fancy-looking trains?
Or the castles and towers?
Grant Bertonneau, Grade 3
Our Lady of the Snows School, NV

Rex
T Rex Rex Rex.
It eats other dinosaurs.
Munch, munch, munch, munch.
He eats dinosaurs for lunch.
Gordon Gray III, Grade 2
Mission Grade School, MT

I Used To...
I used to give my dog a bath.
but now I don't give my dog a bath
because he doesn't like water.

I used to give my cats a bath
but now I don't give my cats a bath
because they scratch.

I used to eat apple pie
but now I don't eat pie
because I don't like it.

I used to play at my house
but now I go to play with my friends.
China Loaisiga, Grade 3
Acacia Elementary School, AZ

The Scariest Thing
The scariest thing
I have ever done
is when I was a baby.
I had three
open heart surgeries.
I died for two minutes.
It was the scariest thing.
have you ever done that?
Michael Bass, Grade 2
Acacia Elementary School, AZ

Statue of Liberty
S tay and be welcome
T he states welcome you to be here.
A tlantic Ocean,
T ake this permission to stay,
U nited States of America,
E llis Island.

O nly the Statue of Liberty
F reedom is in the United States.

L iberty stands for you.
I stay here to have freedom.
B e worthy and stay,
E nd your old life.
R edo your life and stay.
T he United States is a home.
Y ou have a chance here.
Michael Mercado, Grade 3
Lafayette Elementary School, CA

Spring Things
Spring is so lovely
It's as sweet as honey
There are yellows and greens
If you know what I mean
There are pinks and blues
And somebody loves you
Bees are buzzing
Kids are running
Hummingbirds fly high in the sky
They flitter by and by
That's what happens in spring
Madeline Wells, Grade 3
Finley Oates Elementary School, TX

Anger
Anger is red like hot lava.
It dashes through my mind
like a rhino charging at a person.
It makes me feel mad
like a ferocious tiger.
Ryan Winchell, Grade 2
Northridge Elementary School, CO

Make Kameron

Make my face as big as a full moon,
Illustrate my eyes as small as the letter O,
Design my eyebrows like a rainbow going down,
Color my cheeks as pink as a tutu,
Create my lips as red as juicy strawberries,
Trace my nose as pointy as a unicorn's horn,
Picture my skin as brown as soil,
Complete my teeth as white as an ice cube,
Draw my neck as long as an elephant's trunk.
Outline my ears as big as an eraser,
After that make the background outside with a swimming pool,
Then do my hair as curly as the telephone wire.

Kameron Fantroy, Grade 3
Briargrove Elementary School, TX

Tornado

I can see a massive destructive tornado up close,
Closer than other people can. I'm scared.
I run to get a better view.
I see it I start to run back.
I fall down but I wake.
It was all a dream!
But my mom shaking me,
Trying to wake me up.
I can see the panic in her eyes.
I ask her what was going on.
I go outside and I see a tornado!

Chris Allen, Grade 3
Writers in the Schools Program, TX

A Spring Morning

I sway in the light breeze of a spring morning.
As bright yellow streams of joy, rise in the sky,
And all different colors start to brighten the fields.
There is noise all around,
And all different colors, flying across the morning sky.
And beautiful white water fills the sky full.
And furry little animals, popping out of their dark homes,
Where they slept during the winter.
And then this beautiful season must end.
Then all the bright colors from the trees
Start to drift down to the solid green fields.

Meghan H. Hughes, Grade 3
Phoenix Christian Academy, AZ

Basketball Is…
Basketball is breathtaking.
Basketball is a tremendous game.
Basketball is a very hard sport to play.
Basketball is like soccer, only you use your hand.

That's what I think basketball is like.

Zack Carter, Grade 3
Fort Vannoy Elementary School, OR

Sacred Mountain
Mount Blanca
Sacred Mountain lies to the east
White shell, rising sun, whistling prayers, pure form
Remembering our elders teachings, songs of harmony, spiritually
Sacred Mountain
Mount Taylor
Sacred mountain lies to the south
Blue shell, turquoise, reaches the sky with understanding
Thank you for letting me remember that today is very important
Sacred Mountain
San Francisco Peak
Sacred Mountain lies to the west
Soaring, stunning, attractive abalone yellow shell
Letting people know you are important, essential, radiance stars
Sacred Mountain
Hespers Mountain
Sacred Mountain lies to the north
Jet and black shell, extreme, tremendous above the ground
Tall, towering, sky-scraping mountain, people look up to you, stars glow
Sacred Mountain

Dawnya Curley, Grade 3
Ganado Primary School, AZ

Sisters
No matter how much we fight and argue about silly things,
I will always love my sister.
No matter how many times she calls me names, I will always love my sister.
No matter how many times she gets her own way, I will always love my sister.
My sister and I are very close friends, forever in my heart;
I will always love my sister.

Sierra Garza, Grade 3
Jackson Elementary School, CA

Weird Creatures

Oh there is a weird creature called a Goolang
and it bites and causes some pain
oh there is a weird creature called a Doolane
it has eighty legs and some people says it lives near Toolane
and there is another thing it is called a Papapain
and this Papapain had a big stain that made him feel vain
and this Papapain wanted to get on a train to Loolain
and drink some fresh water with a little bit of rain.

Peyton Grover, Grade 3
Wiederstein Elementary School, TX

Baby Brother

I like to play with my baby brother.
He is fun to play with.
He is really cute.
I play tag every day because it is fun.
I like to play hide and go seek with my baby brother.

Dylan Favila, Grade 2
Orchard Elementary School, UT

Flying Love

And God made all the animals
That sang and flew around,
And growled and scratched.
And He made the wind that blew
Fierce and strong and the hurricanes
That take down homes,
And the power of God is in all those things.

Air flows and air goes.
Everywhere you hear it rush
To one place and another,
But you still don't know the way it goes.
For the rush of the wind is not made by man
But it is made by God the creator of all things.

God can fly as birds can fly.
Wind can blow as fury can flow
From the sins that people have made.
And the sins will flow everlasting
'Til He washes our sins away.
When the sins wash away, the gospel will come and stay.

James J. C. van der Pol, Grade 3
Christian Community School, CA

What You Hear at the Ocean

When you go to the ocean
you can hear the ocean roaring
going crashing in the sand
and taking things away from the land
while other waves are rolling and fighting
while other waves try to get you
so they get really thunderous.

Michael Garcia, Grade 3
Lincoln Elementary School, CA

Horses Like to Play

Horses like to have people on their backs,
But, I like to wear a backpack.
Horses like to eat apples and hay,
But, I like to play with horses all day.

Miranda Elliot, Grade 1
Community Children's Center, CA

Titi

Pretty animal
lives in trees — it eats fruit
beautiful titi

Caren Sanchez, Grade 3
Lorenzo De Zavala Elementary School, TX

Scorpions

s   b
c   l
o   a
r   z
p   i
i   n
o   g
n
s   in
the hot weather.
Their tales gleaming
in the sunlight.
The ends
of their
tails are   poison.
injected with

Tashi Sanford, Grade 3
Horizons K-8 Alternative Charter School, CO

Giraffes

Giraffes are big.
Giraffes have long necks.
Giraffes have long feet.
Giraffes eat from long trees.
I like giraffes.

Alan Griffin, Kindergarten
Grace School, TX

Rain

Rain, rain
You are so fun indeed
You go drip, drop
On my head
Ouch!

Jordan Breilh, Grade 2
Carden West School, CA

Bats

Bats
Rough, brown
Flying, sucking, sleeping
Bats hang upside down
Vampires

Matthew Ammann, Grade 1
Myatt Elementary School, TX

Cheetahs

Cheetahs
Fast, spotted
Growling, jumping, hunting
Cheetahs eat meat
Cubs

Christopher Ayala, Grade 1
Myatt Elementary School, TX

Monkeys

Monkeys
Furry, silly
Eating, hanging, swinging
Monkeys have babies
Chimps

Bianca Fuentes, Grade 1
Myatt Elementary School, TX

Me

I am a daughter, a sister, a cousin, and a friend, but when I close my eyes…
I am planets far beyond discovery.
I am a mustang stallion as black as midnight galloping in the pasture.
I am a Tamagotchi pet being pampered.
I am cheese pizza hot and fresh burning someone's tongue.
I am Billie Joe rocking my heart out on guitar.
I am a jockey winning the Triple Crown excited and astonished.
I am a Rottweiler chasing the dog catcher.
I am a Chia pet with seeds constantly growing.
When I open my eyes, I am a daughter, a sister, a cousin, and a friend.

Madison Froebe, Grade 3
Open Charter Magnet School, CA

Dangerous Black Hole

I am one of the most dangerous things in space.
I am a black hole.
I was born when an enormous star blew up.
I have gravity a million times more powerful than the Day Star.
The Day Star was a friend of mine until she got new friends, the planets.
I got jealous and went away.
Now I eat the energy of other things by using my gigantic vacuum.
The things just fly into my mouth like the water flying in a tsunami.
I am a dangerous black hole.
Beware…Beware…Beware…!

Benjamin Ting, Grade 3
Miller Elementary School, TX

My Little Sister

My little sister is four years old.
People say she is cute
but they don't know what she does to me when we are alone.
Sometimes when we play she trips and falls
Suddenly she starts crying,
most of the time she is pretending to be hurt only to get attention.
She cries loud.
Other times when we fight we hit each other
and she tries biting me.
But I push her away.
She takes my clothes and hides them.
But she is really great at finding things; we hide under the covers
and twist and turn until we don't know what direction we are facing.
Then there are times we just read and love being sisters.

Tanvi Varadhachary, Grade 3
Horn Academy, TX

Writing

Writing poetry
Wonderful words.
Books.
Feelings using sentence fluency.
Writing is a big experience.
Kathryn Chwalek, Grade 3
Acacia Elementary School, AZ

My Favorite Animal

What is my favorite animal?
It is the spider monkey.
They are hyper and good
swingers too.
They eat healthy food
every day.
That is why I like spider
monkeys you see.
Christopher Cox, Grade 2
Philo T Farnsworth School, UT

Summer

Summer is pretty
When the blossoms are popping
The bees are buzzing.
Monica Moser, Grade 3
Summit Elementary School, UT

Red

Red is the color of a heart.
Red is the first color of the rainbow.
Red is the color of a rose.
Red is the color of sweet cherries.
Red is the color of a Valentine box.
Red is the color of love.
Philip Galerne, Grade 1
Grace School, TX

Winter

Icicles hang free,
Giving more room for snowmen,
Letting kids have fun.
Weston Kolste, Grade 3
Summit Elementary School, UT

Love

Love is pink.
It sounds like a puppy's sweet howl.
It smells like blooming flowers.
It tastes like a wonderful cookie.
It looks like a loving pet.
Love feels like your parents' hugs.
Hallie Walker, Grade 3
Grace School, TX

Turkeys and Chickens

Turkeys
Wild, gobble
Tom, Jenny, Thanksgiving
Bird, feathers, eggs, beak
Clucking, farms, tasty
Rooster, hens
Chickens
Landry Arnold, Grade 1
Armstrong Elementary School, TX

Hermit Crab

When I look at a hermit crab, I see…

Curly spirals, 'round and 'round,
Pinchy feet that scrape the sand,
Big round eyes that stare at me,
Scrabbling feet going back to sea.

That is a hermit crab.
Ian Davoren, Grade 2
Ponderosa Elementary School, CA

I Wonder Why Butterflies Fly?

I wonder why butterflies fly?
Why do they fly so high
in the sky?

Why are their wings many
shades of blue?
I wish I could be a butterfly too.
Yvonne Bass, Grade 2
Spanish Oaks Elementary School, UT

Jump Rope
Jump roping is fun!
You can move the rope quickly.
But you better move your feet fast,
or you might make a mistake and kiss a snake!
"Cinderella" is the cheer. Never fear!
You can do it. It's as easy as the ABC's or 123's.
JUMP! JUMP! JUMP! THUMP! THUMP! THUMP!

Brandi Arning, Grade 2
C C Hardy Elementary School, TX

Alone Is
Alone is sitting in your room because you got in a fight with your friend
Alone is playing by yourself because you got in trouble
Alone is being by yourself when no one is there
Alone is getting lost in the mall
Alone is running away and not knowing where you're going
Alone is not fitting in a group because they don't think you're cool

Cassondra Wessels, Grade 3
Fort Vannoy Elementary School, OR

Morning Vacation
Today is the day of all the days in bed
But not an ordinary day as I unwrap myself out of bed
My legs flying down on the brown carpet

Long sticks dancing around and around
Going like children to the doctor
Crying to leave
Swinging around to the door
Do not move or you will not see
Up down on the floor

Each foot moves its move
Dancing around like a bird
Over the trees

Let's go it's time to go
Let's go to the car
To leave the house
To go to fun

Let's go

Lauren A. Hoffman, Grade 3
Horn Academy, TX

I Wish

I wish
I were a snake in the zoo,
Looking at all the helpless people,
Smudging their faces on the dirty glass.
I could think how helpless are you?

I wish
I were a baseball base
All the people sliding on me
I could say, "Get your big foot off me."

I wish
I were a porcupine,
Poking and prodding animals,
I would never have to go to school,
Or clean my room,
So, for a rodent's sake
Be a porcupine.

Rachel McGill, Grade 3
Daves Avenue Elementary School, CA

Love

I love my dad
Even when he is mad
He takes care of us
And takes me to the bus
My dad loves to sleep
He doesn't have to count sheep
My mom and I think he is strong
We like to hear a song

Damian Cabral, Grade 2
San Jacinto Elementary School, CA

Mountains

Come and explore the mountains.
Can you hear the trees blowing?
Can you see the deer running?
Can you taste the berries growing?
Can you smell the fresh air?
Can you feel the dirt in your hands?

Garrett Beck, Grade 1
Paonia Elementary School, CO

Skiing

Quiet in the woods,
Snow falling off trees,
Puffy, crunchy snow,
Big pants, mittens, snow boots,
Skiing fast like a cheetah.

Grace Castaneda, Kindergarten
Presbyterian School, TX

Snow Dogs

Snow dogs
in the night
Hiding,
Spying,
in a ray of light.
To Alaska
the snow dogs go
in the night.

Brooke Cabin, Grade 2
Brush Creek Elementary School, CO

Medieval to Star Wars

Medieval
Swords, magic
Running, javeling, surviving
Bad past — bright future
Flying, shooting, engineering
Lightsabers, force
Star Wars

Chandler Shannon, Grade 3
Turner Elementary School, TX

Ocean

Dolphins jump
Seagulls gulp
Sea snakes slide
Orcas glide
Sharks bite
Sea horses might
Whales splash
Waves crash

Meleah Conover, Grade 3
Robinson Elementary School, TX

Babies
Babies are so very nice,
but when they are newborns, don't feed them rice!
I wish I could understand their talk,
but trouble alert when they can walk!
Try to catch them and you'll get more than one blister,
I know because I have a baby sister.

Taylor Selbach, Grade 3
Coyote Hills Elementary School, AZ

My Trees
My trees are greener than your trees of course;
'Cause my trees are taller than your trees of course.
When my trees are green,
Your trees are bare.
When my trees are red,
Your trees are dead.
So my trees are greener than you trees of course;
'Cause my trees are taller than your trees of course!

Neelee Brauner, Grade 3
Ober Elementary School, NV

Toppings on Pizza
Rolling the pizza on the floor.
Hang it up on the door.
Get tomatoes and grind them up.
Put them on to eat them up.
Whoops, forgot the cheese is next.
Ooey, gooey, I'm so vexed!
Squaddle, dawdle, do the dance.
Hurry up to be advanced.
Now the toppings, dingalingling.
Pepperoni on the pizza now it's time to do some more.
Now some olives, have some fun.
Do it well so we'll get done.
Brandish, brandish with a knife.
Now make room for the love of my life.
Burning hot chili peppers
Don't you have some Dr. Pepper?
Get this sticky mess off me,
Off the table to the test.
Oh my goodness barf it up.
Don't forget — in the cup.

Amira Hindi and Pilar Birrell, Grade 3
Cottonwood Montessori School, NM

Space, Space

Space, space
What a place
Jupiter, Jupiter
Bigger than Pluto
Sun, run around the sun
Pluto, Pluto
I want a noodle
Mars, Mars
Give me chocolate bars
Saturn, Saturn
It's a pattern
Stars, stars
Circling around Mars
Moon, moon
Is it noon?
Venus, Venus
What a view
Space, space
What a place
Amanda Rudolph, Grade 2
Scenic Park Elementary School, AK

My Dad

My dad is strong
He sings a song
My dad and I go to the mall
Mom tells us to call
He likes to do math
Every day he takes a bath
Dad likes to go to the snow
On Saturdays he always mows
Yavanka Felix, Grade 2
San Jacinto Elementary School, CA

Snakes

Snakes, snakes what I hate
They slither and slap
While you are taking a nap
But I see as much as you see
Just don't end up in a Snake's Belly.
Ian Ermis, Grade 3
Hood Case Elementary School, TX

Colors

Blue stands for the sky,
all lonely but bright.

Orange stands for the sun,
all hot with light,

Green stands for beanstalks,
all lively and green.

Purples stands for bullies,
all evil and mean.

Pink stands for happiness,
all enjoying and good.

Red is for anger
all in bad mood.

Brown is for chocolate,
all melty and yummy.

Yellow's for candy,
all lemony and gummy!
Sol Kim, Grade 3
CB Eaton Elementary School, CA

Submarine

I have been in a submarine
in Disneyland.
I was young.
We went in a cave.
It was neat.
On March 12, 2006
I will go on it again
if it is still there.
I was three the last time
I was on it.
I am eight now.
I can't wait.
Have you ever done that?
Bryce Brettell, Grade 2
Acacia Elementary School, AZ

Window

Through my window I see the ocean.
I see a dolphin with its calf right beside it.
I see the fish swimming about.
Through my window I see a ship above.
I see sharks circling a raft and a scuba diver diving.
I see the water's waves rippling in the light.
Through my window I see the beautiful ocean floor.

Beth Bitterman, Grade 3
Daly Elementary School, MT

Haleema

H aleema likes hamsters
A nd she likes to play with them
L emon is her favorite fruit
E very time when people need help, she helps them.
E verybody likes her.
M oney her dad gives her.
A nd people play with her.

Haleema Ghannam, Grade 2
Phoenix Metro Islamic School, AZ

Window

Through my window I see a mountain.
I see a bird soaring through the sky and lots of trees.
I see the Bitterroot Mountains.
Through my window I see a stream running through the mountains.
I see a bear running and deer all around.
I see the blue sky.
Through my window I see paradise.

Jacob Gouse, Grade 3
Daly Elementary School, MT

Mystery of the Stars

What are those glowing balls of light up high?
Are they spheres of gas or glowing chocolate balls?
The mystery of space is endless!
Some scientists have solved these problems of the universe,
Super giants, supernovas, galaxies, stars!
Black holes, the solar system, constellations!
Maybe you'll research one, discover one or better!
Who knows, who knows, who knows?
You might be a space explorer at heart.

Nathan Leach, Grade 3
Miller Elementary School, TX

Like No Others

I have friends like no others.
My friends help me when I am feeling bad.
They talk to me about things I do not want others to know about.
We have a special bond between us it is like no other.
My friends know me the most.
They know a lot about me and I know a lot about them.
We talk to each other, about what we like and what we are feeling,
What we are going to do after we leave from school.
We want to be together.
I love my friends and they love me.
My friends Shane and Dennis:
We are like brothers.
We are the closet friends to each other.
We Love each other the most.

Bryce Sullivan, Grade 3
McGaugh Elementary School, CA

What About the Sun?

If you would cut the sun in half and touch it,
would you just get a little burn? Of course not!
The sun has a super hot surface that could burn you into ashes!

If you use binoculars to look at the sun, would you see
an orange ball? Of course not! The sun is so bright
that even without binoculars, you would get blind
because of its ultraviolet rays!

If you had an Astronomy test, would you describe the sun
as a Pluto-sized planet? Of course not! The sun is a
medium-sized star that has been burning for five billion years!

If someone asked you what are sunspots,
would you say that they are freckles? Of course not!
The sun's sunspots are the spots that are slightly cooler!

If you think that the sun's energy ONLY recharges your solar-powered calculator,
think again!
The sun's energy is so powerful that the entire solar system uses it.
So if you still think that you can gobble the sun up, well…
Of course not!

Nazia Ahmed, Grade 3
Miller Elementary School, TX

What Is Red?

Red is a stain on your shirt from plopping ripe cherries into your watering mouth.
Red is a rose waiting to bloom in the spring.
Red is Santa's XXL sized suit and a jolly red hat to go with.
Red is a flame coming from a crackling fire on a chilly winter night.
Red is a million dollar ruby waiting to be discovered.
Red is a salmon rushing down the crystal like river.
Red is lush strawberries growing in the warm sun.
Red is a crimson dress being worn to a Christmas ball.
Red is coral being swayed by the sea's strong current.

Tabitha Grayston, Grade 3
CHEP School - West, CA

Fall

The leaves fall and it starts to snow,
it's getting colder and summer has passed,
no more swimming or playing outside,
you wish you had brought your jacket like your mother said,
you feel like you're going to freeeeezze.

Ryan Moss, Grade 3
Academy of Charter Schools, CO

Poetry

P recious
O ut of this world
E xtremely rhythmic
T errifically exciting
R adiant and outrageous
Y oung and bold

Poetry has much to show
and everyone should really know,
that this kind of writing might
open up a seam of light!

Kai Mesman-Hallman and Blair Buchanan, Grade 3
Solana Santa Fe Elementary School, CA

Colors

If I was red, I would be the big A at the Angels stadium,
or the red stripes on the American flag, or a red hot Cheeto.
If I was green, I would be a green leaf or a green pencil.
If I was orange, I would be a Cheeto or the sunset or an orange.
If I were blue, I would be the blue sky or the blue ocean.

Liam Sellers, Grade 2
St Dorothy School, CA

What Blue Is

Blue is a Cub Scout suit.
Blue is Uranus, Pluto and Neptune.
Blue is the sky.
Blue is water in the sea.
Blue is my dog's fur.
Blue is blue fire.
Blue is a plum.
Blue is my pencil.
Blue is ice.
Blue is a time out card.
All these things are blue.
I am blue if I get the flu.

Henrique Oliveira, Grade 2
Talkeetna Elementary School, AK

Art Storm

Brushes up and we all start to paint
in the new world of art.
Paint starts to overflow,
brushes go wild.
My teacher gets crazy
painting on every child.
Colors swirl into pictures.
My best friend turns into a pastel.
I start mixing up a storm.
Bright volcanoes of red.
Dull rain clouds of blue.
A big bolt of bright yellow lightning
strikes on my canvas.
Paint flowing, colors swirling,
volcanoes exploding!
So much is in my mind!

Hayley Krieger, Grade 3
McGaugh Elementary School, CA

Tiger

R-o-o-o-a-a-a-r!
Devouring monkeys.
Running all day.
Tiger.

Sarah Blute, Grade 2
Acacia Elementary School, AZ

The Loon

The snakes are shattering
Wush, Wush,
The snakes are fighting
Crash, Kaboom,
The squirrels are running in the trees,
The birds are chirping in the air,
And the loon is growing in the night.

Carly Sjordal, Grade 3
IDEA School - Fairbanks, AK

The Bull

To shay for the bull,
The tamer waves his red flag
The bull starts charging.

The crowd has gone wild
As the bull charges fast
He misses the flag.

Now it's time for drinks,
And then it's time for eating.
At last it's playtime.

Robert Hugo, Grade 3
Four Peaks Elementary School, AZ

Coral

Coral
Colorful branches
Bravely protecting the ocean
Coral is like a beautiful castle
Can I hide in you?

Brittany Kendall, Grade 1
Paonia Elementary School, CO

Magic

I will make you disappear,
Then I will make you reappear.
I'll make a quarter disappear,
And where is it now?
It's right in your ear.

Angel Andrade, Grade 3
Honey Hollow Elementary School, CA

White

White is the color of a fluffy cloud,
White is the color you can't see when you are loud.

White is the color of a caucasian man's skin,
White is the color of a moccasin.

White is the color that represents bright,
White is the shade of the moon's gleaming light.

When I don't see white I feel dark,
Just like the color of tree bark.

Neil Gupta, Grade 3
Lincoln Elementary School, CA

Boxing Is...

Boxing is bloody noses.
Boxing is fun.
Boxing is getting teeth knocked out with gloves.
Boxing is having black eyes.
Boxing is getting knocked out.
Boxing is flying back against the ropes.
Boxing is hitting the ground faster than you could blink.

Nathen Spooner, Grade 3
Fort Vannoy Elementary School, OR

Camping Fun

When I went to Colorado for my camping trip, we got to go on a little tour.
We stopped by a lake with a little river that was deep, deep, deep.
We played on a little rock.
We had fun.

Kylie Helms, Grade 2
Orchard Elementary School, UT

Alive

Beautiful sunsets when you walk outside,
Sparkling wind that rushes through my hair,
Ocean waves that shine from the morning sun,
Spring flowers that have drops from the early morning rain,
Ruby red roses that I love,
Shivering snowflakes with dazzling crystals,
When cardinals sing...
It's time to brighten my day!

Sela Britton, Grade 3
Four Peaks Elementary School, AZ

Dogs
Dogs
Labs playing
Yellow, brown, black
Hounds running very fast
Fur, paws, tails
Body moving
Jumpy!
Golnesa Safavi, Grade 3
Nordstrom Elementary School, CA

Friendly
I have friends
Being nice
Playing and
Running
Together
I am friendly
Lillie Younkins, Grade 1
Scenic Park Elementary School, AK

Music
Wanna dance
Love to sing
Slow beats fast beats
I love country and rock
It is fun listening to it
You can dance fast and slow
You could listen to country and rock
You could sing and play all day
You could dream of being a star
You could express yourself
You could be a rock person
A jazz or country person
Or you could be anything
You like fast beats
You like slow beats
Lets dance let's sing
Oh let's dance
Oh let's sing
Let's do everything.
Marlo Veronico, Grade 3
Turner Elementary School, TX

Crayon
The crayon reminds me
Of water at the beach
Blue
Use a crayon
To color the water
Brittany Giberson, Grade 1
Fir Grove Elementary School, OR

The Bear
Roaring through the night.
Putting people in much fright.
Approach it with fear.
Bennett Sneddon, Grade 3
Lanai Road Elementary School, CA

I Can't Write a Poem
I can't write a poem
nobody taught me how
I broke my pencil lead
someone stole my poem
they tore my page
it flew outside
I can't go get it
a dog ate it.
Sandra Mendoza, Grade 3
Patton Elementary School, TX

Leaves, Leaves
Leaves fall like flower petals
D
o
w
n
D
o
w
n
to the ground
And they don't even
Make a sound.
Katie Barbur, Kindergarten
Montessori Christian Academy, TX

Love

Love is like a heart saying "Let's never be apart."
For I love you and you love me.
Our love will always be.
Can't you see our love will always be.

Emily Seang, Grade 2
Philo T Farnsworth School, UT

Soccer

Soccer is my favorite sport
It has my name written all over it.
I love soccer because it involves not giving up which I can surely do
it also involves learning quickly and trying your best.
It involves skill and willing to learn.
It involves athleticism which I truly, honestly have.
I have everything that I've just mentioned
so it is good for me.

Danielle Furman, Grade 3
Wonderland Avenue Elementary School, CA

Colors

If I were blue, I would be the shiniest sky in the world.
If I were red, I would be a lovely tulip.
If I were orange, I would be a fancy orange shirt.
If I were yellow, I would be the shining sun in the sky.
If I were pink, I would be a pink rose.
If I were green, I would be the green grass.
If I were red, orange, yellow, green, blue, and purple, I would be a rainbow.

Lauren Parayno, Grade 2
St Dorothy School, CA

The Dragon and Me

The mystical creature flies among us.
Look up and you'll see thee.
Blue and purple wings magical green body big and full of happiness.
I'll talk to thee.
Ask the dragon some questions.
Why is the dragon so happy?
What do you do at night?
He speaks and I listen as he speaks.
Those words so smart.
And yet he whispers in my ear
Loud noises come to hear

Mara, Grade 3
Katherine Delmar Burke School, CA

Snowman

Snowman,
Snowman how good
you look. 4 fingers on
each hand.
Your long stick
arms are so handsome.
Your big fat bottom.
You look so so
so good.
You are the
best snowman I ever
made. I will name you Snowy.
Your cute little buttons. Your
banana shaped smile. We have to run in
and get your carrot nose and black hat.
When we are in the house let's
get some coal for your eyes.

Ali Prevost-Reilly, Grade 1
Kimball School, WA

Nature

Nature smells like flowers that are sweet.
Nature looks like I am free.
Nature sounds like a tiger.
Nature tastes like dirt.

Armando Delgado-Jimenez, Grade 1
Robert L Stevens Elementary School, CA

Jaguars

Jaguars looks vicious,
and they are dangerous cats.
They look black and gray.

Franky Hernandez, Grade 3
Lorenzo De Zavala Elementary School, TX

Cheerful

Cheerful is red.
It sounds like fireworks.
It smells like fresh new roses.
It tastes like ice cream and chocolate cake.
It looks like a beautiful porcelain dish.
Cheerful feels like a soft cozy blanket.

Priyanka Mathur, Grade 1
CLASS Academy, OR

Animals

Animals in jungles,
Animals in the air,
Animals in pastures,
Animals everyWHERE!!
Animals in trees,
Animals in plants,
Animals in oceans,
Animals everyWHERE!
In houses, on streets, in skies,
Poachers vs animals
Go animals, WIN!!!

Jessica Smith, Grade 2
New Emerson School, CO

Meadow Land

I live
in a
Meadow Land
with
flowers and tulips
and green grass
to sleep on
Oh, sweet Meadow Land

Mitch Koch, Grade 1
Ryan Elementary School, CO

Spring

Spring is yellow.
It sounds like birds.
It tastes like apples.
It smells like flowers.
It looks like heaven.
It makes you happy.

Cora Wilke, Grade 3
Daly Elementary School, MT

Hearts

Hearts, hearts, hearts,
Your shape is so beautiful.
Hearts, hearts, hearts, hearts.
Life is full of hearts.

Jolene Martin, Grade 2
Mission Grade School, MT

Sounds by the Sea*
Waves crashing against the seawall,
The sea breeze billowing my hair slightly,
Seagulls singing with the waves.
I feel like I'm at an underwater orchestra's grandest night.
Blue water with green seaweed
Is the scenery for the stage.
I sit in a luxurious shell seat,
And feel the soft and soothing sand between my wiggling toes.
When I go home,
I will always have the memory of the sea,
Because I found a special souvenir shell,
And when I put it to my ear,
I hear the underwater orchestra playing wildly.
Even when I remove the shell,
It is still ring, ring, ringing in my ear.
Mackenzie Grossgold, Grade 3
McGaugh Elementary School, CA
*Dedicated to Mrs. Curtis.

I Remember My Hamster
I remember my hamster's feet running on me
like a cat that is scared
I remember his cheeks like a big hot air balloon
and that he felt like a giant ball of cotton
I remember the sound of my hamster nibbling the bag of his food
Running on his wheel like a car engine's moving
That's what I remember and really liked and loved about my hamster
Dillon Williams, Grade 3
Westwood Charter Elementary School, CA

Nighttime in Spring
Nighttime in Spring
roses parade near the tropical ocean
nighttime in spring
The moon goddess dances on lilies as graceful as a ballerina
nighttime in spring
the river rocks from side to side
nighttime in spring
a twilight zone at the riverbank
nighttime in spring
the flower bed looks like a lavender haze
nighttime in spring
Emmarie Nosal, Grade 3
Horizons K-8 Alternative Charter School, CO

Navajo Hair Bun

Navajo Hair Bun
Grandmas wear Navajo hair bun
Brushing, fixing, tying, fine-looking long hair
Feeling beautiful pretty, and happy about it
Hair Bun
Navajo Hair Bun
Binded by many yarns of different colors
Some are tied tight, loose, high, low, big, and small
Cheerful, joyful, in high spirits about wearing it to a ceremony
Hair Bun
Navajo Hair Bun
Native men and women attire it
Fixing the whole families' hair can be very exasperating
In the old days, young and old alike worn it
Hair Bun
Navajo Hair Bun
Passed on to next generation
Lengthy, silky-smooth, glossy, shiny beautiful hair tied together
Worn to assortments of indigenous ceremonies.
Hair Bun

Kassie Shondee, Grade 3
Ganado Primary School, AZ

I'm a Continent

I am a continent
I hold more than millions of people
I live in the Earth
I am a continent with 7 bodies
I have life because I live on the only planet with life.

I am a continent
I own everything on Earth
I have seven names
Asia, Europe, North America, South America,
Antarctica, Australia, Africa.

I am a continent
I have a river and plants
I have animals all different shapes and sizes
I am a continent.

Alice Yet, Grade 3
Briargrove Elementary School, TX

Birthdays and Hamburgers in a Bun
Birthdays are very fun.
You get cake, presents, and hamburgers in a bun.
Friends and family come over to celebrate.
In the car they'd say, "I cannot wait."
So even though birthdays are very fun,
You have to wait for cake, and eat your hamburgers in a bun.

Sarah Lingle, Grade 3
Robinson Elementary School, TX

Proud
The trees were swaying left to right
And the wind was blowing hard
I could always feel proud of myself
Even right now or tomorrow
As the morning strikes, the sun shows its bright light
The clouds were dancing around
I could just sit on the ground and feel proud of myself
Our eyes would focus on the clouds that would soon disappear
I would watch the sun fade away in a cloud of darkness
I watch the same thing happen every day
Suddenly, I saw the moon shining its brightest light down on me
And when I see the moon it's now always a full moon
The clouds disappeared
Everything around us was as silent as mice

Joanne Lee, Grade 3
Horn Academy, TX

Simone
Once there was no Simone.
And then there was.
Simone's hand curled around Grandpa's finger
Grandpa and little Simone loved each other very much
Simone grew and grew taller and taller
'Til she was big enough to play with Grandpa at the park
Big enough to look grandpa in the eyes
Grandpa grew older and slower and smaller.
Simone and Grandpa loved each other.
Grandpa's hand held onto Simone's.
Then there was no Grandpa
Just emptiness and sadness for a while
Until a tiny paw filled Simone's hand
And sweetness filled the world once again.

Simone Trevas, Grade 3
Horn Academy, TX

I Can't Write a Poem

I left my poem at home.
I forgot about it.
My dog ate my poem.
I lost it.
A caveman took it.

Alex Benge, Grade 3
Patton Elementary School, TX

Hawks

Swooping in graceful movement
Gliding quickly through the sky,
Soaring like a jet,
The hawks fly while searching for prey.
Still gliding it skates on water,
And soars back up with a slimy fish,
Then it suddenly disappears.

Jonathan Gabbert, Grade 3
Sakamoto Elementary School, CA

Colors

If I were green, I would be grass
If I were red, I would be a flame.
If I were gray, I would be an elephant.
If I were orange, I would be a cheeto.
If I were blue, I would be water.
If I were purple, I would be a grape.
If I were brown, I would be dirt.
If I were yellow, I would be the sun.
If I were white, I would be snow.

Carlos R. Garcia, Grade 2
St Dorothy School, CA

Dad

Dad is kind.
Dad helps me with math —
with the hard ones.
Dad buys toys for me.
Dad buys candy for me.
Dad gives me a ride on his bike.
Dad loves me.

Caitlan Valdez, Grade 1
Lee Richmond Elementary School, CA

Dirt Bike

The most important thing
about a dirt bike is it goes fast.
It is cool and fun.
It can jump and climb.
It is fast.
But the most important thing
about a dirt bike is don't wreck!

Wyatt Luedecke, Grade 3
Daly Elementary School, MT

The Butterfly

Happily,
Lightly,
Nicely,
The butterfly
Is flying in the sky.
— Cool!

Courtney Carney, Grade 1
Fir Grove Elementary School, OR

I Want to Be Harriet!

H arriet was a nice girl.
A lso she worked hard.
R isked her life for freedom.
R an to the stations.
I n Pennsylvania she got her freedom.
E very day she rescued people.
T ubman was a slave.

Bayley Marshall, Grade 2
Pinnacle Charter School, CO

Hiding in My Painting

Hiding in my painting,
Happy face,
Pink coral,
A dartboard,
A tremendous skunk warning,
Fingerprints taking over the world.
Let's go camouflage
So the painting can't find us!

Kevin Stallones, Grade 3
Writers in the Schools Program, TX

My Youngest Brother
My youngest brother is Matthew and he is 4 years old.
He's as crazy as a monkey and screams like a little girl

He likes to run around like a dog
then he trips and falls like a baby learning to walk.

So then he starts to cry like the rain falling from the sky.
Then he waddles to my mom like a penguin.

My mom asked, "What happened?"
Then Matthew said, "I fell down!"
After he calmed down
It started all over again the next day.

Megan Yen, Grade 3
Horn Academy, TX

If I Put This Mask On
If I had the eagle mask on.
I will have the power to fly faster than the wind.
I will have the power to turn into any flying animals.
I would look around the city in the air.
I will go to school early each day by flying fast.
I think I should take this mask off now good bye!

Gabriel Roa, Grade 3
Briargrove Elementary School, TX

When I Am Asleep
When I am awake I am a half-sister, a daughter, a cousin, a friend, a best friend,
a great, great granddaughter, and a niece, but when I am asleep I am much,
much more.
I am a heart shattering to pieces.
I am a teddy bear cuddling a baby.
I am a cradle rocking side to side.
I am an unrolled sleeping bag.
I am a playground crowding up with kids.
I am a hospital bed hoping I will not be brought out.
I am a plane crawling in the air to New York City.
I am a mat tumbling down stairs.
I am a trash bag flowing through the garden and picking up trash.
I am a watering can watering plants, flowers, and herbs.
But when I wake up from my dreams, I am a half-sister, a daughter, a cousin,
a friend, a best friend, a great, great granddaughter, and a niece.

Amandla Stenberg, Grade 2
Open Charter Magnet School, CA

Cotton Candy

Cotton candy
Fluffy soft
Melts when chewed
It's really really good
Candy
Caitlin Scalise, Grade 3
Elmira Elementary School, OR

Yasmine

Y arn is my favorite thing
A lligator is my favorite animal
S 'more is my favorite food
M ints are my favorite candy
I gloos are my favorite place
N oorhan is my favorite friend
E nglish is my favorite subject.
Yasmine Addo, Grade 2
Phoenix Metro Islamic School, AZ

Dinosaurs

Dinosaurs, dinosaurs, dinosaurs,
Why do you eat dinosaur eggs?
Crunch, crunch, crunch, crunch.
Eggs are good.
Tough Snow, Grade 2
Mission Grade School, MT

Fireworks

Fireworks were superb
Fireworks are explosives, Boom!
Fireworks are awesome
Devin Komen, Grade 3
Gold Canyon Elementary School, AZ

Spectacular Spring

Spectacular spring
Cheerful, humid
Blossoming, lovely, breezy
Fragrance flying through the bright sky
Absolute color
Madison Macy, Grade 3
Morningside School, MT

Colors

If I was red I'd be a beautiful rose.
If I was orange I'd be a nice butterfly.
If I was yellow I'd be a sparkling sun.
If I was green I'd be growing grass.
If I was blue I'd be blue sky and sea.
If I was purple I'd be a sweet grape.
If I was pink I'd be a wonderful rose.
If I was tan I'd be lotion.
If I was black I'd be a pretty bird.
If I was brown I'd be a tall tree.
Janessa Kalo, Grade 3
St Dorothy School, CA

Sky

Skies are bright.
Skies are blue.
Clouds are sweet
and so are you.
Randy Song, Grade 3
Cahuenga Elementary School, CA

Jack Frost

He is like a snake
always sneaking up on me
making me cold
Eliza McCall, Grade 3
Our Lady of the Snows School, NV

The Ocean Breeze

The ocean breeze
Is what I feel like,
It is what I am
And what I see.
It soars over me
And through me.
When I'm sad
It shivers me
And when I'm happy
It warms me up.
It is just what I am.
Maggie Svendsen, Grade 3
Katherine Delmar Burke School, CA

The Man on the Beach
Each beach I go to I say a figure of speech and eat a peach and teach.
Then I reach for a leach and screech with a bleached peach.
The next beach I go to I will not say a speech or teach.
I will not reach for a leach or eat a peach or screech with a bleached peach.

Barrett Connelly, Grade 3
Sacred Heart Elementary School, CA

I Am
I am a basketball player who loves to shoot baskets
I wonder how many people are in this world
I hear lots of voices singing
I see lots of pretty faces
I want a ring for my birthday
I am a basketball player you loves to shoot baskets

I pretend I am a teacher that teaches fourth grade
I feel the wet rain dripping on my head
I touch gross green slime that slips out my hand
I worry about what can happen if you take drugs
I cry when I leave my grandma's house
I am a basketball player who loves to shoot baskets

I understand math now and how to regroup
I say I am going to try my best in school
I dream that I'm really smart
I try my best in school when I do a test
I hope I get to see my grandma soon
I am a basketball player who loves to shoot baskets

Shaalin Days-Hawkins, Grade 3
San Onofre Elementary School, CA

I Feel Happy When
I feel happy when the wind is blowing
Past my skin and the daffodils are swaying
Across the wind in the green grassy hills of Oregon;
When the waves of the ocean are swirling
Back and forth in the water
When the daffodils sing
Across the grass hills and sigh
When my toes are stiff in the air
The daffodils sing lovely songs
While swaying across the wind

Alexis Victoria Gonzalez, Grade 3
Coeur d'Alene Avenue Elementary School, CA

Halloween Scare
Headless horse men
Scoops through the night.
Oh my, oh my, what a fright.
Werewolves howl oh my gosh,
Oh man now they bit Josh.
Oh great it's the vampire lord.
But since this is fake,
I'm totally bored.

(snap fingers to get the rhythm)
Jay Neal, Grade 2
Brush Creek Elementary School, CO

Spring
Spring is here,
let the birds sing,
and let the bells ring.

Spring is here,
let the bees sting,
and let's do anything
to have a good time in spring.

I love spring!
Michael Nguyen, Grade 3
Montessori Learning Institute, TX

Trees
Brown, orange colored leaves
Ants crawling on the dark trunk
Birds are making nests
Brooklyn Perez, Grade 3
Willard Elementary School, CA

Butterfly
Butterfly
on my nose
tickles me.
Funny days are here.
I am loving it.
JoAnna Balcazar, Grade 1
Lee Richmond Elementary School, CA

The Swings
The swings
Go back
And forth
And fast and scary
It feels like
You're falling
When I go up it looks like
I'm going to touch the sky
When you swing
The air is touching you and
The air is fresh and
You feel relaxed
When you're swinging
When the swing is swinging
You can go sometimes to the sides
And you can twist and
Go around in circles and
Sometimes you can get hurt and
The only thing that matters is
That you have fun
Angel Juarez, Grade 3
Edison Elementary School, CA

Day and Night
Day
Light, beautiful
Living, playing, learning
Day light — black night
Sleeping, dreaming, snoring
Dark, stars
Night
Matilde Mikolon, Grade 3
Turner Elementary School, TX

Brontosaurus
A brontosaurus
was a herbivore
until it got extinct
by a meteor
for millions of years.
Diego Olivo, Grade 2
Acacia Elementary School, AZ

My Closet Is...the Enchanting Night Sky
My closet is the enchanting night sky,
The hangers are stars shining and glistening wonderfully,
The falling stars are the hangers falling with a great, big "Bang!"
The night sky is captivating.

The beautiful silver moon is the bright shirt,
The tennis shoes are the planets that fill the sky,
The swaying socks that blow in my closet create the cool breeze,
The purse is the bird trying to find his way home,
My belt is an asteroid belt,
The Big Dipper is as big as the wall in my closet,
The night sky is captivating.

My ring, sitting in my jewelry box, shines like the moonlit sky,
My flowing earrings are the bursting comets,
The Little Dipper is the headband that is round and long,
The shoelaces create the Milky Way,
The doors are the passageways that lead to the night sky,
My closet, that is the night sky, is captivating.

Katherine Roush, Grade 3
The Mirman School, CA

Who I Am
I am a detective, looking for a stolen micro chip.
I am a leader, making a plan for finding bad guys.
I am a scientist, making awesome inventions.
I am a boy, with lots of ideas and dreams.

Kyle Morris, Grade 3
Stanbridge Academy, CA

What Do Trees Remember
Trees remember the colorful dots of flowers
They remember catching the sun through leaves
The feel of birds making a nest out of sticks
The taste of cool water
The swish of wind when an owl flies by at night
They remember the hum of busy bees working
The feel of the bear leaning against it, waiting for honey
Trees remember the stillness of night and the moon shining straight at them
They remember the happy chirping of a new bird being hatched
They remember the sight of hills, so far away
And the calmness of the river

Sarah Wu, Grade 3
Westwood Charter Elementary School, CA

Markers

The markers are colorful.

They have
caps like hats.

They have
points like tacks.

Dustin Jones, Grade 1
Fir Grove Elementary School, OR

Warning!

Warning:
If you come across a tiger,
Don't throw a rock at him
For your desire.
Don't look at his playful smile.
Be careful not to hug him.
Because if you do, he might bite you
On the back.
As nice as he can be
He might use you as a stool.
And whenever you meet a tiger,
He's always ready for you
To be his dinner!

Julia Floyd, Grade 3
River Oaks Baptist School, TX

Summer

Summer is when,
The children come out to play.
It is when,
They have field trips and crafts.

Also swimming lessons,
Some of us have vacation.
If you're home,
You can go to the store,
And buy some seeds,
And plant them with your
Mom or alone!

Vishnu Narayana, Grade 1
Montessori School of Downtown, TX

Soccer and Football

Soccer
Soccer ball, goal
Kicking, passing, blocking
Playing, losing, getting hurt
Punting, catching, throwing
Footballs, touchdowns
Football.

Hailey Akin, Grade 3
Turner Elementary School, TX

My Dog

My dog is white.
He likes to play
hide-n-seek with me.
He likes to lick me.
He likes to run with me.
His name is
DRAGON!

Angel Buerquis, Grade 1
Lee Richmond Elementary School, CA

My House

When I come home
I hear my dogs barking,
And my cat meowing.
I see my dogs and my cats,
I also see my neighbors.
I smell brownies, cookies
And leftover food.
It tastes so good and sweet.
I feel like I'm on a cloud.

Morgan Paisley, Grade 3
Four Peaks Elementary School, AZ

Swimming Pool

Smiling blue turquoise and
Blue eye beating the sun
The edges are white
In the middle
It is sapphire water.

Katie Younglove, Grade 2
Heatherwood Elementary School, CO

Grandma's Hogan

Grandma's Hogan
The floor covered with fine brown dirt
Hexagon walls stacks of cedar logs, pile on top of each other
Stack of woods continue up the ceiling forming a small dome
Sh'ma' sani' hooghan' (Grandma's Hogan)
Grandma's Hogan
As the door facing eastward to waiting for sun's blessing
Sheepskin lying on the floor used as bedding
Square cast iron stove is in the middle of the room for heating and cooking
Sh'ma' sani' hooghan' (Grandma's Hogan)
Grandma's Hogan
Weaving loom standing tall and proud
Full of colors, designs, shapes, and patterns
Grandmother sits alone, stringing her design in and out through the wrap
Sh'ma' sani' hooghan' (Grandma's Hogan)
Grandma's Hogan
Blessed by the Four Sacred Mountains and Holy People
Singing and prayers filled the room with herbal smoke
Grandmother sits besides the medicine man as he prays in the night skies
Sh'ma' sani' hooghan' (Grandma's Hogan)

Cody Cleveland, Grade 3
Ganado Primary School, AZ

People

Black, white, brown
People eat different.
People smell different.
People chew with their mouth open, some don't.
People use different soap.
Some are allergic to cats.
Some are allergic to cats and dogs.
Some people are allergic to all animals.

Zachary Hausinger, Grade 3
Gause Intermediate School, WA

Northern Lights

Hello, I am the Northern Lights.
I am the most beautiful thing in the entire galaxy.
That's what I think at least.
Anyway, I usually show up at the North Pole at night
so you can see my beautiful colors.
So now you know a tiny bit more about me.

Sarah Farley, Grade 3
Miller Elementary School, TX

One by One
I wish their souls could run free,
But their innocent souls are trapped behind barbed wire.
Count how many lost
One by one.
The once happy people now at the power of cold-blooded monsters.
All the little girls and boys,
Women and men dying,
One by one.
All it adds up to is six million lost.
Hearts broken, tears,
Nazis tried to ruin their lives
But didn't break their souls.

Cameron Busby, Grade 3
W V Whitmore Elementary School, AZ

All About Me
When I wake up, I see sunshine and it makes me think about myself.
I am a lemon with a twist.
I am a dew drop full of mist.
I am a child full of bliss.
I am a hug and kiss.
I am a beautiful flower.
I am a drum, full of power.
I am a baby book full of happy memories.
I am silly cartoons on TVs.
When it's time for bed, I look at the sunset: the different colors —
pink, yellow, red.
Or orange — remind me of all I am inside.

Christen Wynne, Grade 2
Open Charter Magnet School, CA

Flowers in Spring
Flowers come in any color — orange, green, and blue.
It is all very true.
Flowers grow everywhere — windowsill, garden, and pots.
Some even have spots.
Flowers are exciting to watch when the wind blew.
Over the years, they grew.
They also look like one of the pinwheels I saw.
One got shredded into straw.

Patrick Kjelshus, Grade 3
Froid Elementary School, MT

Astroworld

Here at Astroworld for a water slide
Standing third in line
We saw the next boat come up
We got on and dropped
My mom and I screamed
We heard a KABOOM
We all got soaking wet
We got off
And sunset come upon us
My mom and I heard other people screaming behind us
As the sun went down
The noise faded
And we went home
And went to sleep.

Devin Tebo, Grade 3
Horn Academy, TX

Chief Manuelito

Chief Manuelito
A grandfather who was wise and brave
Was a great influence as a leader and spokesman for the Navajos
He had signed many treaties to protect and aid his people
Hast'ii Ch'il Haajini' (Chief Manuelito)
Chief Manuelito
Born for the Folded Arm clans
One of the Great War leaders of the Navajo Nation
Young warrior who fought many battles as his stories are cherished
Hast'ii Ch'il Haajini' (Chief Manuelito)
Chief Manuelito
With a long life of learning
He had seen a brighter future in his mind for his people
Words of wisdom, anyone who limits her vision to memories of yesterday
is already dead
Hast'ii Ch'il Haajini' (Chief Manuelito)

Tekaela Wyaco, Grade 3
Ganado Primary School, AZ

Rivers

Rivers are blazing breathtaking blue.
They have glaze like glazed donuts on the waters too.
It's like ghosts are haunting the waters
And they say BOO!!

Clare Messenger, Grade 3
Daves Avenue Elementary School, CA

Baboon
The male monkeys fight.
Baboons eat eggs, fruit, and roots.
They live on the ground.
Maria Torres, Grade 3
Lorenzo De Zavala Elementary School, TX

All About Green
Green is the color of the leaves that fall.
Green is the color of a beautiful frog.
Green is the color of my dress that I wear.
Green is the color that I really adore.
Esmeralda Millan, Grade 2
Lincoln Elementary School, CA

Gymnastics
Flips, cart wheels, handstands, too,
Gymnastics is really fun to do!
Judges rate you on your score,
Horizontal bars and much more!
Take a chance, just try this sport,
Who knows! It may even be your sort!
If you try and be gymnastical,
I'm pretty sure you'll feel fantastical!
Stephanie May, Grade 3
Solana Santa Fe Elementary School, CA

Fairies
Fluttering wings,
Their hearts sweetly sing,
Laughing souls,
Through the sunrise for morning strolls,
A shimmer in the eye,
Fairies do fly,
Everywhere,
Golden hearts and hair.
Lauren Howard, Grade 3
Namaqua Elementary School, CO

Bird
A beautiful bird
with pretty colored feathers
that has a long beak
Allyandra Panchoo, Grade 3
Lorenzo De Zavala Elementary School, TX

Winter Is Over
Winter is over
now it is spring.
Plant all your flowers,
water the trees.
Soon will be summer,
but now it is spring.
Zachary Quiros, Grade 3
Grace School, TX

Mountains
Tall trees
Cool breeze
Rushing waters
Snowy winters
Fall winds
Great views
Summer heat
Aspen trees
Nick Crawford, Grade 3
Grace School, TX

Colors
Red is a firetruck
Yellow is a cute duck
Blue is the color of the sea
Black is the stripes of a bee
Gray is the silver of a key
Green is the color of a pea
Orange is a sweet fruit
Colors are so cute.
Connor Gallardo, Grade 2
Grace School, TX

Macaroni Noodles
Macaroni noodles everywhere,
Dancing head to toe!

Gurgles in my stomach!
Gurgles...
Buurrp...
Excuse me!
Jessie Bellmire, Grade 1
New Emerson School, CO

Colors

Red is my special Christmas ornament.
Orange is the big butterfly that hangs above my bed.
Yellow is the little sunflowers in my garden.
Green is the big trees in my front yard.
Blue is the wallpaper in my room.
Purple is my special squishy pillow.

Jordyn Behan, Grade 1
Grace School, TX

Mummies

Mummies have funerals because they're all dead.
You may want to burn them but instead
they need mummification for their next life
or else they will be caught up in a lot of strife.
They also need amulets which are also called jewels.
Pharaohs get enough to fill up big pools.

Josh Vaught, Grade 3
Four Peaks Elementary School, AZ

My Closet Is…a Winter Wonderland

My closet is a winter wonderland,
My shirts create the breezy wind,
My pants are as white as the snowballs,
My watches are all the icicles,
My belt is a long dog sled,
Fast dogs that are my running shoes are pulling my sled,
My hat is the ice king's shiny castle,
My closet is a winter wonderland.

The icy walls of the castle, which are my closet walls, charm me,
My trophy, the ice king, is always inviting me for a visit,
My tennis racket is the brave knight protecting me,
My closet is so full of fantasy.

The ice king gives me a potion that makes me fly into the blue sky,
I soar over the tundra that is a white fluffy blanket,
I walk across the frosty snow,
Panting for breath, I fly through the open sky,
I fly and see my closet,
I dance in happiness,
And suddenly, I jump out of my closet,
I'm home at last!

Varun Pakanati, Grade 3
The Mirman School, CA

God Rocks

I have God in my heart.
He has power.
He created the Earth.
I think He is cool.
And everybody should believe in Him.
He died on the cross for you and me.
I think God rocks.

Cooper Brown, Grade 3
Kootenai Valley Christian School, MT

Peanuts

P eople
E at
A pples and
N uts
U ntil
T he
S ummer

Ruby Grossman, Grade 1
Cottonwood Montessori School, NM

Mom and Pop

Mom makes me feel loved
like a happy child.
Their love races through me
like fast lightning.
I can always count on Pop.
Mom's hair is white
like a soft cuddly cloud.
Their fountain sounds soft
like a soothing colorful waterfall.
Pop has a great
sense of humor.
Mom's cookies smell sweet
like a chocolaty world.
Their hands feel smooth
like a soft warm pillow.
Pop's tea tastes sweet
like a sugary heaven.
I love Mom and Pop!

Whit Davis, Grade 3
River Oaks Baptist School, TX

Life of a Dragon

Dragon! Dragon! Where thy be
Burning down the big oak tree?
Like a shadow in the night
Trees ablaze the color bright
Nesting in the embers
Then soaring off again,
Away from light

Alexandra Hashagen, Grade 3
Katherine Delmar Burke School, CA

Spring Oh Spring

Spring oh spring
I love spring!
It is a wonderful season.
It is so fun when spring comes.
It gets warmer and warmer
as the season goes by.
You can play on the swing set
and play on the slide.
You can fly kites
when it's windy.
Spring oh spring!

Ciarra Tate, Grade 2
Walsh Elementary School, CO

Unicorns

Unicorns jumping, unicorns flying,
Unicorns falling, unicorns slipping
Unicorns everywhere.
Unicorns soaring, unicorns gliding,
Unicorns floating, unicorns sighing,
Unicorns everywhere

Trista Ortiz, Grade 2
Sierra Vista Elementary School, CA

Spring

Flowers and trees bloom
Sunny and warm air is here
Animals come out
Fun is near

Arielle Radparvar, Grade 3
Lanai Road Elementary School, CA

Planets

Jolly Jackie Jackson jumped on Jupiter
Mean Mary Megan married a monkey on Mercury
Victorious Vivian Vera viewed a violet violin on Venus
Sassy Sabina Smith shook seven serpents on Saturn
Marvelous Mickey Mouse migrated to magical Mars
Exciting Ella Evensworth eats eight extraordinary elephants on Earth
Untidy Ursula Umbridge used umbrellas under Uranus
Naughty Nellie Nipper noticed nine nests on Neptune
Playful Peggy Patrick pictured playful puppies on Pluto

Jackie Schaeffer, Grade 3
Wonderland Avenue Elementary School, CA

Yei' Be' Chei' Dancers

Giant Grandfather
Dancing, walking, stomping, rhythms
Woman and man dance together around the fire
Will be blessed and sanctified in a forceful spiritual way
Yei'Be'Chei' (Giant Grandfather)
Giant Grandfather
Dancing, walking, stomping, rhythms
Dance like a spirit and strength of mind in the air
You will grow up and dance like the Giant Grandfather
Yei'Be'Chei' (Giant Grandfather)
Giant Grandfather
Dancing, walking, stomping, rhythms
As you find your way in a spirit
Soaring high above like an eagle
Yei'Be'Chei' (Giant Grandfather)
Giant Grandfather
Dancing, walking, stomping, rhythms
A feather in the wind, dancing, floating swiftly
Children crying, people giving or running from them
Yei'Be'Chei' (Giant Grandfather)

Nalani Shirley, Grade 2
Ganado Primary School, AZ

Tropical Island

Coconut, pineapple and bananas
a smash of juicy fruits colorful and good.
On this tropical island there are juicy, sweet and weird fruits
delicious and perfect too.
On this tropical island there is everything to do.

Yassi Roberts, Grade 3
Katherine Delmar Burke School, CA

My Brothers

I have two brothers.
Sometimes they're mean.
They make me mad.
I like it when they're clean.

They're mostly nice.
They care about me.
I like them a lot,
When they make me tea.

Michael cheers me up when I'm sad
But sometimes he just makes me mad

Daniel is the best of all
I like him most when we play ball
Sharon Ghalchi, Grade 3
Woodcrest School, CA

Flowers Are Mothers

As kind as a yellow gerber daisy.
As interesting as a red poppy.
As surprised as a white lily.
As fast as a purple ranunculus.
As sad as a pink hibiscus.
As honest as a blue delphinium.
Is my mother.
Sophia Frankel, Grade 3
CLASS Academy, OR

Different World

If phoenixes ruled the sky
And hippocampuses ruled the sea,
And dragons breathed on mountains
Oh, what would the world be?

If that really happened,
You see,
Endangered we'd be
Endangered we'd be
That's what the world would be.
Julia Chang, Grade 3
Lincoln Elementary School, CA

I Am

I am a
walking
talking
making
baking
kid.

I am a
shouting
cartoon watching
fast food eating
slurping
girl.

I am a
fast running
toy buying
airplane drawer
person.
Tori Luckadue, Grade 3
Briargrove Elementary School, TX

Run and Play

I love to run.
I love to play.
On a wonderful day.
I run in March. I run in May.
I play, I play, I play!
Then I say, "What a beautiful day!"
Do you love to run in May?
Do you say what a lovely day?
Michelle Nava, Grade 3
Honey Hollow Elementary School, CA

The Books

The books like to cook,
And they met a nook,
and they looked at the nook,
and the nook looked at the book,
and the nook gobbled up the book.
Cameron Klein, Grade 1
New Emerson School, CO

Live the Lights

'Tis time to tell the story of people who lived the lights.
Whom wore pants of glittered gold and rainbow belts to hold them up,
Just as the Northern Lights hold their lives.
Whom the glow children played with light balls and
Whom combed the red streaks of doll hair.
Whom ate the green light of grass.
    The Northern Lights.

Cora Rothenberger, Grade 3
New Emerson School, CO

Flowers

Flowers, red, yellow, pink or blue
I like the smell. Do you like it too?
There are so many kinds I can't name them all;
some are big and some are real small.
Butterflies and bees in the bright sun
drinking their nectar one by one.
You can give them to a special someone
or you can pick them just for fun.
You can buy them in a bouquet
or plant them on a sunny day.
You can put flowers in a vase
or plant them in a warm rainy place.
Each state has a flower, be careful not to pick it
because if you do, you might get a ticket.
We miss them in winter when the weather is cold
but welcome them in spring with their faces of gold.
Daisies violets and beautiful roses
the wonderful smell pleases our noses.
Pick some or plant some then you will see what a joy flowers can be!

Sarah Elmore, Grade 3
Turner Elementary School, TX

The Autumn Cub

There is a special autumn that comes every four years;
It is called The Autumn Cub;
The leaves wrestle as they climb down their tree;
They eat honey as they fall to the ground;
They change color as they grow up;
They will give a weak growl in the wind
as they go to sleep;
until spring when they are reborn.

Katelyn Dinkel, Grade 3
Kyrene De Las Brisas School, AZ

I Love My Cat

I love my cat
She is so soft
I pet her and she purrs.
I love her
She loves me
We are happy together.
She is nice
and I think that while I pet her.
Keaton Bullen, Grade 1
Fort Worth Country Day School, TX

Music Is My Life

Flip Flop Flippity Flop.
Sing so softly in the
Morning air.

Sing with the wind
Rustling in your hair.
Feel the sweetness
That's in you.

Feel how else you
Could possibly be.
Feel how you will sing
To the beat.

Sing along to the morning beat.
Feel the sensation
Of music.
Devan, Grade 3
Katherine Delmar Burke School, CA

Kaleigh

K ind and nice
A lways on target
L ikable
E ntertaining
I nviting
G reat in school
H appy a lot of the time.
Kaleigh Beach, Grade 3
Turner Elementary School, TX

Math

I love school
it is the best
but math is better
than all the rest
I like art
and spelling too
But math is more fun;
it challenges you
fractions, decimals
numbers galore
division, subtraction
addition and more
there are so many things
you can do with math
it's even better
than taking a bath.
So dip in and have some fun
because math is for
EVERYONE!
Jason Sanderlin, Grade 3
Spring Creek Elementary School, WY

Mexico

M y favorite place that is
E normous, and
X -tra fun very
I mpressive
C ool but
O ld
Enrique Villalon, Grade 3
Emerson Elementary School, TX

When Dragon Finds Spirit

He found a crystal.
He killed a dragon.
The Spirit.
The dragon came back alive,
He kept him,
The Spirit.
They became best friends.
Brian Blake, Kindergarten
Jacob Wismer Elementary School, OR

Happy Mother's Day

On Mother's Day, I'll tell my mother,
Happy Mother's Day I'll give my mother
a card and a present.
Then I'll tell my mother, it's Happy Mother's Day.

Rudy Aguilera, Grade 3
Midland Elementary School, CA

My Sister Claire

My sister Claire,
sometimes annoying,
sometimes playful.
No matter what,
I'll love her to infinity.

She likes when I come home from school.
She enjoys the presents that I made for her at school.
I paint pictures of things that she likes.
Without her, my life wouldn't be much fun.

Nolan Hunt, Grade 3
Stanbridge Academy, CA

Ghost Riders in the Sky

An old cowboy went riding out on a dark and windy night,
He heard a moan that he thought wasn't right.
Then he saw a horse in the sky go by then he thought,

Ghost riders in the sky.
He followed the horse through the night.
He rode on with all his might until he died
And became a ghost rider in the sky.

Sienna Holmes, Grade 3
Wonderland Avenue Elementary School, CA

Tutie Frutie

Juicy sweet bitter scrumptious yummy orange divine.
Juicy watery goodness big round and plump.
Take a bite and it's an orange.
Juicy small green and purple.
Yummy.
Take a bite and it's a grape.
Juicy sweet yellow tropical fruit.
Take a bite and it's a pineapple.

Isabelle, Grade 3
Katherine Delmar Burke School, CA

If I Were...

If I were green I would be the shining leaves on a tree.
If I were brown I would be a tree trunk tall and strong.
If I were blue I would be the big blue sky.
If I were pink I would be a pink flamingo.
If I were gold I would be a golden retriever puppy.
If I were orange I would be the sunset on a summer night.
If I were red I would be hot lava.
If I were purple I would be the grapes on a vine.

Rebecca Prunty, Grade 3
St Dorothy School, CA

My Korean Heritage Presentation

At my Korean heritage presentation I was very nervous,
My mom helped me so she was at my service.

I performed a Korean dance with fans,
To hold the fans I used my hands.

Japchae was the food I brought,
It was supposed to be hot but by the time everyone was done it was not.

I brought the Korean currency called won,
Now all my won is gone.

We had a fun and exciting feast,
Some people were playing with their food trying to be a beast.

I taught the class five phrases,
A lot of people gave me gazes.

When I was done I felt so proud,
I felt as puffy as a cloud.

Annabelle Lee, Grade 2
The Pegasus School, CA

The Still Sounds at Nighttime

The still sounds at nighttime, when raccoons tippy toe through the yards. The
still sounds at nighttime, when deer leap over fences. The still sounds at
nighttime, when birds are lying in the cool nighttime breeze. The still sounds at
nighttime, in spring, fall, winter, and summer. The still sounds at nighttime.

Madeline Weiss, Grade 2
Horizons K-8 Alternative Charter School, CO

Victoria's Face

Draw my head as round as a round egg.
Doodle my hair as straight as a horse's tail.
Sketch my eyebrows as straight as a strip of paper.
Color my eyelashes as curved as a wave coming in shore.
Shape my eyes as blue as the sweet ocean.
Turn my nose as small as a tiny tomato.
Do my mouth as pretty as a bright flower.
I'll illustrate my teeth as white fluffy snowflakes.
Outline my ears as tiny as a small eraser.

Victoria Vincent, Grade 3
Briargrove Elementary School, TX

Colors

If I were red, I would be an apple or cherries
or a beautiful rose or a flame who warms people.
If I were blue I would be the sky.
If I were orange, I would be an orange or a peach.
If I were pink, I would be an eraser or a ball.
If I were purple, I would be some grapes.
If I were green, I would be a leaf.

Emily Weise, Grade 2
St Dorothy School, CA

Las Positas Creek

Plants and trees, honeybees in the watershed;
Soda can, little man in the watershed;
We got out of our house;
And went to the Las Positas Creek Trail;
There we saw a little creek;
With two hills on the side of it;
And we got closer;
We saw two birds and three ducklings swimming;
There were four blue and green rocks;
On the trail that we got;
We threw rocks into the muddy creek;
Animal tracks were in the trail;
We saw all kinds of leaves;
Along the creek;
Blue flowers and white flowers;
Lined the creek;
So many things that amaze me;
What a wonderful place to be!

Varsha Ramakrishnan, Grade 2
Henry P Mohr Elementary School, CA

Baseball
BAM!
The ball is hit!
It look's like a homerun!
Is it?
It is a homerun!
The Tigers win the game!
The people go wild!
Logan Rudig, Grade 2
Frontier Valley Elementary School, CO

Winter
Winter
Snowy, cold
Shiver, snow angels, throw snowballs
Winter is fun.
Icy
Mitchell Nelson, Grade 3
Zuni Elementary Magnet School, NM

Stars, Stars
I am stars.
I could be big.
I could be small.
I'm hot.
When I die,
I explode.
I can make constellations.
I could also be the sun.
And that's all I'm saying now.
Jared Brown, Grade 2
Acacia Elementary School, AZ

Catfish and Cats
Catfish
Water, swimming
Eating, fins, swishing
Large, scales, whiskers, fur
Meowing, purring, pouncing
Chasing, running
Cats
Tina Lin, Grade 1
Armstrong Elementary School, TX

This Is Me!
I am a
Basketball slamming
Volleyball bumping
Karate chopping
Softball batting champion

I am a
Snowboard jumping
Game playing
Animal loving
Active doing kid

I am a
Smart reading
Homework doing
Cool checking
Science investigating student

I am a
Bike riding
Rollerblade rolling
Wave swimming girl
Brooklyn Vincent, Grade 3
Briargrove Elementary School, TX

I'm Not Hungry
When I got home,
I picked up the phone.
It was my mom ready to dine.
She said, "It's time."
I said, "Oh my."
Because I had stopped for a cone.
Kristen Drake, Grade 2
C C Hardy Elementary School, TX

The Sky
The sky is blue,
The sky is high,
The sky is anything,
Your mind can find.
Cori Long, Grade 2
Redwood Christian School, CA

Window

Through my window I see a soccer ball.
I see a coach with brown hair and kids running around.
I see the kids playing well.
Through my window I see another team.
I see a coach and adults.
I see the kids winning.
Through my window I see a soccer game.

Marcus Hall, Grade 3
Daly Elementary School, MT

Window

Through my window I see a dog
I see a cat and a dog
I see the cat and the dog jump and flip
Through my window I see a cat scamp around and play
I see the dog run away
Through my window I see the cat stay and play!

Marina McGourty, Grade 3
Daly Elementary School, MT

My Closet Is an Erupting Volcano

My closet is an erupting volcano,
Where socks are the fiery rocks,
Shirts are as dark and as cloudy as smoke,
A tall pile of coats is a dark brown volcano,
The air smells of smoke,
The air tastes like smoke,
This can only mean one thing,
The heaping of books suddenly topple over in my closet!
The volcano is erupting!
"Boom, bang, bam!"

Jackets are boiling hot lava,
The lava comes tumbling out of the volcano as fast as a speeding cheetah,
Look! The hangers are burning trees,
I can hear the clock that is a howling eagle,
The eagle is screeching as loud as a fire alarm,
I can hear the toy people screaming, "Aaaaah,"
I touch the hot lava, "Ouch!"
Bye, bye erupting volcano,
When I shut my closet door, the magic ends,
Poof!

Skylar Deutsch, Grade 3
The Mirman School, CA

Eraser
like a cookie,
little,
slimy and cool,
bouncy.
Delaney Barr, Grade 2
Edmonds Homeschool Resource Center, WA

Yellow
Yellow is the color of the bright sun.
Yellow is the color of a pretty sunflower.
Yellow is the color of a smiley face.
Yellow is the color of a folder in my desk.
Yellow is the color of my dad's shirt.
Makenna Roberds, Grade 1
Grace School, TX

Green
Green is the color of the summer grass.
Green is the color of tasty grapes.
Green is the color of leaves in spring.
Green is the color of a yummy lime.
Green is the color of a chameleon's scales.
Green is the color of a poison dart frog.
Daniel Cho, Grade 1
Grace School, TX

Things I Like About the World
Looking at stars remind me of smiley faces
Sometimes, I see my dad's face there.
The sun shining warm on my face
The smell of red and purple roses and
Fry bread cooking on the stove…
These things I like about the world.
LaRee Vest-Manuelito, Grade 3
Four Peaks Elementary School, AZ

Moon Cheese
I wonder if the moon is made out of cheese?
Can you tell me please?
Is the moon made out of cheese?
Is there a man up there named Sneeze?
Is the moon made out of cheese?
Madison Lambiase, Grade 1
St Mark's Day School, TX

Bats…Bats…Bats
B ats
A irborne
T iny
S mall

B lack
A ctive
T errific
S ilent

B rown
A dorable
T iny
S mart
Alek Rakow, Grade 2
Carden West School, CA

Snakes
Slinky, scaly, snakes
slimy and cool slithering
gracefully climbing.
Haiden Collins, Grade 1
Highland Park School, MT

My Mom
I love my mom
and she loves me
we keep happy company
Kylie LeBarre, Kindergarten
Hollister SDA School, CA

Word Play
Swinging of swings
Bouncing of balls
Playing of kids
the ground smiles
grounds smiling
is unusual
but…

NOT for a PLAYGROUND!!
Madison Wright, Grade 3
Lyons Elementary School, CO

Petals of a Daisy

When I wake in the morning, the first thing I see is a daisy.
The petals of the daisy remind me of the members of my family.
I am one of those petals.
I am a soccer ball soaring into the goal.
I am thumbs on a controller tapping a lot of buttons.
I am a joke jar exploding with funny things.
I am a sponge cleaning the kitchen.
I am a basketball flying into the basket.
I am a pencil writing on a piece of paper.
I am a speedy rocket flying around in the air.
I am a game piece moving from space to space.
I am a remote flipping from channel to channel.
At night, when the daisy closes its petals and I go to sleep,
I think even more about myself.

Taylor Dinwiddie, Grade 3
Open Charter Magnet School, CA

Chocolate Chip Cookies

Chocolate chip cookies are good and sweet
I know you love them better than wheat.
Wheat smells like feet.
Warm chocolate chip cookies are good and great.
Kennedy loves chocolate chip cookies
As long as they're good and sweet.

Ariannah De La Ossa, Grade 3
Hollister SDA School, CA

The Voice of Moon

The voice of moon sparkles in the night.
The hands of the sky carry me into the clouds.
The tongue of the sun licks me with warmth.
The song of the stars twinkle in my eyes.
The shoulders of the river peek out of the water.
The ear of the plants listen to the animal sounds.
The melody of the piano carries me away in music.
The leaves of the trees fall in my hands.
The whisper of fire flames in my ear.
The noise of my brother gives me hope.
The bark of my dog gives me peace.
The sweetness of my cats gives me love.
The branches on the trees wave to me.
The voice of the moon brings me happiness.

Hannah Harkness, Grade 3
CLASS Academy, OR

Sea Lion
Sky
sun
Ocean
Beach
Sand rock
The sea lion
sleeps lazily
like crowns.
Briant Shen, Kindergarten
Mission Valley Elementary School, CA

Spring
Spring is a flower season.
I like to smell flowers.
People have picnics and fly kites.
High school girls and boys run track.
Elementary boys play baseball.
When you have picnics,
you can hear bees buzzing
and flies going around muzzing.
Halbert Alvarez, Grade 2
Walsh Elementary School, CO

All About Me
M y favorite sport is tennis
A mazing soccer player
R ocks are my collection
Y ellow and red are favorite colors
A lways try to be helpful
M y favorite food is pizza
Maryam Nassar, Grade 3
Camptonville Academy, CA

Spring
Flowers grow in the spring.
Birdies sing in the spring.
Frogs croak in the spring.
I do something in the spring.
I read inside from a book,
About the birds in the spring.
Jesica Banker, Grade 1
Community Children's Center, CA

Christmas
Christmas at my house
is so beautifying

I love to hear my family
pray and sing

We wake up in the morning light
it fills my day with joy

We thank our Father up above
for all the wonderful toys

I love to eat the food we make
it gets me energized

I do not really have to
get myself compromised

We say "Happy Birthday" to Jesus
and then we watch our shows

I hope you have a great Christmas
Because that's how our Christmas goes!
Hunter Cunningham, Grade 3
Rice Canyon Elementary School, CA

My Sister Esra
I like my sister.
Because she is cute
And hugs me
When I come from school.
And she kisses me
And she is the best.
She laughs a lot.
And she likes playing
And she likes dogs
And she likes the park
And slides and swings
And she likes playing
What I'm playing
Hussain Ahmad, Grade 3
Phoenix Metro Islamic School, AZ

What a Dolphin Remembers

A dolphin remembers the sound of little fish
rushing not to get caught by the dolphin
It remembers the sound of the waves hitting the beach
A dolphin remembers the sound of other dolphins
saying come here we have gossip
The sound of its mother telling it to come
A dolphin remembers the sound of crabs walking along
the soft sand of the deep
A dolphin remembers the splish and splash of when it jumps up
and out of the water
The sound of people swimming
A dolphin remembers everything about its life.

Mariana Garcia, Grade 3
Westwood Charter Elementary School, CA

My Life

When I look at myself in a mirror and close my eyes
I am a silly cat making silly faces.
I am a brain full of math facts.
I am an angry mouth that screams.
I am a ladybug sharing my food with my fly friend.
I am a bunk bed that kids sleep on.
I am legs in the air upside down.
I am a soccer ball rolling in a goal.
I am clothes on a kid jogging around the track.
I am arms hugging my family.
But when I open my eyes, I am me.

Samantha Fernandez, Grade 2
Open Charter Magnet School, CA

My Teacher

My teacher is great!
She is very dear.
She says to us, "You make me melt like an ice cream."
In her class, we can't break the rules,
We can often sing, act and dance.
She teaches phonics,
Reads us stories,
Teaches us math and Chinese too.
She lets us lie down on a pillow,
When she plays her piano.
My teacher is great!

Pranav Nagarajan, Kindergarten
Forest Park Elementary School, CA

I Like Flowers

When I smell
The flowers
I think that
I'm a flower
Getting energy from
The sun and
Getting food from
The rain
When I feel happy
I think of a
Wonderful flower
But when I feel sad
I think that
I'm an old flower

Anitza Serafin, Grade 3
Edison Elementary School, CA

Star Bright, Star Light

Stars shine high in the sky.
Stars are fireballs.
You can only see stars at night.
Stars are very bright.
Some stars shoot through the sky.

Colin Hubbard, Grade 2
Acacia Elementary School, AZ

Leaf

Green
Wet
Black
Soft

Evan Richardson, Grade 1
Fir Grove Elementary School, OR

Vacation

I can't stop smiling.
We're going in six months.
Splash Mountain is my favorite ride.
I've never been on Space Mountain.
I can't wait.

Kyle Stewart, Grade 2
Frontier Valley Elementary School, CO

Beach Day

When the sand blows at the beach
Crabs speak

Some clang, some clamp,
Some speak

Sand sings
Shells shine

Toes sleep and wiggle
At the sand

Salt in the water
Swims and paddles

Shells shine
Water crashes

When the people go suddenly
Then the crabs are quiet again

Gabriela Diaz, Grade 3
Horn Academy, TX

Winter

Winter
Snowy, blowzy
Playing, snow fights
Playing fun games in winter.
Icy

Julianne Olguin, Grade 3
Zuni Elementary Magnet School, NM

Bow and Arrows

Bow
Wooden, curved
Strong, weapon, tall
Carving, archers, Indians, short
Pointing, flaming, shooting
Triangular, sharp
Arrows

Avi Steinberg, Grade 1
Armstrong Elementary School, TX

Window
Through my window I see Silverwood.
I see cotton candy and a wet, fun water park.
I see the wave pool and the water tower.
Through my window I see the Timber of Terror roller coaster.
    It was amazing.
I see bumper cars and carnival games.
I see the prizes at night that you can buy.
Through my window I see the wonderful world.

Shaylan Mohn, Grade 3
Daly Elementary School, MT

P.E., I Love You
P.E., I love you you're so fun to play,
I'm lucky we don't have to pay.
P.E., I really love you, I wish I had you for my own.
Too bad I'm at home.
I can't wait 'til I go to you.
I can't wait 'til I move.
P.E., I love you, you're like a zoo.
And you're really cool.
Too bad you're in my imagination.
Because I'm not at that station.

Mario Sandoval, Grade 3
Midland Elementary School, CA

My Face
Color my skin as tan as caramel.
Draw my head as round as a plate.
Create my hair as blond as the sand on a beach.
Illustrate my eyes as blue as a clean pool.
Trace my nose as pointy as a party hat.
Shade my mouth as red as a flame.
Outline my teeth as white as a clean piece of paper.
Shade my background as blue as the ocean.

Jenny Bobo, Grade 3
Briargrove Elementary School, TX

Thankful
The things that I am thankful for: food, family, and pets.
I am thankful for food because it keeps me healthy.
I am thankful for my family because I love them.
I am thankful for my pets because I love them, too.

Zeke Renner, Grade 1
Mound Valley Rural School, NV

Mom
Pretty like a red rose,
Likes to wear red shorts and blue pants at work,
Has curly hair,
I wish I was pretty,
Like her,
Her voice is soft,
She does not yell at me,
She smells like strawberry and grapes,
My mom is pretty,
Like my sister's baby,
Cora

Alyssa Tsosie, Grade 2
Ganado Primary School, AZ

An Old Doll
Yesterday I went to my grandma's and grandpa's house
And my grandma opened a chest.
It had a lot of things in it.
I saw two dolls in it.
I told my grandma that I thought they were cute.
She let me have them.
But, I can't until my room is clean and organized.
Then I can have them.

Savannah Tittle, Grade 2
Orchard Elementary School, UT

Hades
Hades, Greek god of the Underworld,
Watches over the land of the dead.
Son of the Titans Cronus and Rhea, brother of Zeus and Poseidon,
husband to Persephone.
Powerful, merciful, wealthy and lonely,
He cares for all the dead souls who have paid an obolo to the ferryman,
Charon, to cross the river Styx,
Who must meet the terrible three-headed dog Cerberus that guards his dark gates.
Hades is lord of all the wealth beneath the earth — gold, silver, copper.
He fears nothing because all eventually come to his kingdom.
He loves the beautiful Persephone, daughter of Demeter, goddess of the harvest,
But he must wait patiently for nine months through spring, summer and fall
To see his lovely wife for the three months of winter.

Shayna Begay, Grade 2
East Valley Academy, AZ

Singing

I love to sing.
When I sing a song,
My heart feels so strong.
My favorite song is *The Beat of my Heart*,
Because I like Hilary Duff,
And all of her stuff.
I want to be a singer in the Kindergarten Circus.
I can sing, dance, and do cartwheels.
And just be like Hilary Duff!

Sarah Catherine Vanderbloemen, Kindergarten
Presbyterian School, TX

Me

When I am alone with myself, my imagination takes over.
I am a football on fire, thrown over and over.
I am all the toys a kid desires.
I am toys scattered around the room.
I am a sharp pencil doing geometry.
I am a loud laugh coming out of a big mouth.
I am someone who loves to do a lot of nice things for people.
I am imaginative ideas bursting out.
I am footballs, basketballs, and baseballs all together.
And when my imagination stops, I go outside and play.

Ryan Indelicato, Grade 3
Open Charter Magnet School, CA

October Surprises

October has Halloween and Halloween is very fun
Because you can get candy.
You go over to a friend's and have a party.
You can also go trick or treating with your family.
October has lots of stuff waiting for you.
You also give the candy.
October Surprises!

Fiona Bennett, Grade 2
St Mark's Day School, TX

The Disappearing Ice Cream

I lost my ice cream. Where did it go?
Did it melt? No. Did it fall? No.
Wait, I forgot. I haven't bought it yet.
Good bye ice cream truck. Good bye ice cream.

Kaylee Huntley, Grade 3
Academy of Charter Schools, CO

Spring
Rainy, oh rainy.
Spring is a time of year
with April flowers on their way,
green grass, sunny days, windy days.
Animals come out of their den,
bees gather nectar to make honey,
butterflies fly around.
Baseball season is starting,
people fly kites and have picnics.
Spring, oh spring is wonderful!
Montana Cook, Grade 2
Walsh Elementary School, CO

New Chicks and Cub Polar Bears
Cub
soft, white
freezing, fishing, snowed
milk, Arctic, sand, Maryland,
nesting, feeding, fishing,
fluffy, gray
Chick
Narisse Trippel, Grade 2
South Side Elementary School, WY

Outside in the Wild
Outside in the wild
Where the forest glows
The paint of air is a spirit of gold.
Flowers are there.
Bluebonnets in the forest glow.
Zoey Dugat-Burge, Grade 1
Montessori Learning Institute, TX

The Eagle
Fastly,
Quickly,
Madly,
The eagle
Was flying in the sky.
— Wow!
Byron Bass, Grade 1
Fir Grove Elementary School, OR

Sounds of the Radio:
Ba-ba-beating
Talking
Singing
Rapping
Screaming
Background noising
news talking
Jazz saxophoning
Hummmmming
Alex Barnes, Grade 3
Cubberley Elementary School, CA

Cowboy Job
When I see a cowboy with a rope,
And a gun or two,
Then I hear them sing their song,
"Yippie I O, Little Doggies."
When they catch a cow.
They take it to the train.
It's then sent off to the ranch.
When I see a cowboy with a rope,
And a gun or two,
Then I hear them sing their song,
"Yippie I O, Little Doggies."
Christian Neils, Grade 3
Kootenai Valley Christian School, MT

Dear Sparkling Lights,
When I plug
You in
I feel
Excitement coming
FLASH!
So bright
Colors
Twinkling in the dark
Spreading all the
Bright colors
To the world.
Sarah Baines, Grade 2
Heatherwood Elementary School, CO

The Nice Dragon

There once was a dragon so tender and mild.
He loved to play ball with kids.
He loved to run from here to there.
He had a friend named Eli.
He loved to draw pictures.
He loved to write stories.
He wrote a poem called "The Dragon and the Mummy."
He loved to read it.
One day he died because he was very sick.

Jakob Snider, Grade 3
St John of San Francisco Orthodox Academy, CA

I Am a Girl

I'd like to tell you that I am a girl, a sister, and I have a family.
But that's not all I have to say.
I am a stretchy rubber band.
I am a vacuum cleaning a house.
I am a lion deep in the wild, roaring out madness.
I am a light blue sky up high with clouds floating around me.
I am feet of a horse galloping across the finish line.
I am a skinny chapter book on a bookshelf in a little wooden house.
I am a silver rock in the desert lying on dusty sand.
I am a white crystal, shining in a blue velvet bag.
I am a knife cutting fruit in the kitchen.
I am a pencil writing in a diary, about everything that happens.
I am a bunny eating lettuce and hopping as high as I can.
I am a pepperoni pizza on Friday.
I am a hug, warm like a blanket for your bed.
I am a type writer typing lists and stories for children.
I've told enough about me.
To know the rest you need to know me.
I am happy to be Lia Peña

Lia Peña-Ochoa, Grade 3
Open Charter Magnet School, CA

Red

Red is the color of fire flashing bright with the smoke spreading in the sky.
Red is the color of shoes that you wear.
Red is the color of your heart that is full of love.
Red is the color of the marker that you use to draw a rainbow.
Red is the color of paint, red as the strawberries that are so sweet that you eat.

Jonathan Torres, Grade 2
Lincoln Elementary School, CA

Books

Books you can read,
Books you can write,
Books you can listen to
Even at night.

Some books are scary,
Some books are sad,
Some books are happy
And make me feel glad.

Some books are fiction,
Some books teach history,
Some books are make-believe,
Some solve a mystery.

Books can be big,
Books can be small,
Whatever the size,
I like them all!
Alexa Milliner, Grade 3
Home School, UT

Dad

Plays basketball
plays soccer ball
plays football
plays catch with me
plays kickball
plays volleyball
plays with me and
makes me happy!
Samantha Cardens, Grade 1
Lee Richmond Elementary School, CA

Snake

I once saw a snake, it was very big.
It wore a very cool wig.
In a flash it ate a Twix flavored cake.
And ended up with a belly ache.
As it wiggled away dancing a jig.
Tara Ballew, Grade 2
C C Hardy Elementary School, TX

The Snow Tiger

The snow tiger running,
all dressed in white.

It rises in the night,
and sleeps in the light.

They may look small,
but are of very great might.

The blackness in its fur are it's stripes,
dark as night.

I don't know,
but they might have great sight.
Evin Hurlin, Grade 2
Bridlemile Elementary School, OR

Money

Money, money, money
Money is the best.
I have money.
My piggie bank is blue.

Do you like money?
I like money.
Money is cool.
MONEY MAKES ME HAPPY.
Michelle Hernandez, Grade 3
Honey Hollow Elementary School, CA

Happy

Happy makes me think
of the color red
like an apple.
It rushes through me
like a cheetah.
It makes me feel excited
about myself
like a laughing hyena.
Then I want to explode.
Robert Klamo, Grade 2
Northridge Elementary School, CO

Starry Night

As I sit alone by my window on this starry night
The stars are bright no telephone wires to get in my way
As I sit alone so quiet the only things I hear
Are my calm and the crickets chattering along.
When I was little my mom would say
"The crickets? They keep the monsters away."
As the fireflys light the night sky
So I start to listen again I hear a whistle sound
I look and see the wind blowing the daffodils
And it is making a cool noise and I feel that I am weightless
And floating on this starry night I see the gleaming moon
Who is shining brightly and I feel that it is alive
Talking and staring at me on this starry night.

Kaiya Peralta, Grade 3
Coeur d'Alene Avenue Elementary School, CA

Perfect Line

I can't make a sign if I don't draw a perfect line
I have to draw the line so I can make a perfect sign
First I start out straight, then the teacher calls me and I ruin the perfect line
And if I ruin the line I can't make a perfect sign
Now I am mad unexpectedly somebody pops up and says "Are you trying to draw
a perfect line to make a perfect sign?"
I say, "Yes," then they say use a piece of paper.
3 more sides to go!

Claire Hobika, Grade 3
New Emerson School, CO

German Dodge Ball

When I was playing German Dodge Ball,
The teams were really unfair,
Someone almost pegged me and I made a great fall,
Then I realized I was the only one there,

I was a pretzel, twisting and turning,
When I was playing there was a flash of lightning,
After the game my heart was burning,
I didn't care, but it was a little frightening,

It is a little rough on my knee,
German Dodge ball is fine for me.

Nathan Slattery, Grade 3
Daves Avenue Elementary School, CA

The Bee
Buzz went the bee
Why are you looking at me?
I'm the one who gives you your honey
So you should be proud of me
Sophie Frank, Grade 3
Wonderland Avenue Elementary School, CA

Mom
My mom is nice when she smiles at me.
My mom is so beautiful when she fixes my hair.
I love the way she laughs and plays.
My mom is so special to me.
Ashley Walthing, Grade 2
Lincoln Elementary School, CA

Soccer
Soccer is fun.
We get to play in the sun.
I kick and score.
Now I have to do more.
I play soccer every year.
Don't have any fear.
Two years in a row the rules are the same.
Now I have to get back to the game.
Monica Roberts, Grade 2
St Mark's Day School, TX

My Dad
My dad is a frog on a log.
He jumps over bumps.
He mumbles and his stomach grumbles.
I think he's perfectly handsome.
He's nice
And is good at catching mice.
I love him.
He loves me too.
Dad, a hardworking brave dirty man.
Takes me everywhere he can.
He's very strong.
He loves me,
Even when I'm wrong.
That's why he is the best dad ever.
Rosamaria Segura, Grade 3
Lincoln Elementary School, CA

Degus
Degus
friendly, small
cute, jumping, furry
running, funny
fun!
Kayla Irish, Grade 1
Highland Park School, MT

Dogs
Dogs
Brown, soft
Play, eat, lick
Dogs like to run
Puppies
Brandi Hayes, Grade 1
Myatt Elementary School, TX

The School Bus Ride
I like riding the school bus
Everyday at 7:25.
I ride the bus,
So, I do!
And you will too!
Toot! Toot!
Robert Snyder, Grade 2
New Emerson School, CO

Dogs and Cats
Dogs bark *arf arf*
Cats meow *m-e-o-w*
Dogs and cats fight a lot
They don't know when to stop.

They think they are cool
But they are just fools
And they don't go to school.

They don't go to the bath pool
They don't wash their paws
They are very funny!
Dillon Coleman, Grade 1
New Emerson School, CO

The Lily

The lily lays still on the vine.
It is cold from the cool shower.
It smells good after the cool shower.
Now the sun comes out and warms the sweet flower.

Brittney Thliveris, Grade 1
Paonia Elementary School, CO

Window

Through my window I see a rainforest shining in the sun.
I see a still pond and a lion cleaning her cub.
I see the mountains gleaming in white.
Through my window I see an elephant roaming around.
I see a windy river and a zebra eating grass.
I see the lake with a crocodile in it.
Through my window I see a rainforest.

Eric Matt, Grade 3
Daly Elementary School, MT

Powers

You don't know about all that I wish.
I wish that I had more powers.

Did you know that the only powers we have are…
Powers to
move,
see,
and love.

Nathan Gale, Grade 2
Orchard Elementary School, UT

Spring Is Here

Spring is the time of year
when animals come out from hibernation.
It is time for calving season for my family.
Calves are finally lying on the ground.
We get to play outside longer with our friends and our pets.
We can even play at the park and at home.
It is a time to hunt for Easter eggs
and sing some songs about Easter.
You can get stuff from the Easter bunny.
Spring is here.

Samantha Steward, Grade 2
Walsh Elementary School, CO

Eagle*

I am an eagle
Flying in the air
So fear me.
I am an eagle
Building a nest
Don't look at me
Make my home.
I am an eagle
Resting in leaves.
I hope a whale won't attack me.
Ahhh! Bye-bye

Arturo Prieto, Grade 3
Writers in the Schools Program, TX
*Inspired by a Cherokee warrior song

Halloween

Tonight is scary.
It is Halloween tonight.
Better say "trick or treat!"

Aaron Rahberger, Grade 3
Four Peaks Elementary School, AZ

My Wonderful Parakeet

Every morning I hear
my parakeet chirping.
It makes me feel happy
when I hear my parakeet
chirping in the morning.
My parakeet is like a rainbow
because it has a lot of
bright colors.
He is bright green
like the stem of a flower
and yellow as a flower
and it is black as a spider
and it is blue and brown.
The feathers of my parakeet
feel soft and smooth.
When you touch him
he bites you hard.

Ivan Nunez, Grade 3
Edison Elementary School, CA

Dragon

Dragon in the sky
Soaring, flying, screaming in the air,
Green as grass, as long as a field,
Moving like a snake,
Strong, spiky head,
Keeper of the Earth,
King of the heavens.
My, oh my, I wish I could fly
Like the dragon in the sky.

Robert Ritchey, Grade 3
Writers in the Schools Program, TX

Rodeo, Rodeo

Rodeo's fun.
Me in Jr. Rodeo,
My family cheering.

I go fast up the arena.
My horse Bandet close to the calf.
I throw the rope.
I catch.
I stop.

The rope breaks off my saddle horn.
I win!

Rio Lee, Grade 3
Acacia Elementary School, AZ

Raindrops

Rain falls flop flop
Rain falls plop plop
Raindrops drop drop
Raindrops hear the sound
Raining cats and dogs
Rains like fairy dust
Sprinkles on your face
Stings your face
Splish splash in the puddles
Wet cool fun
Fun fun fun

Gaby Bruce, Grade 3
Katherine Delmar Burke School, CA

Silver
Silver is very, very shiny.
It might startle you.
A lot of kings and queens have this wonderful thing.
Silver makes you VERY rich.
But beware if you have too much.

Evan Kim, Grade 1
Solana Santa Fe Elementary School, CA

How to Make a Delicious Dragon
First take a globe
And make its head soaring through oceans.

Take a licorice rope and put it in a circle for eyes,
Cut one in half for pupils.

Take icicles for teeth.
Take a Laffy Taffy for the tongue.

Melt Jolly Ranchers for the fire breath.
Use a slice of watermelon for the mouth.

Cut the ends of two watermelons.
Then stick them together for the stomach.

Take smashed Skittles for hands and feet.
Use lollipops for the scales.
And there you have your dragon.

Kristen Autrey, Grade 3
Parker Elementary School, TX

Penguins and Puppies
Penguins and puppies are most similar you know.
Penguins like to run and slide and puppies like to bark and roll.
Puppies are most playful and penguins can swim real fast,
But what I don't understand is why penguins can't flap their wings
And fly real high, up in the sky.
Puppies are most wild and very cuddly you know
And sometimes they play hard and rough,
But they don't mean to hurt you though
Don't you see that penguins and puppies are alike,
Don't you think so?

Ellyssa Collinsworth, Grade 3
Robinson Elementary School, TX

Soccer

I love soccer.
Soccer is cool, fun, exciting and most of all
About sportsmanship and making new friends.
I like soccer, you should and everybody should.

Katherine Kupp, Grade 2
University Park Elementary School, TX

Draw My Face

Do my face as oval as an egg.
Doodle my hair as brown as a grizzly bear
and as wavy as a wave in the ocean.
P.S. I have long hair!
Draw my eyebrows as curvy as a shrimp.
Create my eyes as round as a buzzing beetle.
Create my eyelashes as curly as a piggy's tail.
Make my nose as curvy as a bridge.
Sketch my mouth as happy as a chicken.
Do my neck as round as a tree trunk in the woods.
Doodle my ears as curvy as a tree branch.
You are done!

Almudena Robledo, Grade 3
Briargrove Elementary School, TX

The Question

My teacher gave me a question one day
It was very hard and terrible
I screamed my head off
Screaming and shouting I was in quite a bit of trouble
My teacher told me to quiet down
How could I do that if I was in such a bit of misery
I struggled and thought what is the answer
So soon I figured the answer
I was asleep.

Joshua Sanchez, Grade 3
Robinson Elementary School, TX

Bloom

B eautiful beginner
L aying on a hill waiting
O n a new flower to explode
O utstanding thing happened a
M agical day finally came a kindness flower awakened.

Maria Glover, Grade 3
Emerson Elementary School, TX

100 Bugs

I see 100 caterpillars crawling at night.
I see 100 spiders having a fight.
I see 100 ants trying to get into my pants.
I see 100 butterflies high in the air.
I see 100 moths, each only have one hair.
I see 100 ladybug giving some hugs.
I see 100 bees drinking a gardener's tea
I see 100 big tarantulas climbing a tree.
I see 100 grasshoppers jumping happily.
I see 100 worms in the middle of their first term.
I see 100 little beetles looking for some needles.
You see this poem is 100 words because of me.

Jigar Shah, Grade 3
CB Eaton Elementary School, CA

The Dream

As I stumble by a bushy snake hissing and slithering slowly, I see a tornado of fire.
It's whipping the wind, spinning like dancing leaves.
I hear screaming. My mom's flying in the tornado!
I run to help her but my mom is spinning madly in the middle of it now.
I see a black hole at the bottom. I grab her.
My mom turns into fire. I scream.
I yell, "Please don't take my life. It means more than gold.
It means more than silver. It is my right to live, to run, to play."
I fall on my knees but I cannot live without family.
I fall...
It is morning. My dog is pawing me for food.
I smile. It was all a dream.

Elisabeth Gray, Grade 3
Writers in the Schools Program, TX

Cutler

Chocolate brown with soft fur,
Fat and fun and playful.
He likes to lick everyone,
And he likes to run in the warm sun.
He's a smart dog and loves to do tricks,
Like jumping in the air to catch sticks.
He is older than me, I think he is ten.
Cutler is a good old friend
And always ready to play with me, until I say, "The End!"

Natalie Luther, Kindergarten
Presbyterian School, TX

Cousin

Cousin,
I like when
    we play together.
I like when
    we sit together.
I like when
    we play soccer.
I like when
    we went to the fair
    and played
    shoot the bottle.
I like when
    we went home
    together.
Julio Arevalo, Grade 1
Lee Richmond Elementary School, CA

Dinosaur

Dinosaur.
The tallest one of all.
Plant-eating dinosaur
roaming free.
Greatest of them all.
Mighty dinosaur
so big and tall.
Nothing bigger than it.
Brontosaurus.
Dakota Hiser, Grade 2
Acacia Elementary School, AZ

Mr. Lincoln

Abraham Lincoln was a strong leader
He lead our country strong and pure
He was our sixteenth president
Abe was such a pleasure!

Abraham Lincoln had a nickname
It was Honest Abe
He was a very good man
He was never to blame!
Kennedy Scherwinski, Grade 3
Canyon Rim Elementary School, CA

If I Was a Lion

If I was a lion
I would rule the jungle,
If I was a lion
I would scare people,
If I was a lion
I would eat other animals,
If I was a lion
I would eat people.
Zanen Montoya, Grade 2
Manzano Christian School, NM

Yellow

Yellow is sunshine
And autumn leaves too.
Yellow is a summer day,
When all the birds coo.
Yellow is a sunflower
Tall and bright.
Yellow is the moon
That gives us light at night.
Yellow is the stars
Way up high.
Yellow is sweet
Like an apple pie.
Yellow is a sunny color
As bright as the sky.
Shivani Mouleeswaran, Grade 3
Lincoln Elementary School, CA

Gaylen*

G reat mushroom soup maker.
A lways loves me.
Y ou would think she's beautiful.
L oves my sister.
E verybody in my family loves her.
N ever yells at me.
Jarren Worthen, Grade 2
Thomas Edison Charter School, UT
*Dedicated to my mom.

Index

Index

Index

Index

Author Autograph Page

Author Autograph Page

Author Autograph Page

Author Autograph Page

Author Autograph Page

Author Autograph Page

Author Autograph Page

Author Autograph Page